Men, Masculinity
and the Media

RESEARCH ON MEN AND MASCULINITIES SERIES

Series Editor:
MICHAEL S. KIMMEL, SUNY Stony Brook

Contemporary research on men and masculinity, informed by recent feminist thought and intellectual breakthroughs of women's studies and the women's movement, treats masculinity not as a normative referent but as a problematic gender construct. This series of interdisciplinary, edited volumes attempts to understand men and masculinity through this lens, providing a comprehensive understanding of gender and gender relationships in the contemporary world.

Men, Masculinity, and the Media

Edited by Steve Craig

SAGE PUBLICATIONS
International Educational and Professional Publisher
Newbury Park   London   New Delhi

For information address:

SAGE Publications, Inc.
2455 Teller Road
Newbury Park, California 91320

SAGE Publications Ltd.
6 Bonhill Street
London EC2A 4PU
United Kingdom

SAGE Publications India Pvt. Ltd.
M-32 Market
Greater Kailash I
New Delhi 110 048 India

Printed in the United States of America

Library of Congress Cataloging-in-Publication Data

Men, masculinity, and the media / edited by Steve Craig.
      p. cm. — (research on men and masculinities; vol. 1)
  Includes bibliographical references and index.
  ISBN 0-8039-4162-5 (cl). — ISBN 0-8039-4163-3 (pb)
  1. Men in mass media. 2. Masculinity (Psychology) I. Craig, Steve, 1947- . II. Series.
P94.5.M44M46 1992
305.31—dc20   91-44222
                                        CIP

92 93 94 95 96 10 9 8 7 6 5 4 3 2 1

Sage Production Editor: Judith L. Hunter

Contents

Acknowledgments

An anthology is, of course, a group effort, and many people had a hand in helping to produce the words that follow. On behalf of the contributors, I would like to thank all those who assisted the authors with the preparation of their chapters.

In addition, special appreciation goes to Elizabeth George, who spent many tedious hours working to combine all the chapter bibliographies into a single list. Scholars who find the composite reference list a valuable source for their future research owe her their thanks.

As series editor, Michael Kimmel made many suggestions and contributions that have served to strengthen the work. In addition, his theoretical perspectives on men's studies formed the essential framework necessary to unify scholars from different traditions and backgrounds under a central theme. His enthusiasm and encouragement were also much appreciated.

At Sage, Mitch Allen was the guide who helped navigate the maze of seemingly endless details that must be attended to before a volume reaches the reader. I am grateful for his straightforward advice and assistance.

Finally, thanks also go to the University of Maine, which supported this project in several important ways.

Foreword

This volume inaugurates the Sage Series on Men and Masculinity Research. The purpose of the series is to gather together the finest empirical research in the social sciences that focuses on the experiences of men in contemporary society.

Following the pioneering research of feminist scholars over the past two decades, social scientists have come to recognize gender as one of the primary axes around which social life is organized. Gender is now seen as equally central as class and race, both at the macro, structural level of the allocation and distribution of rewards in a hierarchical society, and at the micro, psychological level of individual identity formation and interpersonal interaction.

Social scientists distinguish gender from sex. Sex refers to biology, the biological dimorphic division of male and female; gender refers to the cultural meanings that are attributed to those biological differences. Although biological sex varies little, the cultural meanings of gender vary enormously. Thus we speak of gender as socially constructed; the definitions of masculinity and femininity as the products of the interplay among a variety of social forces. In particular, we understand gender to vary spatially (from one culture to another); temporally (within any one culture over historical time); and longitudinally (through any individual's life course). Finally, we understand that different groups within any culture may define masculinity and femininity differently, according to subcultural definition; race, ethnicity, age, class, sexuality, and region of the country all affect our different gender definition. Thus it is more accurate to speak of "masculinities" and "femininities" than to posit a monolithic gender construct. It is the goal of this series to explore the varieties of men's experiences, remaining mindful of specific differences among men, and also aware of the mechanisms of power that inform both men's relations with women and men's relations with other men.

If masculinity is socially constructed, one of the primary elements in that construction is the representations of manhood that we see daily in the mass media. The media portray a wide variety of masculine images, informing us about the positive characteristics toward which we should aspire and warning against the negative facets of personality that we must avoid. Media representations tell us who we are, who we should be, and who we should avoid.

Steve Craig's volume, *Men, Masculinity, and the Media*, gathers together articles that deal with a variety of topics and a variety of media. Empirical articles range from discussions of men's friendships on prime-time television and in war movies, to images of men in comic books, beer commercials, and heavy metal music videos. Throughout, there is a concern with two dominant themes in the recent social science literature on masculinities: power and difference. Several articles underscore that media representations of ideal manhood serve to perpetuate gender inequality; others explore the intersection of gender inequality with other forms of inequality, such as race or ethnicity. Other authors note the variety of images of men, and the ways in which other features of social life are called into play in the service of the construction of representation of masculinity. Masculinities are constructed through media representation, these essays suggest; changing the definitions of manhood will require a serious confrontation with images of power as well as structural realities of power in social life.

MICHAEL S. KIMMEL
Series Editor

1

Considering Men and the Media

STEVE CRAIG

Over the past three decades, the women's movement has focused attention on the role of the media in helping to shape attitudes about gender and behavior. Media scholars have responded to the questions raised with a variety of approaches, from content analyses of gender portrayals, to critical work grounded in psychoanalytic, economic, or cultural studies theory.

But as might be expected, most feminist analyses of the media have focused on women. In fact, men and masculinity have frequently been treated as the "norm" and men's portrayals in the media have often been seen as unproblematic or even exemplary (Durkin, 1985a). But feminist theory's concept of a socially constructed gender suggests that the analysis of men and masculinity will also provide valuable insight into social relationships. For example, how can we understand the social forces involved in patriarchy without understanding the gendering of men?

A few scholars have already begun to examine men and masculinity more critically, and "men's studies" has emerged as a name for the cross-disciplinary study concerned with these issues. Yet men's studies has only begun to have an impact on media research, and so far, only a few scholars have published work that focuses on the media and their relationship to men *as men*. This volume attempts to address this shortcoming by bringing together new work on men, masculinity, and the media.

The Idea of Men's Studies

Men's studies represents the collective work of scholars from many disciplines who have found the concepts and insights of feminist theory useful in the exploration of male gendering. The amount of this research has grown to the extent that in 1985, August published a bibliography on the subject. The work of such authors and editors as David and Brannon (1976), Pleck and Pleck (1980), Brod (1987), and Kimmel (1987a) constitutes an impressive body of new theory, criticism, and research on men and masculinity.

Men's studies is clearly the offspring of not only feminist theory, but also the social awareness brought on by the women's movement. As a result, men's studies is largely pro-feminist in its approach. In fact, most men's studies research seeks to extend and expand the insights into gender relationships offered by feminist thought. Kimmel has aptly described the focus:

> Men's studies responds to the shifting social and intellectual contexts in the study of gender and attempts to treat masculinity not as the normative refer-ent against which standards are assessed but as a problematic gender con-struct. Inspired by the academic breakthroughs of women's studies, men's studies addresses similar questions to the study of men and masculinity. As women's studies has radically revised the traditional academic canon, men's studies seeks to use that revision as the basis for its exploration of men and masculinity. Men's studies seeks neither to replace nor to supplant women's studies; quite the contrary. Men's studies seeks to buttress, to augment women's studies, to complete the radically redrawn portrait of gender that women's studies have begun. (Kimmel, 1987d, pp. 10-11)

Gender as a Social Construct

One of the key concepts of feminist theory—and of men's studies—is that gender is a concept that is socially constructed. Scholars are careful to differentiate between *sex*, a distinction based on biological differences, and *gender*, a term used to describe characteristics society ascribes to persons of one sex or the other. Drawing on economic, linguistic, psycho-analytic, and sociological approaches grounded in structuralism, criti-cal theorists argue that men and women are acculturated into their gender roles. Most (if not all) behavior commonly associated with gender is seen as learned rather than innate, and biological theories that see gender dif-ferences as "natural" are themselves considered to be the product of these cultural distinctions. Masculinity and femininity can then be examined as sets of social expectations, created and maintained in a patriarchal society.

Therefore, for men's studies, masculinity becomes a focus of inquiry. Masculinity is what a culture expects of its men. In modern American culture, part of this expectation is that men will participate in and support patriarchy, and the traditional characteristics of masculinity are made to seem so correct and natural that men find the domination and exploitation of women and other men to be not only expected, but actually demanded. Men who find it difficult or objectionable to fit into the patterns of traditional masculinity often find themselves castigated and alienated.

Some key questions about masculinity immediately arise. How is masculinity defined? What is the function of masculinity in today's society? Does the cultural definition of masculinity change from time to time and place to place? If so, is it changing today? How do boys (and men) learn what constitutes appropriate masculine behavior? What is the relationship between masculinity and patriarchy? What aspects of masculinity promote the exploitation of others? Can masculinity be redefined to promote a freer and more democratic society?

Men, Masculinity, and Media Study

Since the popular media have long been considered to have an important role in defining and shaping American culture, it follows that the media should be one focus of any study of men and masculinity. The chapters in Part One look at past media research on men and masculinity. Parts Two through Four are aimed at examining how the media serve to construct masculinities, that is, how men and their relationships have been portrayed in the media and the role these portrayals play in the cultural definition of masculinity. Part Five seeks to investigate how men read the media. Do men have a gendered way of seeing the world? If so, how does this affect the meaning they make from the media?

In selecting chapters for inclusion in this anthology, the editor has sought to present some of the newest research and ideas concerning men, masculinity, and the media. The chapters' authors have approached their subjects from a variety of research philosophies and critical traditions, although feminist theory, and especially feminist film criticism, has clearly been a major influence on many. A variety of media are examined, from comic books and rock music to film and television. In each case, however, the authors have sought to explore the nature of the American definition of masculinity and the role of the media in shaping, reinforcing, and even changing that definition.

In Chapters 2 and 3, Fred Fejes and Diana Saco, respectively, examine some of the past media research on which our current perspectives are based. They have found that most previous work has not been directed specifically at men as men, but rather as men in the context of other social factors. For example, Fejes points out that "the concern about pornography is essentially a concern about male sexuality." In structuring their reviews, Fejes and Saco have chosen to differentiate between two major philosophical and methodological approaches to the past research. They argue that traditional empirical research has generally viewed masculinity as "fact," whereas critical research has usually seen masculinity as socially constructed "signs." Under the category of "masculinity as fact," Fejes reviews those studies that seek to report and quantify observations about male portrayals and behaviors. He specifically finds that this work can be classified into two groups: research on sex roles and the media, and research on pornography. Saco reviews the critical work on men that has grown from the newer traditions of linguistics, semiotics, cultural studies, and feminism, in which gender is analyzed as a social construct. Her inquiry focuses on "how masculinity is constructed, within sign systems, as 'given' and 'obvious.'" She finds that this literature, much of it an outgrowth of film criticism, has been clustered around three major approaches: the psychoanalytic, the textual, and the Marxist-influenced.

If masculinity is to be conceived of as a social construct, what role do the media play in formulating it? How do men (and women) learn what behaviors are "manly"? Part Two presents three case studies of how masculinity is defined in different media contexts.

In their chapter, "Metal Men and Glamour Boys," Stan Denski and David Sholle look at the representation of masculinity in performances by heavy metal rock groups. Arguing that gender differences may be best understood in terms of codes of performance, they examine the heavy metal subculture and analyze the role of gender display as a fundamental attribute.

Norma Pecora looks at masculinity in the persona of the comic book superhero. Her chapter, "Superman/Superboys/Supermen," details the part such heroes play in forming the image of masculinity (and femininity) for adolescent boys. She finds that both Superman and the newer superheroes present a fundamentally patriarchal view of the world, where the good guys are predominantly middle-class white males who seek justice through vigilantism. Women and people of color are mostly relegated to either invisibility or traditional roles.

In "Beer Commercials: A Manual on Masculinity," Lance Strate presents a mythic analysis of television beer commercials. Aimed almost exclusively at men, beer ads exploit traditional images of masculinity to promote their products. But, Strate argues, they also "constitute a guide for becoming a man, a rule book for appropriate male behavior, in short, a manual on masculinity."

An essential element in the role of the media in defining masculinity is how men are portrayed in their relationships with other men. How have the media treated such portrayals? Are these images of men changing? Part Three looks at these questions.

In her chapter, "Buddies and Pals," Lynn Spangler takes a historical look at male friendships as they have been represented on prime-time television. Drawing on past social research on same-sex friendships, Spangler finds that action programming has tended to portray men *doing* together rather than *being* together. Situation comedies, on the other hand, have often portrayed more intimate relationships.

Father-son relationships in poor black families is the subject of Venise Berry's chapter, "From *Good Times* to *The Cosby Show*." Berry questioned a group of low-income black youth on what they thought of the very different father figures portrayed in the title programs. She found that although her respondents considered the shows to be representative of real-life situations, they adapted their definition of masculinity to fit their own experiences, indicating the limited power of such portrayals to influence the perceptions of a non-mainstream audience.

Ralph Donald investigates popular representations of male relationships in war in his chapter, "Masculinity and Machismo in Hollywood's War Films." Portraying military service as a modern rite of passage for American boys, most war movies have promoted heroic violence as the true hallmark of manhood. Donald concludes with a comparison between masculinity as promoted in sports and that in war films, and offers an analysis of the concepts of competition and winning as promoted in both venues.

The three chapters in Part Four seek to investigate the role of the media in reinforcing male dominance and power. Diane Barthel's chapter, "When Men Put on Appearances: Advertising and the Social Construction of Masculinity," takes a look at men's advertising, arguing that ads contribute a good deal to our socially constructed definition of masculinity.

In "Men and the News Media," David Croteau and William Hoynes report on their analysis of the guests on ABC's *Nightline* program over a period of two and a half years. They find that these "newsmakers" are overwhelmingly white males with elite backgrounds. They argue that this supports the contention that American news is dominated by a narrow perspective controlled not just by men, but by men who are part of the "culture of power."

Turning to sports, Don Sabo and Sue Curry Jansen offer a critical analysis of media portrayals of athletes and athletic events. In "Images of Men in Sport Media," they review past research and criticism of sport and point out that mediated sport remains a nearly all-male province, clearly structured to reinforce patriarchal concepts of masculinity. They also examine the particular contradictions surrounding the black male athlete, whom the system at once both valorizes and excludes.

Much recent critical analysis has focused on the activities of the audience as readers. How do men respond to mediated images of masculinity? How much of an impact can changing portrayals of men's roles actually have on the audience? The chapters in Part Five focus on discussions of men as audience.

Robert Hanke begins the section with "Redesigning Men: Hegemonic Masculinity in Transition," arguing that television, in its attempt to reach multiple audiences, presents a variety of images of masculinity. These social definitions may then be embraced, ignored, negotiated, or resisted by viewers.

This theme is continued in Clay Steinman's analysis of the television show *Evening Shade* in his chapter, "Gaze Out of Bounds: Men Watching Men on Television." Drawing on Mulvey's concept of the "male gaze," Steinman examines how heterosexual males respond to portrayals of attractive men. In his analysis, he raises important questions about the way gender is imaged by a medium that economics requires please both male and female audiences.

Gender imaging is further explored from a perspective outside the United States in "The Transatlantic Gaze: Masculinities, Youth, and the American Imaginary," by Jeff Hearn and Antonio Melechi. Writing from the perspective of European media scholarship, they argue that the worldwide dominance of the U.S. media results in an international Americanization of gender images. They see the Hollywood film, and especially the Western, as the medium by which America projected its version of rugged, violent masculinity to the rest of the world.

Finally, a bibliography at the end of the book represents the composite reference list of all the chapter contributors. It should serve as a useful starting point for those who find in these chapters ideas worth further research. Gender study has offered important insights into the way media and culture interact. It is our hope that this book will serve to demonstrate new ways these insights can be applied.

2

Masculinity as Fact

A Review of Empirical Mass Communication Research on Masculinity

FRED J. FEJES

In media studies, the topic of masculinity is only at the very earliest stages of emerging as a research area in its own right. Compared to the study of women and the media, one finds few studies explicitly addressing the interrelationship between the media and social definitions of masculinity. For example, in review of the empirical literature of the past decade, the author was able to locate only five items that focused primarily on men and masculinity (Cantor, 1990; Gray, 1986; Meyers, 1980; Postman, Nystrom, Strate, & Weingarter, 1987; Skelly & Lundstrom, 1981) and two of these were qualitative in nature.

This is not to suggest, however, that media studies has totally ignored the topic of masculinity. Two major areas of empirical research contribute to a knowledge of masculinity and mass communications. First, there is the research that focuses on sex roles and the media. This area of research deals both with the investigation of the type of images of men presented in the media and the effects such portrayals have on an individual's notion of his or her own gender. Although researchers in masculinity question the entire efficacy of using the sex-role perspective in studying masculinity and gender (Davies & Harré, 1990; Kimmel, 1987d; Pleck, 1982; Stacey & Thorne 1985), the sex-role research in mass communication provides the only major empirical analysis within the social science perspective that treats the issue of masculinity and the media. Major reviews of the research on sex roles and the mass media can be found in Durkin (1985a, 1985b), Busby (1985) and Gunter (1986). Second, the empirical research on pornography presents another exploration of masculinity. The concern about pornography is essentially a concern about male sexuality. In most research on pornography the subjects are generally male, and the goal of the research is to study the male response to sexualized images.

A reading of the research in these two areas will emphasize what the literature presents on the subject of masculinity. In most cases the topic of masculinity was not the major, or even a secondary topic of these studies. As a result the author had to attempt a reading of the work in which he had to construct the masculinity subtext. While there are problems with this kind of approach, it does show that, taken as a whole, research on sex roles and pornography does present a coherent discourse about masculinity.

Sex-Role Research and Masculinity

Content

The bulk of media and sex-role research has been a traditional analysis of manifest media content that examines the way male and female sex roles have been portrayed. As noted by Durkin, such research has "concentrated on the female role and the male sex role tends to be illustrated by default, and is often assumed to be the converse of whatever characteristics are identified as associated with the female stereotype" (1985a, p. 110). A further reservation is that most analyses emphasize the differences rather than the similarities found between the sex roles. Again as noted by Durkin, while male and female may be commonly portrayed in the media differently in some areas, such as occupation, they are often both portrayed as similar in other areas, such as intelligence, yet such similarities are not often the subject of research. The implications of the differences can be better understood only in the context of the overall picture of both differences and similarities.

Broadcasting

Within the study of television programming, one consistent finding is that in terms of simple frequency, television is a male-dominated medium with more portrayals of men than women (Butler & Paisley, 1980, p. 78; Durkin, 1985a) and with men placed more often in starring roles (Dominick, 1979). Beyond the dominance in simple frequency, men are more likely to be found in action/drama programming and less likely to be found in situation comedies and soap operas (Greenberg, Simmons, Hogan, & Atkin, 1980; Gunter, 1986, p. 8; Miles, 1975; Miller & Reeves, 1976). Thus viewers tend to see men in programming contexts that emphasize action and drama at the expense of humor, emotions or interpersonal relationships.

In terms of occupation, men are more likely to be shown as employed in higher status jobs (Barcus, 1983; Durkin, 1985a) and are less likely to be shown in a home environment (Downs, 1981). Moreover, they tend to be employed in occupations that are traditionally defined as male occupations (lawyers, ministers, doctors) (Seggar & Wheeler, 1973).

Other aspects of the portrayal of men in television reveal that men are less likely to be shown as being married (Manes & Melnyk, 1974; McNeil, 1975), generally shown as being older, and less likely to be shown involved in a romantic relationship (Downing, 1974; Durkin, 1985a; Signorielli, 1982). Men are portrayed as being more dominant than females (Lemon, 1978), more likely to engage in acts of violence (Gerbner, 1972; Potter & Ware, 1987), and more likely to give or receive responses and to be involved in the reinforcement or punishment of behavior, thus being depicted as possessors of both power and status through the greater control of rewards and punishment (Downs & Gowan, 1980). A study of prime-time humor revealed that, because of their greater number on television, men were more often the object of humor or disparagement, although males were more likely to disparage females than the reverse (Suls & Gastoff, 1981).

Examining the visual portrayal of men on television, one study found in commercial television programming a tendency to portray men in terms of close face shots as opposed to full body shots, as was the case for the portrayal of women (Copeland, 1989). The author suggests that this example of "face-ism" may be a manifestation of deeply rooted cultural myths of men, pictorially represented by their faces, as intellect, and women, pictorially represented by their bodies, as heart or emotion.

Compared to women, men drove, drank, and smoked more, used firearms, did athletic things, and made more business calls. They made more plans for themselves and others and were more likely to be involved in problem solving (Downs, 1981; Henderson & Greenberg,

1980; Greenberg, Richards, & Henderson, 1980). A study of the portrayal of men and women on noncommercial public television showed little difference between that medium and commercial television in regard to the representation of men. The only major difference noted was in an equal distribution between men and women in the initiating of action (Matelski, 1985).

Based on these empirical studies, it is evident that men, as portrayed on adult television, do not deviate much from the traditional patriarchal notion of men and masculinity. Men are powerful and successful, occupy high-status positions, initiate action and act from the basis of rational mind as opposed to emotions, are found more in the world of things as opposed to family and relationships, and organize their lives around problem solving.

Moreover, the masculinity portrayed on television is a white, middle-class heterosexual masculinity. For example, Gray (1986), in a study of the portrayal of black men in situation comedies, argues that television presents an assimilationist image of the black man that is far from the reality of most black Americans. Cantor (1990), in a review of the research on the portrayal of families on television, noted that in situation comedies that revolve around a family, there are few stereotypical macho men. She found, however, that class was an important determinant in how father/husband figures were portrayed. Working-class father/husbands were generally portrayed as clumsy, awkward, and inept, with the wife dominating as the primary decision maker. In situation comedies involving a middle-class family, the husband is portrayed as kind, sensitive, caring and domesticated, in many ways an idealized figure that is equally unrealistic.

Regarding sexual orientation, although there has been no empirical study on the presentation of gay men in the media, the negative stereotypical presentation of both gay men and lesbians is so well recognized that gay and lesbian organizations such as the Gay and Lesbian Alliance Against Defamation (GLAAD) have come into existence to work for the elimination of such presentations (see also Montgomery, 1981). Even when gay men are presented in a sympathetic manner, the central focus is on the heterosexual characters' response and acceptance of the gay characters' homosexuality. The gay characters are totally defined by their "problem" (Gross, 1989; Henry 1987). Programming that presents a gay character's homosexuality in a non-problematic manner is exceptional and is usually relegated to pay cable channels or public television.

The portrayal of men in television programming aimed at children does not vary significantly from that of adult programming, with males greatly outnumbering females and occupying high-prestige occupations (Busby, 1985; Durkin, 1985a; Schechtman, 1978). A small number of studies attempting to assess the behavior of the male characters likewise find little difference between children's programming and adult programming. Males are portrayed as aggressive, constructively engaged in building and planning activities, and less willing to defer to others' plan or suggestions (Sternglanz & Serbin, 1974). Moreover, males more often display problem-solving ability, activity, and autonomy (McArthur & Eisen, 1976). A more recent study of child characters found that boys are consistently shown as more active, aggressive, rational and unhappy. Likewise, boy characters engaged in traditional male activities, such as playing sports, going places, and making mischief, while the girl characters talked on the telephone, read, and helped with the housework (Peirce, 1989). A study of children's educational television showed little difference in that medium in the portrayal of males (Dohrmann, 1975).

Advertising

Research dealing with advertising shows similar evidence of a high degree of stereotyped presentations of gender roles. Again this research tends to be organized primarily around a concern over the portrayal of women; the first major study of sex roles and advertising was undertaken by the National Organization for Women (NOW) in 1972 (Hennessee & Nicholson, 1972). Compared to gender portrayals on television, which tend to be affected by plot and character aspects, the portrayal of men and women in advertising tends to be far more blatant in its sexual stereotypes. This is due in large to the fact that the products advertised are aimed at target male and female audiences, thus resulting in a higher level of specificity in sex-role portrayals.

Research conducted in the 1970s laid out the basic aspects of the advertising portrayal of men. Overall, men were portrayed as more autonomous than women, with men being portrayed in many different occupations as compared to women being shown mainly as housewives and mothers. Men were far more likely to be shown advertising alcohol, vehicles, or business products while women were found mostly in advertisements for domestic products. Men were far more likely to be shown outdoors or in business settings while women were shown primarily in domestic settings (Dominick & Rauch, 1972; Schneider &

Schneider, 1979). Men are far more often portrayed as authorities (McArthur & Resko, 1975). Moreover, voice-overs, advertising narrations carrying the connotations of authority, are overwhelming male (Courtney & Whipple, 1974).

These findings tended to be confirmed with few variations by subsequent research in the 1970s and early 1980s. While some studies reported a greater balance in male and female voice-overs and product representatives, female voice-overs were mainly confined to food, household products, and feminine care products, while male voices were associated with a wide range of products (Knill, Peach, Pursey, Gilpin, & Perloff, 1981; Maracek, Piliavin, Fitzsimmons, Krogh, Leader, & Trudell, 1978; Meyers, 1980; O'Donnell & O'Donnell, 1978).

More recent studies suggest some changes. Ferrante, Haynes, and Kingsley (1988), replicating the 1972 study of Dominick and Rauch, reported significant declines in portrayal of men's traditional roles, such as husband, father, athlete, and construction worker. Other recent studies of television advertising (Bretl & Cantor, 1988; Lovdal, 1989) show similar findings. One of the few studies of radio advertising (Melton & Fowler, 1987) reported that, as in television, the male voice tends to be the dominant voice in commercials, with 1,382 single male narrator commercials counted, compared to 144 female narrator commercials.

A qualitative analysis of 40 beer commercials found a very strong relationship between drinking and a stereotypical view of masculinity (Postman et al., 1987). The drinking of beer is related to challenge, risk, and mastery over nature, technology, others, and the self. Strong emotions and displays of affection are eschewed while solidarity with other men is stressed. Women are portrayed as a mere audience for male activities. Furthermore, boys are initiated into the community of men by their ability to drink. Men who are sensitive, thoughtful, scholarly, gay, or complex are not present in beer commercials.

By comparison to the research on commercials on adults, the research on commercials aimed at children is not extensive. Generally, while the majority of ads aimed at children contain both boys and girls, boys are the dominant characters (Macklin & Kolbe, 1983). Ads aimed at boys have far more activity than those aimed at girls and contain more aggressive behavior (Verna, 1975; Welch, Huston-Stein, Wright, & Plehal, 1979). A study of the traits associated with boy and girl characters portrayed in children's advertising indicated that boys were typically shown to be active, aggressive, rational, and unhappy (Peirce, 1989). Production characteristics of the ads were also gender-linked. Male voice-overs were predominant in male-oriented and neutral ads, and male-oriented ads were far louder than either female-oriented or neutral ads. Even the form of the ads was different. As noted in one study, "The commercials directed at boys contained highly active toys, varied scenes, high rates of camera cuts and high levels of sounds effects and loud music. . . . Commercials directed at girls had frequent fades, dissolves and background music" (Welch et al., 1979, p. 206).

Research on the portrayal of gender in advertising in other countries tends to duplicate the findings of American research. In studies of British television (Harris & Stobart, 1986; Livingstone & Green, 1986; Manstead & McCulloch, 1981) reported that males were typically portrayed as having expertise and authority, as being objective and knowledgeable about reasons for buying particular products, as occupying roles that are autonomous, and as being concerned with the practical consequences of product purchases. A study of British radio advertising found similar results (Furnham & Schofield, 1986). A study of Italian television found that medium to be very similar to British television in the portrayal of men (Furnham & Voli, 1989). A comparative study (Gilly, 1988) of sex-role portrayals in television advertising in Australia, Mexico, and the United States revealed that while the commercials of all three countries contained traditional stereotypes, Australian commercials were less stereotyped on a number of different factors, such as occupation, setting, marital status, whether a man or woman acted as a spokesperson and their credibility for that role, and whether they were recipients or providers of aid. Mexican commercials, on the other hand, were the most stereotyped on all the factors studied.

The portrayal of men in print advertising has also received attention. Skelly and Lundstrom (1981) used a scale designed to measure the level of sexual stereotyping in an analysis of 660 magazine ads from 1959, 1969, and 1979 to determine whether there was any change in the portrayal of men in print advertising over the two decades. They found a small and gradual movement toward the nonsexist portrayal of men over the 20-year period. Lysonski's study (1985) of sex roles in British magazine advertising showed similar results. Looking at a sample of ads from British magazines in 1976 and 1983, he concluded that while the sex-stereotyping had decreased slightly, men still are more likely to be depicted in themes of sex appeal, as career-oriented, and in activities and life outside the home.

Other studies suggest little or no change. While the percentage of women portrayed in business suits increased from 1963 to 1983, there was no significant difference in the way men were portrayed in a business setting (Saunders & Stead, 1986). A study of computer ads in magazines showed that men appeared in such advertisements almost twice as often as women; were overrepresented as managers, experts, and technicians; and were portrayed as more active and accepting of new computer technology (Ware & Stuck, 1985). Massé & Rosenblum (1988), utilizing Erving Goffman's approach (1979) to the study of gender and body positioning in advertising, analyzed 564 ads from 1984 editions of three male-oriented and three female-oriented magazines. In male-oriented magazines, males tended to be portrayed in a dominant stance; were less likely to be shown smiling; were less likely to be touching one another, themselves, or an object; and gazed full-faced at the viewer or an object, but not at others. In female-oriented magazines, the portrayal was similar, except that men were more likely to touch and gaze at others. As noted by the authors, "The 'self' in men's magazines is a figure who does not defer. Unsmilingly, he touches objects rather than people, and he gazes outward at the viewer, apparently oblivious to those in the frame who gaze at and touch him. With some qualification, this is the same man we will see in women's magazines" (p. 139).

Other Media

The portrayal of men in other media forms, such as photography, has also been examined. A study (Luebke, 1989) of gender division in persons shown in newspaper pictures revealed that photos of men outnumbered women in all sections of the newspaper except lifestyle pages. In a gatekeeper study of newspaper sports photos, Wanta and Leggett (1989) examined sports photographs of the 1987 Wimbledon Tennis Tournament sent over the Associated Press (AP) wire and compared those with the photos that were then actually used by eight newspapers. The authors found that newspaper sports editors tended to select photos of women that showed them in emotional and helpless states and rejected those photos of men that showed them similarly. Studies of portrait photographs (Mills, 1984; Ragan, 1982) from high school and university yearbooks found that males smiled less than females, canted their heads less than females, suggesting an appearance of dominance, and wore glasses more often than females, suggesting more intelligence and industriousness.

A study (Thomas, 1986) of gender and social class coding in photographs in heterosexual erotic magazines (*Playboy, Penthouse, Mandate, Playgirl,* and so on) found that in magazines aimed at upwardly mobile heterosexual males, women were portrayed in a highly sexualized and idealized manner. Their physical attributes and beauty were uncommon and there was a great deal of photographic manipulation (airbrushing, lighting, and so on) of the figures. On the other hand, magazines aimed at heterosexual females showed men with average physical attributes, and the degree of photographic manipulation was nowhere near as great. The male image in the female erotics was mostly that of a reasonably attractive average man who was seemingly willing to be photographed nude and "who apparently need(ed) no artifice, seductiveness or specialness to enhance his appeal" (p. 110). In contrast, the images of men found in homosexual erotica was comparable to the image of women found in erotica aimed at the upwardly mobile heterosexual male in that men had uncommon physical attributes and were of above-average attractiveness. Thus, it seems that erotica aimed at males, either hetersexual or homosexual, rely upon an idealized image of sexuality and sexual attractiveness.

Analysis of comics revealed typical differences in the portrayal of gender. Replicating a 1974 study, Brabant and Mooney (1986) analyzed the portrayals of males and females in four popular family-oriented Sunday comic strips in 1984 and found that the change in the role of male and females in the Sunday comics over the decade were minimal, with males still portrayed in a fairly tradition manner. Another study (Thaler, 1987) analyzed the relationship between comic characters and stereotypical masculine and feminine traits. The author found that masculine traits were most closely associated with those characters defined traditionally as heroes. The author's data suggest that the more comic a character, the greater the gender inversion.

Music

There have been a number of studies focusing on the analysis of gender in popular music. One study of the top record sales of various music groups from 1955 to 1984 shows that male individual artists and groups overwhelmingly dominated the musical scene (Wells, 1986). Research in the area of male sex-role representation in music lyrics presents contradictory findings. Some researchers find that males conform to stereotypical images (Freudiger & Almquist, 1978). Others have shown that while females conform to the traditional female image, men are often portrayed as being emotionally dependent and loving (Hyden & McCandless, 1983).

The genre of the music seems to be an important factor. Saucier (1986) studied male and female portrayals in country and western music and found that, in contrast to almost all nonmusic media genres, the love relationship is clearly the most important element in the lives of the male and female characters portrayed in the lyrics. While a woman's status is derived from her ability to get and keep a man, a man's status is derived from his ability to provide for his woman and family, as well as his ability to satisfy his woman. Appropriate women's roles are those of lover, wife, and mother—never as a worker or career woman. The men's roles were less clearly defined, but when mentioned were those of lover and provider. For both, work is secondary and unsatisfactory.

Analyses of music videos, while focusing primarily on the portrayal of women, show that the portrayal of men is highly stereotypical. One study (Vincent, Davis, & Boruszkowski, 1987), of 900 music videos aired in 1985, revealed that one-third of them contained violence with man-to-man or man-to-object acts of violence dominating. The authors found that men were portrayed as relating to and treating women in very sexist ways. An analysis of MTV music videos aired in 1984, which focused on the portrayal of gender and race, found that 83% had white male singers or bands led by white males. Examining a number of different content categories, including race, occupation, activity, social and sexual behavior, and overall tone of the video, the authors conclude: "White men, primarily by virtue of their greater numbers, are the center of attention and power and are more often aggressive and hostile than helpful and cooperative" (Brown & Campbell, 1986, p. 104).

Film

Traditionally, film content has received little attention from social scientists, and much of the discussion of masculinity has been done from a qualitative interpretive perspective. The study of the hero in Hollywood cinema has been a staple in film courses and has formed the basis for the study of masculinity. One of the earlier major studies of masculinity in film is Joan Mellen's *Big Bad Wolves* (1977), a qualitative analysis of five decades of American films. Mellen argues that the image of masculinity presented in film is not only very traditional, but also so idealized as to be unattainable. Two major studies on gay masculinity and film (Dyer, 1984; Russo, 1987) not only examine the kinds of negative stereotypes of gays found in film, but also explore the numerous gay subtexts. It was from these subtexts that earlier generations of gays, isolated from one another and with very few live role models, developed images about who they were. Dyer's and Russo's work suggest that the role of media in gay identity-formation and socialization is greater than that among heterosexuals. However, as Dyer points out, since the 1970s there have been other emerging sources of knowledge about gays, such as those found in gay bars, in local gay communities, and in public figures who have come out, which have provided gays the wherewithal to resist the dominant heterosexual construction of gay sexuality found in film and other media.

Effects

While content studies show fairly conclusively that the media replicate and reinforce traditional versions of masculinity, the question of the impact of the media is a far less settled question. The number of empirical studies examining the issue of effects is small, and their conclusions have been heavily criticized. The underlying issue in such studies is to what extent media content has an impact on the sex-role attitudes and behavior of the members of the audience. Given that people are affected by their entire environment and thus affected by notions of masculinity and femininity present in the family, school, church, and larger social environment, the task of isolating the effects of the media is a difficult one.

The effects studies have focused primarily on the impact of television on the sex-role development of children, with the goal of empirically demonstrating whether children acquire important information about sex roles from media, primarily television, which they then integrate into their own behavior and attitudes.

Unfortunately, the research is not very conclusive. Studies (Cheles-Miller, 1975; Frueh & McGhee, 1975; McGhee 1975; McGhee & Frueh, 1980; Meyer, 1980; Morgan, 1982; Perloff, 1977; Zuckerman, Singer, & Singer, 1980) have examined the correlation between television viewing and the degree to which children have stereotypical notions of masculinity and femininity and men's and women's roles. Such studies either have been criticized as using faulty empirical measures of sex-role development or have showed very modest associations between viewing patterns and sex-role stereotypes (Durkin, 1985b). A number of experimental studies (Barkley, Ullman, Otto, & Brecht, 1977; Cobb, Stevens-Long, & Goldstein, 1982; Cordua, McGraw, & Drabman, 1979; Drabman, Robertson, Patterson, Jarvie, Hammer, & Cordua, 1981; Miller

& Reeves, 1976), which allow for the greater control and manipulation of content and viewing variables, likewise have been inconclusive.

Overall, this research on children does not lend very much support to the idea of television as having a strong impact. It does show that the information, and the attitudes and conceptions of masculinity and femininity that children bring to television, play an important part in how they interpret what they see and what they do with it. This research does provide evidence of child television viewers as active participants in the construction of the meaning of the programming, and not simply passive recipients of media messages about sex roles. These results fit into current notions in media of audience response as being active, with audience members selectively attending to different aspects of media programming and formulating individualized meanings of program content.

Pornography

As noted above, most of the empirical media research subsumes the issue of masculinity in a discussion of sex roles that often has, as its ultimate goal, a focus on the female role. The research on pornography, however, is one area of empirical media research in which the basic focus is on heterosexual male sexuality.

In contrast to the literature on sex roles, there is very little research on the content of pornography or how that content has changed over the years. The common view is that prior to 1970, what pornography was available tended to be "soft-core" and nonviolent. During the sexually permissive 1970s and early 1980s, both the amount of pornography increased and the nature changed, with the content becoming more explicit and containing more images of degradation and violence toward women. There is, however, little empirical research to confirm this widely accepted view.

Reviewing the few existing studies on content (Malamuth & Spinner, 1980; Palys, 1986; Scott, 1985; Slade, 1984; Smith, 1976), Donnerstein, Linz, and Penrod (1987, p. 91) conclude that it is difficult to say that pornography overall has become more violent in recent years. While the absolute amount of violent and nonviolent pornography has obviously increased, there is no solid evidence that it has become more violent. Furthermore, as Brown and Bryant (1990) note, pornographic films tend to portray a lesser frequency of violence than do other media forms.

In contrast to the sex-role research, the bulk of the research on pornography is focused on effects and consists of experiments and studies conducted by behavioral psychologists and communication researchers, who study subjects' reactions to pornography under varying conditions. In a comprehensive review of this literature Donnerstein, Linz, and Penrod conclude that the main problem about pornography is that sexually explicit material, when linked to violence and positive outcomes (e.g., a woman initially resisting a rape, but then showing that she enjoys it), result in not only a desensitization in most male viewers toward victims of sexual violence but also a rise in willingness on the part of male viewers to be violent toward women. Other researchers, studying pornography that was nonviolent but nonetheless abusive and dehumanizing in content, found that such material had similar effects on the test subjects (Check & Guloien, 1989; Zillman & Bryant, 1982, 1984).

The notion of masculinity that emerges from this literature is that men have a different sexual nature from women. In men, sex and aggression are linked, and men have more difficulty then women in controlling their sexual and aggressive drives (McCormick, 1978). Some researchers (Zillman & Weaver, 1989) have argued that the factor that best explains the typical male response to pornography is the *macho personality constellation* (Mosher & Sirkin, 1984), consisting of the following three interrelated components: (a) calloused sex attitudes toward women, (b) celebration of male aggressiveness, and (c) fascination with danger —attributes that men are socialized into during adolescence.

Studies that move beyond laboratory settings present a similar picture. While unpublished studies conducted by Baron and Straus (cited in Donnerstein, Linz, & Penrod, 1987, pp. 66-68) show that levels of consumption of selected pornographic magazines and incidence of rape are positively related, these researchers suggest that a third variable, "hypermasculine" sexual and sex-role orientation, underlie this relationship. In another study, Scott (1985) found that, while there was no relationship between state-by-state rape reports and consumption of pornography, there was a positive relationship between rape reports and consumption of outdoor magazines, such as *Field and Stream* and *American Rifleman*.

Conclusion

The empirical research on sex roles and pornography, although differing in terms of focus, provides an account of the presentation of masculinity in the media. The sex-role research shows that media content presents a heavily stereotypical view of masculinity, yet such a conclusion has to be tempered with the lack of solid evidence that such media stereotypes have a direct effect on an individual man's notion of his masculinity. The research on pornography, on the other hand, presents fairly convincing evidence that the media, in this case pornography that is violent and/or degrading to women, has a heavy impact on a man's notion of his own masculinity. The literature suggests that after a man has viewed violent and/or degrading pornography, callousness toward women becomes an important part of his sense of masculinity.

Beyond these two bodies of empirical research, the research issues associated with masculinity and the media have only barely been addressed. Far greater attention needs to be paid to exploring in a systematic way, which is not dependent on a sex-role model, the images of masculinity that are presented through the media. More attention needs to be paid to how audiences, particularly adult male audiences, use these images in the construction and maintenance of their own notions of masculinity. If media effects research is any guide, one would expect to find that members of the audience "read" media messages about masculinity in a highly individualistic fashion, supporting the notion that there are many masculinities. Such knowledge about audience response to and use of media messages about masculinity would have to go beyond the narrow laboratory methods and findings of the pornography research and examine how such messages are incorporated into one's everyday ideas and behavior.

The paucity of empirical media research on masculinity at this point represents a challenge and an opportunity to media researchers to contribute not only to a growing new area of research, but also to the examination and redefinition of one of the fundamental ways we define and act out our reality.

3

Masculinity as Signs

Poststructuralist Feminist
Approaches to the Study of Gender[1]

DIANA SACO

Our commonsense understandings of gender share with traditional social science studies the view that masculinity is a fact of nature. As interpretive genealogical analyses of these discourses show, however, academic and popular discourses work to naturalize the very concept that has been so unproblematically embraced as fact. What is at issue in these interpretive analyses is the *facticity* of masculinity—how masculinity is constructed, within sign systems, as given and obvious. Masculinity as signs contributes as much to the reality of gender differences as do the physical differences that have led traditional researchers to ascribe "masculinity" to men and "femininity" to women. Whatever the physical differences between men and women, ascriptions like "masculine" constitute human beings as particular kinds of subjects. The symbolic sign system within which masculinity and femininity are coded oppositions is not *other* to this process; this symbolic system—of which language is one important component—is what makes the constitution of masculine and feminine subjects possible.

In recent years some researchers in the field of men's studies have moved toward a notion of masculinity as signs. This research, however, has not gone far enough: It has lacked a theoretical orientation for addressing how it is that gender differences are constituted or *realized* in our culture. Two theoretical concepts in particular are, I think, necessary to this understanding. First, *subjectivities* need to be understood as symbolic categories that emerge out of particular discourses: For example, masculinity and femininity are two subject positions made possible by the discourse of gender, and we can well imagine androgyny as another possibility. Second, *identity* should be regarded as a composite term signifying the multiple subjectivities that comprise one's sense of who one is.

The possibility of multiple subject positions enabled by different discourses means also that some subjectivities may contradict others. Moreover, because not all discourses are equal with respect to what human beings *as subjects* may have invested in them, some subject positions are more compelling than others. For example, once upon a time in our culture, the subjectivities of "mother" and "worker" were contradictory. And, arguably, the first of these subject positions, "mother," was more naturalized: That is, mother seemed the more natural symbolic ascription for women, given discourses about biological destiny, the cult of motherhood, and patriarchy. The tension between "mother" and "worker" demanded the renegotiation of women's social identity, where "renegotiation" is understood as a lopsided or asymmetric mediation between two or more unequal subject positions. One of the ways this tension has been resolved (albeit, provisionally) is through the current social identity of "the working mother."

Given the historical incommensurability of some subject positions, therefore, identity is best understood not as a product, but as a process that involves the constant negotiation and renegotiation of multiple subjectivities in which human beings have unequal investments. Identity is the feigned product of interested intersubjective mediations. The dual nature of identity—its concomitant *presentness* and *becomingness*—derives from these endless mediations and is what makes identity fluid: at once defined and redefined, at once real and (re)presented.

In contrast to many researchers in the field of men's studies, poststructuralist feminists have explicitly embraced and expanded this notion of identity. In what follows, I survey some of their work and propose a synthesis for understanding how masculinity as signs is realized. I begin by outlining a poststructuralist feminist orientation in contrast to more limited interpretive approaches, like Erving Goffman's (1979) work on gender display. This is followed by a survey of literature by feminists and feminist-influenced researchers who have adopted the orientation I outline.[2] For analytical purposes, I divide this literature into three components: psychoanalytic, textual, and Marxist-influenced. These should be regarded as ideal types inasmuch as each of these terms addresses a particular set of relations to the exclusion of other sets of relations; in practice, however, the theorists whose works I discuss under each of these categories would stress that the production of meaning in film or television is a complex process involving a combination of psychological, textual, and intersubjective relations. To better understand this complex process, I argue for an analytical approach that draws from all three of these components.

Masculinity as Signs

The approach, which I am calling *masculinity as signs*, is based on a set of related assumptions that differ significantly from those underlying traditional social science approaches. It begins with the notion that gender differences are symbolic categories for ascribing subjectivities onto human beings. When we say that someone is "masculine," we are claiming something about that human being as subject. We might also make the additional claims that "he" is "straight," "black," "upper-middle-class," "hard-working," and "a proctologist." Taken together, these subjectivities (of gender, sexual orientation, race, class, personality traits, and occupation) comprise a human being's social identity. This identity, however, is neither essential to human beings, nor given by dint of anatomical features. To push the point even further, let me note that wherever people wear clothes, what remains hidden—namely, anatomical features—is usually inferred from the information or signs we do see. These signs (e.g., style of clothing, mannerisms, and so on) are coded as either feminine or masculine, and they help to mark a human being as a gendered subject.

Second, the masculinity-as-signs approach assumes that film, television, and other media help to constitute gender difference, rather than simply reflect or represent that difference. Consequently, researchers in this area sometimes speak in terms of the *(re)presentations of gender*. This phrase parenthetically conveys the idea that gender is constructed through the media (presented) as if it were direct knowledge of real objects (as if it were representation). Direct knowledge is called into question: The subjective characteristics that we ascribe to human beings cannot help but be mediated through symbolic sign systems.

Finally, this approach rests on a relational and, hence, fluid conception of masculinity. In claiming that masculinity is constructed through sign systems, researchers in this area draw from the theoretical work of

Ferdinand de Saussure (1974), a structural linguist who argued that the meaning of a particular sign is ambiguous because meaning is the product of how a sign differs from other signs in a field. The Sausserian concept of *meaning in difference* conveys the relational character of meaning. What is rejected by this is the dogma that meaning inheres in the sign itself: A correspondence theory of language, for example, maintains that every sign refers to a particular object (its referent). Saussure's relational theory of meaning—that is, *semiotics*—denies language this simple, referential property. Theorists who adhere to a semiotic understanding of language argue that every (re)presentation is comprised of a set of relations among signs in a field. "Masculinity" becomes a meaningful category by dint of a given set of relations among signs in every (re)presentation of masculinity. Or as feminist theorist Teresa de Lauretis argues, "The construction of gender is both the product and the process of its representation" (1987, p. 5). The approach I am outlining, therefore, marks a shift from analysis of the representations of real gender differences to analysis of gender differences as (re)presentations: or to put it another way, from the *signs of masculinity* to *masculinity as signs*.

This approach has been realized only partially in men's studies research on masculinity in the media. To date, much of this work has been limited to studies of changing trends in how men are depicted in the media. Wernick (1987), for example, maintains that in the past 40 years, three significant changes in advertising have contributed to the softening of the male image (p. 280). He notes that the family has been displaced by peer groups as loci of male affiliations; masculinist conceptions of technology have given way to more feminized ones (e.g., user-friendly technology); and masculinity defined in terms of the sexual gaze has yielded somewhat to masculinity defined as object of desire. He concludes that "men, like women, are [now] encouraged to focus their energies not on realizing themselves as self-activating subjects, but on maximizing their value as tokens of exchange" (p. 295). Wernick's analysis provides an adequate description of changing mores, but falls short of an explanation of how it is that advertisements encourage men to become, in Wernick's terms, "tokens of exchange."

This essay, like many others in the men's studies field, draws from theoretical work, which, I want to argue, has limited analytical utility. Erving Goffman's (1979) analysis of gender displays in advertisements has been cited often in this field and therefore merits consideration. Goffman argues that the performance of gender in social situations is analogous to the display of gender in media texts. The *actor* or *model* who displays a particular gender is distinct from the *character* or *subject* produced by this display (p. 13). The subject is what the picture or representation is about, what is produced by the picture. According to Goffman, the gender display that an actor makes is evidence of the actor's *alignment*, which Goffman defines as "the position [the actor] seems prepared to take up in what is about to happen in a social situation" (p. 1). Read this way, then, gender displays are socially functional because they tell participants in the immediate context how an actor (a person) wishes to be identified: Information about human beings as subjects (and hence social identity) is encoded in such displays. Moreover, as particular displays become ritualized, we learn to read them as displays of, for example, masculinity.

Davies and Harré (1990) argue that Goffman's notion of alignment is limited in important ways. They maintain that while Goffman uses alignment to convey the notion that meaning is produced relationally in particular social situations, the relevant relationships, for Goffman, are between the actor's conception of himself and *his* conception of what sort of person the viewer is. Therefore, the position that the actor is prepared to take up in a given social situation (his alignment) is determined by the actor prior to the display and helps to shape that display (Davies & Harré, 1990, p. 55). For this reason, Davies and Harré read Goffman's notion of alignment as simply another version of role theory. As they point out, the concept of "role" (used particularly in sex-role studies and some content analyses) follows from the metaphorical treatment of human interaction as a "prestructured play" (p. 53). Role researchers treat individuals, in turn, as actors who learn when and where to step into the particular roles predetermined by these sociocultural plays.

In contrast to this, Davies and Harré offer the concept of "subject position," which replaces the metaphor of the prestructured play with the metaphor of an "unfolding narrative" (p. 53). This second metaphor conveys the notion that actors' alignments, or the subject positions they step into in particular social situations, "are actual relations jointly produced in the very act of conversing" (p. 55), or for that matter, in the very acts of reading or of viewing. If we are to understand how masculinity is realized, we need a theoretical orientation that addresses the very process of subject positioning. This process, as I have already suggested, involves three significant sets of relations. In the next section, I discuss the first of these.

Psychological Relations and Cinematic Address

Laura Mulvey's (1975) "Visual Pleasure and Narrative Cinema" is a well known work in the area of feminist psychoanalytic film studies. Drawing from Freudian theory, Mulvey attempts to explain how it is that the spectator's subjectivity is constructed through processes of visual pleasure at work in mainstream films. Her focus is intentional: Part of Mulvey's argument is that mainstream films adhere to a particular narrative structure of relationships. Her aim is to deconstruct these relationships and show how classical narrative cinema, to use Althusser's (1971) terms, *hails* or *interpellates* spectators into a "masculine" subject position.[3]

Mulvey argues that the sequence of "looks" in classical narrative cinema—that is, that the spectator looks, the camera looks, the male character looks, and the female character *is looked at*—sets into motion a series of unconscious psychological mechanisms that constitute the film spectator as a gendered subject. The spectator sees through the eye of the camera, which in turn sees through the eye/I of the character who activates the look. According to Mulvey, the character possessing the look in classical narrative cinema is almost always marked as male. The masculine subject emerges through two primary processes working in tandem: narcissistic *identification* with male characters and *objectification* of female characters. These processes transform "the look" into a sexual "gaze." The female object of the gaze, according to Mulvey, calls forth both feelings of desire and memories of the primal scene that opens the Oedipal drama. In her sexual difference, her lack of a penis, the woman created in the film text becomes a reminder of what may happen to the male: She signifies the threat of castration.

Mulvey argues that the male unconscious seeks two forms of *scopophilia* (visual pleasure), which work to lessen the displeasure associated with castration anxiety. *Voyeurism*, the first of these forms, involves a process whereby the object of the gaze is made responsible for the viewer's anxiety. The voyeuristic gaze, therefore, is controlling, for it seeks to exercise power over its object by marking "her" as "the bearer of guilt" (Mulvey, 1975, p. 11); and the gaze is sadistic, insofar as it also marks the object as punishable. For Mulvey, this process is typified by the devaluation, punishment, or salvation that follows from the treatment of the female image as guilty in, for example, film noire. *Fetishism,* the second form of visual pleasure, involves the disavowal of the castration threat through the adoption of a fetish object (a fragment of the female image or the entire image as spectacle) to stand in for the penis. Rather than controlling and wanting to punish the female object of desire, the fetishist raises the object of desire to the level of spectacle. According to Mulvey, fetishism leads to the over-valuation of the female image, as typified in the cult of the female movie star (pp. 13-14).

Others have extended Mulvey's thesis by looking at what happens when a male character is made the object of desire (e.g., Flitterman, 1985). Neale (1982, 1983) raises this issue from the standpoint of spectators who identify themselves as masculine and argues that objectification of the male image elicits homoerotic desire. Hence, the male object of desire is as disruptive to self-identified male spectators as is the image of woman. Neale concludes that patriarchy depends not only on the repression of woman "to give order and meaning to the world" (Mulvey, 1975, p. 6), but also on the repression of homosexual desire. This argument suggests that the dominant address of classical narrative cinema is not only masculine (to reiterate Mulvey's point) but also heterosexual.

Green (1984) challenges Neale's argument. He suggests that some narrative structures, like melodrama, may open up spaces for other forms of identification: for example, with female characters. In narratives where self-identified male spectators are encouraged to identify with female characters and to objectify male characters, the homosexual threat need not surface. What Green denies, in other words, is Mulvey's and Neale's contention that spectators are always forced into a masculine subject position. In this sense, Green moves closer to a poststructuralist orientation. He avows the possibility of multiple forms of address and the concomitant multiple subject positions into which spectators are hailed.

Rodowick (1982) pushes the notion of multiple subject positions still further by suggesting that Mulvey fails to acknowledge a second possibility evident in her own analysis. Rodowick returns to Freud's work to reveal that:

> [T]he structure of vision which is the foundation of pleasure in looking contains both active and passive components. This structure is maintained not only in the *act* of the look, but also in the *return* of the look from the imaginary other in which that vision is verified. (1982, p. 7, his emphasis)

Rodowick then shows how Mulvey's analysis sidesteps further discussion of this second component of the look. As I noted above, Mulvey associates voyeurism with mastery or control of the female object: The aim is to exercise power over the object of the gaze by marking her as punishable. Hence, voyeurism is active and sadistic. But what Mulvey fails to mention, according to Rodowick, is that fetishism is a phenomenon that Freud would regard "as passive submission to the object: in sum, *masochism*" (p. 7, Rodowick's emphasis).

The displacement of voyeurism with masochism marks an important shift toward a poststructuralist orientation in psychoanalytic film theory. The concept of voyeurism links male desire with sadism, and male subjectivity with masculinity. Masochism, on the other hand, uncouples the male from both sadism and masculinity. This uncoupling signals a shift from the notion that identity is relatively fixed to the idea that identity is fluid precisely because it is a process involving multiple subject positionings.

Psychoanalytic film theory, however, does not go far enough; it still explains the construction of subjectivity solely in terms of a process of interpellation. Cinematic address alone, however, cannot account for this construction. The possibility for intervention by the spectator must remain open; that is, we need a theoretical orientation that can account for the ways in which spectators may consciously resist the dominant cinematic address. Without the possibility for intervention, projects like Mulvey's become untenable, for how could she account her reading of classical narratives against the grain, as it were? This is the issue I turn to in the next section.

Textual Relations and Decoding

Researchers influenced by Roland Barthes' work on codes focus on the process of reading or decoding a text. According to O'Sullivan, Hartley, Saunders, and Fiske (1983), a textual code "is a system of signs governed by rules agreed (explicitly or implicitly) between members of the using culture" (p. 36). The rules that readers/viewers learn help them to attribute particular meanings to signs given the relationships between signs in a text. In his early work Barthes (1972) focuses on *cultural codes*, which he describes as dominant or conventional ways of reading the signs in a text. But because several different codes may come into play in the process of reading a text, Barthes (1974, 1975) later identifies a more active role for the reader. He suggests that the act of reading can involve an interpretive strategy that transforms the text or (re)writes it. Readers have a number of options for reading texts: They may adopt conventional or dominant codes, negotiated codes, or oppositional codes (Hall, 1980) in the process of reading, thereby producing a multiplicity of possible meanings. Reading, therefore, is a "writerly" process (Barthes, 1974) because it can involve the production of plural texts, with different meanings. In this sense, then, shared meanings are possible only because of conventionalized ways of reading.

In their analysis of the James Bond image, Bennett and Woollacott (1987) use the term *reading competence* to describe the kind of learning that makes it possible for readers and viewers of Bond novels and films to "read" this image in a particular way. They argue that female spectators who have become familiar with the particular conventions of the romance novel will bring that competence to bear in their viewing of a Bond film. What emerges from this is a reading of the masculine image (Bond) as both desirable (i.e., the "romance hero" who holds out the promise of love) and unattainable (i.e., not the marrying kind, given his "'liberated' male sexuality" [1987, p. 228]). This way of reading may, of course, conform with the dominant mode in which female spectators are addressed by Bond films (to reiterate the psychoanalytic argument), but the crucial point here is that a spectator's willingness to step into a privileged subject position is at least in part dependent upon her way of reading. As Bennett and Woollacott's notion of reading competence makes clear, the way a reader decodes a text will contribute to the meanings of gender ascribed to particular images.

In her analysis of *Miami Vice*, Schwichtenberg (1986) examines the processes of decoding that may be used to read less conventional male images. Drawing from the work of postmodern theorist Jean Baudrillard, Schwichtenberg argues that Don Johnson's body functions as a "cipher of style" (p. 58). A cipher can be a kind of writing, or it can be a numerical figure for zero or nothing. Schwichtenberg uses the term in both these senses to mean an empty sign with no substance or physical-world referent: a "cool, transparent product of simulation" (p. 58). In this analysis, Schwichtenberg moves away from the semiotic focus on coded oppositions, which help to anchor otherwise floating signs and make them referential by dint of their relation to other signs in a *relatively* closed field. In contrast to this notion of anchoring, Schwichtenberg suggests that the Johnson/Crockett image, particularly in stylized music-video segments, is disengaged from conventional coded oppositions, making the image more ambiguous. These music-video stylizations, however, do provide viewers with cues about how to read nonconventional images. Schwichtberg suggests that the image of the male figure in motion is combined with music and rhythm to provide a "sensualization of movement (in dancing, walking, driving) linked to a romanticized notion of male freedom of movement within the public domain" (p. 63). In the absence of conventional codes, therefore, viewers may turn to other stylized modes of reading; in the process, however, the non-fixity of signs may be foregrounded.

In a similar vein, Willis (1989) analyzes the images of masculinity constructed against the postmodern urban backdrop in the film, *To Live and Die in L.A.* Willis argues that the film's endless circulation in and among a variety of stylish spaces makes identification difficult for the spectator. The construction of relatively fixed identities depends on spatial and temporal continuity: Classical cinematic codes like the 180 degree rule provide this continuity. By pinning down a "space" within the narrative structure that provides a point of reference or signposts for the spectator, conventional codes limit the number of possible relationships between signs, making them at least provisionally referential (meaningful). In other words, conventional codes provide a medium for linking dominant forms of address with how spectators read/view a film, which in turn makes it possible for spectators to step into particular subject positions. Excesses of spatial cues, however, confound the spectator by providing too many, and perhaps contradictory, signposts. One sign refers to another, which refers to another in an endless circulation of meanings; the end or relative fixity of the referential act is not supplied here. In films like *To Live and Die in L.A.*, therefore, masculinity as signs reveals itself as all-style-and-no-substance, forcing the spectator either to ignore some of the cues provided or to accept the notion that identity is an "unworkable fiction."[4]

The semiotic literature on textual relations and processes of decoding provides us with a framework for thinking about how readers might use codes and, perhaps, resist dominant modes of address.[5] In the absence of an understanding of what it is that makes resistance and intervention possible, however, the semiotic literature suggests that "reading otherwise" is always a conscious option, a fundamental property of readers and viewers. While I do not necessarily want to deny this, I want to suggest a framework for understanding why and when some readers may decode texts differently. And for this, we need a way of understanding how readers and viewers are constructed *before*, and not just during, the process of decoding.

Spectators already have identities (albeit, tenuous ones) before coming to a film: They are already marked as particular kinds of subjects (e.g., masculine, white, heterosexual, Anglo-Saxon, and so on). In order to think about how masculinity as signs is realized in, for example, the process of viewing a film, we need an orientation that focuses on how it is that our prior experiences with and investments in multiple subject positions mediate our understandings of particular subjectivities like masculinity. Experience informs and also limits understanding. In the next section, I focus on this process of mediation among multiple subjectivities.

Intersubjective Relations and Investments

Researchers influenced by Marxist theory combine a focus on systems of cultural production and consumption with an understanding of social identity. This focus provides a corrective for what some theorists regard as serious omissions in exclusively psychoanalytic and textual analyses. Gaines (1986), for example, notes that the increasing focus on the structured text provided by psychoanalytic approaches in feminist film theory has signaled a movement away from social, historical, and, of course, economic questions about the conditions of textual production and reception, as well as questions about concrete readers (e.g., their sex, their socioeconomic status, their sexual orientation, and so on). Gaines suggests that Marxist approaches can help address these limitations in significant ways.

This is not to suggest that Marxist contributions to the study of masculinity as signs amounts to the simple addition of class and race to a mixture of approaches. Inasmuch as orthodox Marxism relegates culture to the realm of the epiphenomenal and regards the economic base as determinant, it provides no language, as it were, for talking about the sociocultural construction of gender. Clearly, some reformulation of key concepts has been needed in order to apply Marxist concerns to questions about sociocultural constructions. Such reformulations have been provided by Gramsci and Althusser. (I have already suggested ways in which Althusser's notion of interpellation has contributed to analyses of masculinity.) The Gramscian notion of hegemony has been adopted and expanded by men's studies researchers interested in investigating the ways in which particular realizations of masculinity have remained dominant. This has led to the study of "hegemonic masculinity"

(Carrigan, Connell, & Lee, 1987), and to analyses of how this operates in popular television programs.

In his analysis of *thirtysomething*, for example, Hanke (1990) suggests that what is unique about this show is that it purportedly gives a progressive image of masculinity, in contrast to the macho male image presented in many action/adventure or law enforcement series. Male characters in *thirtysomething* are coded with traditionally feminine characteristics, such as being more open to domestic concerns and interpersonal relations. Yet Hanke warns that such new images should not be taken as evidence of the displacement of dominant discourses about gender. Rather, they can be seen as representing an attempt to modify elements within the discourse of hegemonic masculinity without explicitly addressing questions of power, other gender inequalities, and capitalist work relations also enabled, in part, by that discourse. These modifications in various aspects of hegemonic masculinity work to recuperate it by making it more adaptable to contemporary social conditions and more able to accommodate counterhegemonic discourses, such as feminist and gay/lesbian positions.

As Hanke himself points out, however, his analysis is a "tentative step toward understanding the process of hegemonic masculinity" (1990, p. 245). He notes that:

> These social definitions of masculinity may be activated, resisted, or ignored by some viewers and not others; different strategies of representational practice may articulate [link] in different ways to historically specific "subject" positions, social identities, or social formations. (1990, p. 245)

I have already suggested two processes—address and decoding—for understanding how representational practices are linked, at the microlevel, to subject positions, and hence how these practices become realized. I want to suggest a third process that might help us understand what Hanke points out but does not really explain—namely, why some viewers and not others activate, resist, or ignore particular social definitions of masculinity. This third process involves the interested negotiation between multiple subject positions. Furthermore, this negotiation is interested because of the unequal discursive *investments* that human beings have in different subject positions.

In her discussion of Wendy Hollway's concept of *investments*, De Lauretis (1987) attempts to chart a theoretical space for understanding how human beings mediate contradictory and unequal subject positions. According to De Lauretis:

> [W]hat makes one take up a [subject] position in a certain discourse rather than another is an "investment" . . . something between an emotional commitment and a vested interest, in the relative power (satisfaction, reward, payoff) which that position promises (but does not necessarily fulfill). (1987, p. 16)

Investment in a particular discourse implies also investment in a particular way of reading and understanding the things we experience. Consequently, our investments may militate against our being subjectified by a dominant mode of textual address, but they also limit the number of ways in which we can read a text. Investments in multiple subject positions can, I think, help us understand how it is that new understandings of gender are realized—-or else resisted. For example, the concomitant investments that women have had in the subject positions of "mother" and "worker" can help to explain the emergence of "the working mother" as a new social identity available to women; this development has required some modifications in dominant discourses on, for example, motherhood.

A number of recent Marxist-influenced studies of masculinity have attempted to wrestle with the notion that multiple subjectivities and our differential investments in them mediate our understandings of gender. The essays collected in the British anthology, *Male Order: Unwrapping Masculinity* (Chapman and Rutherford, 1988), reflect this concern. In Mercer and Julien (1988), for example, the authors examine Robert Mapplethorpe's photographs of black male nudes and provide the three-dimensional analysis I have been proposing here. Drawing from Mulvey's work, they argue that the potential homosexual disruption caused by the male spectator's looking at his *sameness*, as embodied in the image of another male, is avoided through a discourse of racial *difference*. In their concern with racist codes, they move beyond Mulvey's framework and suggest that these photographs hail the white spectator as scrutinizer, and code the black male image as the object of scrutiny, rather than the object of desire.

In addition to these concerns with psychoanalytic and textual relations, however, Mercer and Julien mention, as well, their own ambivalence as black, gay men who find themselves wanting to look at these images, despite the racist coding (p. 152). In this way, then, they implicitly point to a set of contradictions that emerges out of their multiple subject positionings: As "blacks," they perhaps do not want to look; as "men," they perhaps should not want to look; and perhaps it is as "gay men" that they find themselves wanting to look. Given their own ambivalence, Mercer and Julien argue that, "we need to re-think how boundaries of race, class, gender and sexuality are constantly crossed and negotiated in the commonplace cultural construction of one's social identity" (1988, p. 101).

This need is especially acute in the study of pornography. Here, a number of issues have surfaced in ways that have, I think, obscured rather than clarified our understanding of the construction of identity. One key issue in the pornography debate involves the extent to which pornography is about gender. Intellectuals on all sides of the debate accept the notion that pornography involves the explicit depiction of various kinds of sexual practices (though clearly there is considerable debate about which sexual practices get to count as pornography). Those who argue that pornography is also about gender make the additional claim that sexuality and gender are interdependent symbolic categories. Radical anti-porn feminists, for example, argue that masculinity is defined by the male sexual desire to possess women (Dworkin, 1981). Pornography, in turn, is what makes this equation between sex and gender possible:

> [T]he sexualized subordination of women to men *is* the sex-gender system. In a dual motion, gender becomes sexual as sexuality is gendered, and pornography is central to the process through which this occurs. (MacKinnon, 1987, p. 81.)

Because of the many ways in which pornography constructs "male" sexuality as the active, controlling, and powerful penetration of "female" sexual objects who "ask for it," pornography, according to this view, evinces particular, sexualized notions of masculinity and femininity.

Furthermore, MacKinnon dismisses the idea that lesbian sexuality "solves" the problem of gendered sexuality:

> Unaddressed [in this notion that lesbian sexuality liberates women from gender inequality] is whether sexuality is so gendermarked as to carry dominance and submission with it regardless of the gender of the immediate participants. I tend to think so. (1987, p. 68)

The problem with MacKinnon's position is that it makes gender and sexuality virtually synonymous symbolic categories and hence, indistinct subject positionings. This denies the possibility that contradictions may emerge between gender and sexuality. The case of lesbian sadomasochism is, perhaps, the most obvious example of what MacKinnon might regard as "gendermarked" lesbian sexuality, for clearly, patterns of dominance and submission are involved. But even this obvious case raises serious doubts about MacKinnon's notion of gendermarking. In lesbian and gay subcultures, "gender bending" practices like "camp" serve an important social and political function: Lesbians and gay men engage in and interpret these practices as modes of resistance against dominant conceptions of masculinity and femininity. Rejecting lesbian sadomasochism as gendermarked ignores the important ways in which even lesbian sadomasochists resist being subjectified as masculine or feminine and engage in gender-bending practices that call these very categories into question. Whatever the patterned "similarities" between the sexuality of lesbian sadomasochists and the dominant mode of (hetero) sexuality depicted in pornography, "lesbian sadomasochists" constitute a significantly different social identity with demonstrably little investment in dominant discourses of gender and (hetero)sexuality.

Although gender and sexuality may operate in tandem to constitute the social identities of some human beings in noncontradictory ways (as MacKinnon maintains), other human beings clearly experience these subject positionings in conflicting ways. From a poststructuralist perspective, therefore, gender and sexuality must remain analytically distinct categories precisely because they constitute distinct (and at times contradictory) subject positions. Does this mean, then, that pornography involves only issues of sexuality? The answer, I think, is clearly no; pornography does involve (re)presentations of "masculinity" and "femininity." The point is that we cannot reject these (re)presentations, as radical feminists do, without first considering the issues of address, decoding, and intersubjective mediations that make these (re)presentations real. What is needed, in other words, is a focus on the actual process of reception.

Kuhn (1985) suggests that the spectators of pornographic films may engage in two possible modes of reception. By focusing exclusively on issues of textual address, however, Kuhn does not really provide an analysis of the actual process of reception. Instead she argues that in the viewing of "soft-core pornography," so defined by dint of the fact that the images are primarily female, the spectator is constructed as voyeur, who engages solely in the process of objectifying the female images. In contrast to this, "hard-core pornography" involves the depiction of male genitalia and hence, the presence of male characters. Following Mulvey, Kuhn suggests that the presence of male characters in hard-core pornography facilitates identification on the part of male spectators. On the basis of this, Kuhn links the structure of hard-core pornography with a process of reception that involves the constitution of masculinity and male sexuality through a process of spectator identification.

Smith (1988), on the other hand, maintains that pornography constantly transgresses the realist conventions on which arguments about spectator identification are based. Hence, for him, pornography may promote "exactly an instability of identificatory positioning in the male spectator" (p. 106). Smith argues, moreover, that the meaning of pornography is mediated through the lived experiences of male viewers. While he does not deny the radical feminist conviction that pornography gives *some* men what they want, Smith wants us to entertain the possibility that other male viewers may register a discrepancy between pornographic fantasies and their own lived experiences. He suggests, in other words, that other men may view pornography as "affectively and effectively addressing the boundaries and limitations of the male body and extending and complicating the peremptory simplicity of male sexual experience" (p. 108).

Like Smith, Ross (1989) argues that the pornographic text is open to other possible modes of reception. Because spectators can and probably do fantasize while viewing pornography, they can produce meanings different from the ones that radical feminists attribute to pornography. Ross does not attempt to outline what those meanings might be. Instead, he calls for ethnographic studies of the ways in which consumers use pornography.

Conclusion

The literature on pornography, in particular, points to the need for research on the actual process of reception. This complex process, I have argued, involves modes of textual address, strategies of decoding, and intersubjective mediations. By focusing on the symbolic character of subjectivities and the multiplicity of social identities, a poststructuralist feminist orientation can, I think, help us unravel and understand this complex process.

In proposing this orientation for studies of masculinity as signs, I have proceeded on the premise that feminist studies and men's studies share a similar concern: namely, to understand how it is that some notions of gender, and not others, gain acceptance in a given culture and become real. The task remaining for future scholars is to incorporate the insights yielded by both feminist and men's studies in order to reveal alternative possibilities for the construction of masculinities not yet realized.

Notes

1. I would like to thank Jacquelyn Zita, David Sylvan, Jennifer Milliken, Fred Fejes, and Lisa Disch for their comments on drafts of this chapter.

2. For a more comprehensive survey of feminist media research (primarily on women in the media) see Steeves (1987).

3. Althusser (1971) uses these terms to talk about the ways in which ideological apparatuses hail persons into certain subject positions: for example, the "Hey, you there!" of the policeman constitutes the person addressed as a particular kind of subject (a "suspect," perhaps) within a particular structure of authority.

4. In his analysis of the multiple roles that Jerry Lewis plays in, for example, *The Nutty Professor*, Bukatman (1988) argues, "The multiplicity of identities in the world of Jerry Lewis belies the existence of identity as anything other than a necessary but unworkable fiction" (p. 203). For a psychoanalytic treatment of this, see Silverman (1989), in which she draws from Lacanian theory to analyze the impossibility of identification in the films of Rainer Werner Fassbinder.

5. As a method of textual analysis, semiotics can tell us only how readers might use codes. This is inferred from the relative openness or closure of a given text. Fiske (1987a), for example, argues that "masculine" television texts like *The A-Team* are less open to multiple readings than "feminine" television texts, which are more open and ambiguous. To find out how readers actually do read certain texts, however, researchers would have to conduct ethnographic analyses like the one undertaken by Radway (1984). Unfortunately, very little work of this kind has been done in studies of masculinity.

4

Metal Men and Glamour Boys

Gender Performance in Heavy Metal

STAN DENSKI
DAVID SHOLLE

Introduction

The focus of this chapter is directed at linking together some recent questions caught up in three rather broad areas of overlapping concern. First, within the literature of *gender studies* (incorporating within its concerns those of an emerging literature of men's studies), recent questions have been directed at the performative character of gender. This position suggests that gender differences may be better understood in terms of culturally transmitted codes of performances than in the more traditional terms of fixed gender identities rooted in nature and biology.

Second, within the literature of *cultural studies*, recent questions have been directed at the development of new theories of the audience, and the complex relationship of the active media consumer to the dominant forms of popular entertainment media in the United States. In a movement away from more deterministic models in which the various mass media represent a "consciousness industry" exerting powerful influence over the thoughts, values, and desires of a faceless and passive mass mass audience, some contemporary cultural theorists (e.g., Fiske, 1987a,

AUTHORS' NOTE: The authors would like to express their thanks to Steve Craig, University of Maine, Orono, and Lisa McLaughlin, University of Kentucky, Lexington, for their help and insights in the completion of this manuscript.

Radway, 1986) have begun to focus attention upon the idea that some of the intersections between audiences and the various popular media may represent sites of resistance. While dominant cultural values may be woven into the fabric of popular entertainment media (e.g., romance novels, situation comedies, pop music, and so on), these scholars argue that some audience members read these media texts "against the grain," such that these readings become sites of struggle with (or resistance to) the dominant power relations of gender, race, and social class. This notion of resistance continues, however, to generate considerable controversy (Sholle, 1990). Some scholars argue that, while the audience may be considerably more active than earlier critical approaches allowed, the oppositional potential of popular media may be significantly overestimated in these recent reformulations.

Third, within the literature of *popular music and communication studies*, recent questions have arisen over the increasing fragmentation within the genres of contemporary popular music. While from the mid-1950s through the mid-1960s contemporary popular music was characterized by a certain homogeneous quality, from the late 1960s through today the number of distinct and identifiable styles, genres, and subgenres has, in effect, exploded. Evidence of this can be found in the changes in contemporary radio formatting, the evolution of music video, the increasing complexity of categories present in the average music store, and recent empirical research into the diversification of popular music and the popular music audience (e.g., Christenson & Peterson, 1988; Denski, 1990).

In this chapter we hope to link together these broad and diverse concerns in an analysis of the representation of masculinity in contemporary heavy metal music. Using a performative theory of gender as a framework, we will examine the constructions and representations of masculinity at work in the subgenre of heavy metal known as "glam metal." Within this framework, we will also reconsider the questions caught up in the reading of glam metal performance as either an embodiment of dominant values, or a site of resistance to the dominant gender relations of contemporary culture.

Heavy Metal

Efforts toward locating the origins of any musical form will unavoidably involve a rich blend of ambiguity and uncertainty; history, in other words, always blurs at the edges. Locating the origins of contemporary heavy metal is no different. In general, we would point to the hard rock styles of bands like The Who; blues-based rock bands like The Rolling Stones; volume- and performance-based psychedelic bands like Cream and The Jimi Hendrix Experience; and the hard-rock-influenced Southern rock sounds of bands like The Allman Brothers, throughout the middle and late 1960s, and, perhaps, culminating with the appearance of Led Zeppelin, the most popular and influential hard rock band of the 1970s. Hibbard and Kaleialoha (1983) describe Led Zeppelin as the primary inspiration for a new style of 1970s hard rock (epitomized in the music of bands like Aerosmith, Alice Cooper, Foreigner, Journey, Thin Lizzie, Heart, and others), and place heavy metal as a genre within this particular stylistic locale.

Heavy metal, as a distinct genre, may be differentiated from its origins in the more general style of hard rock by an emphasis upon four- and eight-bar phrases rather than blues or pop structures. For example, groups like Black Sabbath, Uriah Heep, Judas Priest, AC/DC, The Scorpions, and Iron Maiden differ from their hard rock counterparts in their use of simplistic "very rudimentary harmonies and melodies [and] through the endless repetition of simple chords with extremely short progressions" (1983, p. 113). Throughout the middle- and late-1980s, heavy metal underwent intra-generic transformations, splintering into a variety of subgenres, in some cases openly hostile to one another. The influence of the punk rock movement of the late seventies resulted in the emergence of a genre described by its listeners as "speed metal" or "thrash metal." Characterized by high volume, the absence of ballads, a decrease in the presence of a blues-based influence, and very fast and often intricate rhythms, bands like Metallica and Megadeath eschew the theatrical complexities of costume and stage props associated with other metal varieties. The fans of "speed/thrash" metal define their terrain, in part, through their openly hostile attitude the genre of "pop" or "glam" metal (exemplified by bands like Bon Jovi and Poison).

Where speed/thrash is influenced by punk, "glam metal" bears the influences of the glitter rock movement of the 1970s and performers like the New York Dolls and early David Bowie. Characterized by an elaborate emphasis upon theatrics, expansive staging, and costume, glam seems to, in its preference for slower, more ballad-like composition (for example, Poison's "Every Rose Has Its Thorn"), attracted a wider and more gender-mixed audience. In doing so, the popularity of heavy metal in terms of album sales, and an increased acceptance by radio and music television, has reached record highs, and, ironically, threatened its hard-core base of followers. The marginality of heavy metal and its audience, the lack of acceptance by the popular music mainstream throughout its development and emergence as a distinct genre, created a cult-like status that its fans could participate in and take pleasure in. An increased popularity and wider acceptance of pop and glam metal forms undermines a key use of the music in the establishment of difference and identity in many of its adolescent male fans. The cult-like status of contemporary speed or thrash metal bands like Slayer or Anthrax (and the resultant further delineation of heavy metal into these intra-generic forms) may represent one response to this development.

Until this intra-generic fragmentation of the 1980s, heavy metal enjoyed a certain marginal status in contrast to its mainstream pop music counterparts. Characterized by a general lack of interest on the part of pop radio programmers and a near blanket critical dismissal, this marginality could be understood as partially the result of its almost exclusively white male audience. While gender preferences continue to be exhibited in recent studies (e.g., Christenson & Peterson, 1988; Denski, 1990), there is growing evidence in the results of radio station call-out research (in which potential listeners are played fragments of records over the phone and asked to rate their listenability) to suggest a significant change in the preference of female listeners toward hard-rock and heavy metal genres. For example, under the headline "Fems Take to Hard Rock" in the October 8, 1988, issue of *Billboard* magazine, various call-out research attributes a flourishing of hard-rock and heavy metal acts in the Top 40 to a growing female audience, a phenomenon that has continued into the 1990s.

Heavy metal is often cited as the most straightforwardly coded example of masculine, macho posing in rock 'n' roll (thus the genre of "cockrock"). Yet heavy metal style is, at the same time, increasingly blurred. Heavily marked with feminine elements, glam metal in particular is increasingly attracting a female audience through its emphasis on more nurturing and romantic themes in the context of ballad-like composition and performance. This makes heavy metal an interesting, contradictory phenomenon in terms of its representation of masculinity, and it allows us to examine a number of multilayered relationships in popular culture's play with gender identity.

Throughout the development of heavy metal a distinctive aspect of its internal subculture of followers has been the different expectations that exist for male and female fans. In a recent participant observation study Friesen (1989) observed that males and females conform to a variety of social expectations in order to maintain peer acceptance. Failure to conform to these expectations resulted in a range of sanctions from ridicule to ostracism. The expectations for males, for the most part, represented the conformance to extremely rigid roles:

> Males were expected to emulate certain characteristics (e.g., aggressiveness, independence) in their image, demeanor and argot, and were also expected to practice behaviors that would disassociate themselves from anything feminine. Females, on the other hand, were allowed the option at times to display certain male qualities in addition to female characteristics. (1989, p. 8)

Heavy metal (as music and as cultural style) has undergone various changes. The music and the fans have splintered into subgroups, often around some notion of which "metal" is "really metal." Some fans argue that the music itself has progressed and is capable of making "important" statements (the political themes in the recent music of bands like Metallica and Megadeath are frequently cited as examples). But, nevertheless, a general heavy metal style can be discussed at the level of American mass media audiences. For our purposes, "heavy metal" will be applied to performers who proclaim themselves to be heavy metal and who generally fit into the genres of hard rock or glam metal. The discussion focuses on the situation in the United States, where the issue of working-class identity is of minimal importance for heavy metal fandom. Additionally, through all of this runs further disruptions and tensions across the terrain of masculinity and gender identity. It is to these tensions that the analysis now turns.

Masculinity and the Performance of Gender

On the back cover of Hurricane's "Slave to the Thrill" (an album whose front cover features a naked woman strapped into a frightening-looking machine), the band members appear with teased hair, exposed belly buttons, low-slung pants, and jewelry—various stylistic marks that many rock critics and fans interpret as feminine. This example points to a number of contradictions in the representations of sexual identity that surface in heavy metal style. While male band members take up styles that imply female or homosexual identity, they are identified by most audiences as masculine/macho. What is at question here is the supposed "maleness" of rock 'n' roll and the manner in which it constructs gender, both for its performers and for its audiences. Our primary concern is with the question of what it is that constitutes sexual identity. This is particularly significant for the examination of the performative character of heavy metal: How is it that an adolescent heterosexual male audience identifies with performers who appear to take up the stylistic marks of the feminine? How is that young heterosexual female audiences fantasize over aggressive males in feminine clothes?

If we try to answer these questions by assuming a stable notion of gender (one that remains unchanged throughout history), we are inevitably led to some attempt to read the expression of sex embodied in gender. We will argue that the idea of gender should not be conceived of merely as the cultural inscription of meaning on a pregiven sex. Rather, notions of gender must also take into account the very apparatus of production through which the sexes themselves are established (Butler, 1990).

Until recently the study of gender has employed a sex-role model that has been the target of increasing theoretical criticism for its ahistorical, psychologistic/reductionistic, and apolitical character. Michael Kimmel (1987d) argues that this sex-role paradigm offers very little in the way of theoretical usefulness, reducing gender to an ahistorical static sex-role container into which all biological males and females are forced to fit. The process through which we are fitted into these invariant preexisting roles is also undertheorized as simple "socialization." In all of this what is ignored is the extent to which our conceptualizations of masculine and feminine are relational; that is, the product of gender relations that are historically, culturally, and socially conditioned and constructed. Kimmel argues that:

> Masculinity and femininity are relational constructs, the definition of either depends upon the definition of the other. Although "male" and "female" may have some universal characteristics (and even here the research on biological dimorphism suggests a certain fluidity), one cannot understand the social construction of either masculinity or femininity without reference to the other. (1987d, p. 12)

Looking at heavy metal's taking up of various styles as expressive of an underlying male/female sex, or expressive of an underlying interpretation of sex, leads to two opposed viewpoints. On one hand, we might approach heavy metal as straightforwardly misogynist by simply reading off its surface images and statements. While, on the other hand, we might consider heavy metal (glam metal in particular) as expressive of a resistant parody of straight heterosexuality. Both views, however, simplify the phenomenon in that each assumes an essential truth to sex. Butler (1990) contends that this view is rooted in a *metaphysics of substance*; that is, in taking up either approach, it is assumed that there is, at the center of notions of sexuality/gender, some abiding substance that establishes the self as either man or woman. Instead, the "meaning" of sex must be seen as a form of signification arising from extended social performance.

In this sense then, the body is not "sexed"" in any significant sense prior to its determination within a discourse through which it becomes invested with an "idea" of natural or essential sex (however, it is clear that such a "unity" is in some sense desired in contemporary society). Within a cultural context then, the foremost function of the body is as a signifier of sexual difference. It is in this sense that sexual difference itself is never understandable just as a biological state. Rather, it is a *historically grounded complex ideological terrain* across which are gathered a range of meanings directed toward notions of biological sex, social gender, gender identity, and sexual objectification.

It is the treatment of this heterogeneous set of constructs as an unproblematic and unitary aspect of human subjectivity that results in the identification of each human being as either male or female. Acts, gestures, and desires produce the effect of an internal core or substance, but these are produced on the surface of the body. Such acts are performative; that is, what we read as gender is constructed through a performance that is repeated. Since the reality of gender is created through sustained social performances, the suggestion is that the idea of a true or essential masculinity or femininity is an illusion.

This approach to notions of the body and sexuality, as developed in the work of Butler (1990) and Kuhn (1989), is indebted to the work of French critical theorist, Michel Foucault (1980). Foucault argues that sexuality is not a fixed, natural fact, but is better understood as the "set of effects produced in bodies, behaviors, and social relations by a certain deployment deriving from a complex political technology" (1980, p. 127). This complex cultural apparatus of sexuality results in the production of the binaries of gender and sexual difference as seemingly normal or natural categories. The representations of sexuality within heavy metal will be examined, using this notion of *gender as performance*.

Heavy Metal: Style and Image

As heavy metal has evolved, the music itself has become expressive of an aggressive sexual prowess (Chambers, 1985). This is most evident in the cult of the guitar hero, where technical mastery of the instrument in conjunction with intense volume create a close link between the performer and the (male) audience. The technological power used and represented in heavy metal is one of the primary ways in which the male audience identifies with the masculine pose of the band. The improvisatory pretensions of the heavy metal musician are read as direct signs of mastery and aggressive "attack." As Klaus Meine of The Scorpions describes it: "This music is not played from the head, it's played from here (touches his heart) and here (ditto his groin)" (Drozdowski, 1990, p. 49).

The technological power of heavy metal slides easily into sexual power via a physical mastery of machine by man and the deployment of machine against women. The traditional male dominance of the heavy metal audience may be partly due to this emphasis on technical prowess (especially the guitar solo). Young males identify strongly with the *producerly* role in music as evidenced in concert settings where the audience participate as "air" guitarists, playing imaginary guitar runs in homage to their alter egos performing on the stage. The amplitude of the music and its sheer noise level enhance the connective link between the hero/performer and the imitative fans (Reist & Casey, 1989).

In keeping with these themes of futuristic machines and the warrior hero, heavy metal has acquired curious connections to a variety of visual images and narrative (particularly those associated with heroic sci-fi genres). An entire undercurrent of publication and artistic design has sprung up around these images. Examples can be found in the comic book *Heavy Metal*, heavy metal fanzines, iconography on clothing and tattoos on the body, and in the design of pinball machines, video games, and so on. Within heavy metal it is the heroic and masculine features of science fiction that are emphasized, and, along with this worship of the warrior/hero, technology again is emphasized in the form of machines of great power and destruction. The animated film *Heavy Metal* provides interesting examples of this machine-dominated world. The vignettes that compose the film all rely on young or weak males taking up or conquering machines on their way to sexual initiation with large-breasted women.

These themes are particularly foregrounded in a "Heavy Metal Special Issue" of *Musician* magazine (No. 71, September 1984), the cover of which features Rob Halford, lead singer for Judas Priest, in which his arm is replaced with the massive green illustrated arm of Marvel comic's Incredible Hulk. In the same issue, Bill Flanagan, with tongue planted partially in cheek, asks: "Why do adolescent boys like heavy metal music so much? Wrong. It has nothing to do with sexual frustration or adolescent rebellion, tendencies toward vandalism or the desire to show off. It has to do with comic books" (p. 58). Borrowing primarily from the Marvel inventory, Flanagan provides a list of comparisons that includes: David Bowie as Chameleon Boy; Elvis Costello as Clark Kent; Marshall Crenshaw as Peter Parker; Ozzy Osbourne as the Hulk; Ted Nugent as Wolverine; Joan Jett as Wonder Woman; Dave Lee Roth as Conan; Meat Loaf as The Thing; and Cheap Trick as The Archies. More recently, connections drawn between heavy metal, comic and sci-fi characters, and the spectacle of professional wrestling are suggestive of the collapse of categories and play of signification, the pastiches and bricolage of postmodern popular culture.

Machines of power and desire function as pivotal images in heavy metal performance and iconography, from hot rods and Hogs to cyborgs and robotic dozers. The *power of the machine* and the *power of the hero* are present in the production of the music itself. The heavy metal sound actually requires little in the way of sophisticated equipment, yet every heavy metal band (with the exception of those in the speed/thrash metal genre) will have a drum kit of immense proportions, stacks of amplifiers and processing equipment, and the elaborate theatrical machinery of lighting and pyrotechnics. The band members themselves emulate the heroic gestures and even the narrative moves of the fantasy heroes of sci-fi (and backward sci-fi, e.g., the Conan fantasies). In larger stadium shows, the band members enter a scene of pandemonium and, taking up and taming an immense technological machinery, they physically take up the heroic posture, literally "destroying and tearing up" as they move about the stage with "heavy metal thunder."

These performative aspects of heavy metal lead to what Butler calls the *heterosexualization of desire* (1990, p. 141). This requires and institutes the production of discrete and asymmetrical oppositions between "masculine" and "feminine," where these are understood as expressive attributes of male and female. Thus, the practices of desire are made to follow from sex and gender. This is the domain of "intelligible" genders that heavy metal is heavily invested in maintaining. This is further offered as evidence in support of our assertion that, regardless of a certain level of play with gender signification, heavy metal does not bend gender outside of a dominant view of heterosexual definitions.

The physical look and gesture of the prototypical hard rock heavy metal band is at root an overblown adolescent macho pose. The heavy metal hard rock band is "bad," from the late-night routine of endless groupies, trashed hotel rooms, cases of hard liquor, and drugs (including a preference for heroin, which is not normative outside of hard-rock genres, and, as some players suggest, "separates the men from the boys"), to the onstage prancing and taunting behavior.

The performative/bodily gestures of heavy metal are stereotyped and exaggerated reproductions of aggressive masculine behaviors—fighting and/or protective fear gestures, such as jutting lips, fists forward in the air, back tilted forward, lower pelvis thrust out, and so on; aggressive sexual gestures, such as sticking out the tongue in mock cunnilingus, hoisting of the guitar from the crotch, grabbing and/or stuffing the crotch,[1] mock coitus (usually depicting the man on top and from behind). More important, the heavy metal band carries out this erotic aggression in the context of "being with the boys." The physical contact of band members, the gestures to one another, and the visual gaze and exchange of looks, all signal an attachment to the male gang. Heavy metal band members are individuals, but typically are "band first"; that is, they are identified by male fans as members of a group with an image that defines the group as "bad" in a particular way (whether as hyper-drunks, super-studs, mega-musicians, and such).

The "badness as maleness" of the heavy metal band is expressed then both in the music itself, and in the language used to describe the sound and the making of the sound—for example, thunder, axe, attitude, outlaw, fast and mean, ball-busting, attack, crunch, cook, pump, and so on. One quintessential musical element of heavy metal is the power chord, which conceptually mirrors the entire style of heavy metal. The power chord is not more of a chord, but actually less of one in that it typically uses only the bottom three strings of the guitar. This reduction of the chord to its elemental triad is what creates the type of power that heavy metal has—elemental, singular, direct—the hyper-amplification of simplicity.

Heavy metal has increasingly appropriated elements of style that are traditionally regarded as feminine. Originally, the so-called hippie or long-hair culture blurred gender definitions through its disregard for dominant fashion definitions. This was, of course, primarily expressed in hairstyle, and heavy metal has retained the rebellious "long hair" of the original rock 'n' roll bad-boy bands. But this hairstyle is not directly symbolic of or reflected upon as a gender-blurring operation; instead, it seems to express a general rebelliousness, particularly toward parental authority. As heavy metal promoter Tom Zutat suggest: "That's what the 'heavy metal' bands are now. They're the rebellious kids who say 'fuck you' to the police, to the parents. That's what Elvis did" (Considine, 1990, p. 62).

However, in heavy metal in general and glam metal in particular, the feminine (or what is taken as feminine) has been taken up in a much stronger style. Heavy metal hair is not simply long, it is moussed, teased, dyed, or streaked in a manner that is much more directly gender-coded. In addition, many bands use makeup, particularly lipstick and mascara, not simply for emphasis (as in theatrical makeup), but to soften the face and emphasize the eyes and cheek bones. Makeup use reaches an extreme of masquerade in bands like Kiss and Twisted Sister, where the makeup loses its gendered coding and becomes a means for the creation of another species (tied again to the codes of comics and sci-fi).

Glam styles exaggerate the clothing styles of early heavy metal and progressive rock, adding gender-blurring elements inherited partly from the chameleon traditions of earlier glitter music styles (e.g., Bowie, New York Dolls, and so on). Low-slung denim jeans, leather pants and accessories, open shirts, scarves, jewelry, and such, all blur gender-coded styles. Heavy metal bands extend a curiously macho image, while stylistically feminizing the "male body" (or perhaps "masculinizing the feminine"). As R. Bolan, of the band Skid Row, notes: "Facial hair and heavy metal don't jive" (Raso, 1990, p. 39).

Genders are neither true nor false, but are only produced as the *truth effects* of a discourse that attempts to anchor identity. The notion of an original or primary gender identity is often parodied within the cultural practices of drag and cross-dressing (Butler, 1990, pp. 136-137). Notions of drag play with essentialized descriptions of the body and soul as being outside and inside. Appearance is the outside, it is only what a person looks like. Essence is what a person is on the inside. It is in this manner, then, that notions of drag deconstruct such a dichotomy by trading between feminine and masculine. Butler argues that:

> *In imitating gender, drag implicitly reveals the imitative nature of gender itself—as well as its contingency.* Indeed, part of the pleasure, the giddiness of the performance is in the recognition of a radical contingency in the relation between sex and gender in the face of cultural configurations of causal

unities that are regularly assumed to be natural and necessary. (1990, pp. 137-138)

The emergent question then is: Does heavy metal fit into this imitative parody, or does it fall short of such a subversive discourse? This is a key question for the fans and performers of heavy metal in addressing questions of signifying practices and gender construction as possible sites of struggle across the cultural terrain. Our description thus far leads to a tentative answer.

Contradictorily, heavy metal holds up a model of masculine power and sexual prowess, but not under the rubric of traditional masculine "muscled" power. The "new male" body is an object of desire, an object to be possessed, but in heavy metal's terms, only if one is willing to be possessed. Thus, the glam-styled body is seductive, but seduction is used to seduce the female and control her desire. For the male audience, the feminization of the body marks out a quite different discourse—one that overcomes fear of the feminine by incorporating it.

Heavy Metal: Audience Identification

As noted, a large aspect of heavy metal is its emphasis on "producing rock," and the rock 'n' roll life-style (i.e., the identifications established are between star virtuosos and teenage, male, "would-be" guitar heroes). But as recent analyses have suggested, a growing female audience also exists for this music. Before dealing directly with the gender identification involved in this new division of the audience, a brief look at the social milieu of the heavy metal fans must be undertaken. Straw (1989) has noted that heavy metal tends not to define a subculture in the way that musical movements such as punk or rap do. It is consumed, and lived as consumed, rather then generating a productive subcultural body of fans. Thus heavy metal in the past tended not to generate local band scenes, underground magazines, or serious collectors. It was a *stadium culture*, a music consumed with a minimum of involvement. However, heavy metal has generated a powerful sense of commitment among its fans, who endlessly debate the authenticity of heavy metal and its existence as the "true" form of rock 'n' roll in the age of Madonna, corporate rock, dance music, and New Age.

Heavy metal has tended to be a working-class phenomenon, and there appears to be some correlation between low levels of educational performance and heavy metal fandom. We would suggest, however, that the implication is not that heavy metal is made by and produced for low-class, low-taste audiences, but that it is widely popular with alienated (rather than underprivileged) youth, who view the future as under-opportunitied. It should be emphasized that heavy metal is predominantly white music. Not that it is racist, it simply does not acknowledge difference—that is, rock 'n' rollers are white boys.

As Cashmore (1984) notes, "it would be unfair to call heavy metal conservative: inert would be more accurate" (p. 37). In general, heavy metal does not support the status quo, nor does it want to change it, it just wants to retreat into a world where one can sleep all day and rock all night. Given the male, white, suburban, inert world of heavy metal; how is it that fans—male and female—identify with heavy metal performers in terms of gender? Particularly, how can the contradictions surrounding gender identity be explained in heavy metal? For the male fan, how is it that young, heterosexual, white boys come to identify with performers who border on transvestism? For the female fan, how is it that young heterosexual white girls come to desire macho males styled in gay and female dress who act out adolescent fantasies of misogynist conquest? We have already laid out a basic description that points to one possible answer to each of these questions. At this point we will direct our focus only toward the male audience, leaving the newer female audience to a later examination.

Heavy Metal: Male, Self, Other

The exaggerated male techno-power of heavy metal, along with its obsession with de(re)-romanticizing sexual relations with women, is the key aspect of our description thus far. This seems to point to an adolescent fear of "woman" (growing up) at the core of heavy metal. Young male adolescents remain the primary audience for heavy metal. For young male fans, adolescence is a time of sexual awakening, but a space where fear and loathing mix with desire. These boys are confronted by girls who may be larger, stronger, and smarter than they are, while at the same time these boys are being socialized into the dominant masculine cultural position of pursuer of the female, thus generating a fear of the feminine.

These contradictions and tensions, developed between feelings of powerlessness while wanting to exercise one's growing power, are the elements of the male adolescent experience that heavy metal has traditionally addressed. Faced with intimidating females, the heavy metal fan finds fantasy escape in the aggressive, powerful figures of heavy metal, who sing about and seem to act out an extreme control of woman. The fear and loathing of women expressed in heavy metal music would be merely paranoid and destructive, if it were not for the manner in which desire for women is set within the greater pleasures of male bonding in the gang—rock 'n' roll (and at times even beer) comes before sex in the heavy metal pleasure hierarchy. As Slash, lead guitarist for Guns N' Roses, recalls, "When I was 14 I was over at this girl's house I'd been trying to pick up for months, and she played 'Aerosmith Rocks'; I listened to it eight times and forgot all about her" (Rowland, 1990, p. 32).

These descriptions are in keeping with Irigaray's (1985) explanation of a *phallocentric economy*, or an economy of the *same*. In this view, both the other as well as the same are marked as masculine (the other positioned as simply the negative elaboration of the masculine subject). The result is that the female sex is unrepresentable, incoherent within this signifying system. Further, the female sex is not one in that:

> [I]t eludes the univocal signifying characteristic of the Symbolic, and because it is not a substantive identity, but always and only an undetermined relation of difference to the economy which renders it absent. It is not "one" in the sense that it *is multiple and diffuse in its pleasures and its signifying mode*. (Butler, 1990, p. 103, emphasis added)

A repressed and, hence, disparaged sexuality (a relationship between men and bonds between men) takes place through the heterosexual exchange and distribution of women. This is particularly evident in the movie, *Heavy Metal,* and in music videos where groups of men divide the spoils, that is, the women. This is especially evident in the Motley Crüe video for their song, "Girls, Girls, Girls." In it, the women exotic dancers are obvious targets for exchange, yet function only as visual pleasure. The only physical, bodily pleasure in the video takes place in the exchanges between the male band members.

The feminized appearance of heavy metal bands seems then to not stand as signification of solidarity with feminism and gay rights (a possible "resistant" reading); rather, it is, at the simplest level, a way for straight white performers to inject an element of flamboyance into their performance. At a deeper level, it is a complex practice that at once expresses both a rebellion against straight societal and parental rules, and offers a response to feminine power. By taking the feminine into itself, heavy metal disavows the need for women, thus overcoming the fear of exercising desire.

As Kaplan (1987) notes: "If I possess the feminine myself, it seems to say, then I no longer need to satisfy the desire for woman *outside* myself, thus avoiding the terror of so doing" (p. 93). For the male adolescent fan, this identification with the performer does not result in a desire for the performer, but in a desire to be like the performer. That is, a desire for the ability to masquerade as both fully masculine and yet seductive. The heavy metal performer has everything that the feared adolescent female has, and more. The power of the female is taken up, emptying out any need to desire the female. Instead, the female is sadistically possessed. Grounding her position in psychoanalytic theory, Kaplan argues that the function of male masquerade in heavy metal differs significantly from that of female masquerade in which the layering of accessories upon the body serves to mask the absence of a lack (of the phallus). Instead, the male masquerade functions as an effort to deny that there is any separate sexual difference that would necessitate accepting the possibility of a lack, rendering the feminine "non-male rather than Other" (1987, p. 93).

It seems then that heavy metal's use of the feminine is neither simply a misogynist aggression nor an intentional playing with the boundaries of sexual identity. Rather, it is rooted in a culturally practiced binary division of sexual identity, an identity that cannot hold because the substance of its core is illusory. As a result, the fixed signs of feminine/masculine partly break down. Heavy metal then is, in part, a parody. But it is questionable what this parody does. Is it subversive in any manner? Or is it recirculated as part of the cultural hegemony? Our review of fanzines, and interviews with musicians and fans, seem to point toward the latter conclusion: *Heavy metal may shift some outward signs of gender, but it leaves untouched the constructed core identity of binary sex, and unchallenged the asymmetrical dominant power relations of gender.*

Heavy Metal: Masculinity and the Male Fan

The debate over notions of "resistance" taken up by various scholars (e.g., Condit, 1989; Fiske, 1986; Jenkins, 1988; Radway, 1986; Sholle, 1990; Streeter, 1989) in the literature of contemporary cultural studies has often focused upon the polysemic character of popular media texts. Creating, some studies argue, a "semiotic democracy" (Fiske, 1987a, p. 236), media receivers are able to negotiate among a wide array of decodings and avoid the tyranny of dominant messages. Or are they? In the specific case of heavy metal, notions of polysemy (as they have been developed within the popular cultural studies literature) would imply the widespread ability of metal fans to decode the music's play with gender signification both in a wide variety of different ways, and in opposition to the dominant asymmetrical gender relations that characterize contemporary U.S. culture—to, in effect, resist the hegemony.

Both authors have, for some time, been involved in separate and ongoing ethnographies of musicians and music audiences.[2] The two interviews that were conducted in preparation for this chapter are themselves connected to these larger projects. Two young men were invited to participate in an evening of viewing, listening, and conversation. "Michael" is 23, employed at a local carwash. An avid Led Zeppelin fan, Michael sports a "ZoSo" tattoo on a forearm and is rarely without a Zeppelin T-shirt, jacket patch, or some signifier of his primary musical preference. For Michael, musical preferences appeared primarily connected to various social uses (drinking, drug use, partying, hanging out, and so on), in particular, the role of various musics in his social relations with women. Throughout the evening, Michael's comments seemed to continually move between descriptions of his own musical tastes and the preferences of women with whom he regularly interacts in the local singles bar scene. Of the two respondents, Michael was noticeably more interested in, and critical of, the physical characteristics of the various male band members, often comparing their strong and weak points with his own. At one point, he jokingly admitted that his dislike of Bon Jovi was based less on the band's music then on a certain jealousy over lead singer Jon Bon Jovi's much-touted good looks.

"Art" is 20, currently unemployed, and contemplating the possibility of beginning college classes in the fall. Not yet allowed to actively participate in the local scene of bars and dance clubs, Art differentiated himself from Michael early in our conversation as the more "serious" music fan. "There's music which is made for the purpose of playing in the background while you're having a good time, then there's music which is made for more serious listening," he commented. Aside from his passion for Led Zeppelin, Michael's tastes ranged from metal to country (in particular, the party-all-night music of Hank Williams, Jr.), with no strong feelings one way or the other in response to most of the videos we watched ("If it sounds good on a stereo *loud*, I like it."). In contrast, Art was much more analytical in describing his own personal pantheon of "truly great music." Like so many contemporary 17- to 21-year-olds, Art seemed condemned to the musical tastes of his older brothers, describing a list of performers representative of the heavy rotation play-list of any given "classic rock" radio station ("Pink Floyd, Yes, Traffic, CSN, The Doors . . .").

Both men are high school graduates and both describe music as a very important part of their lives. A "best of" retrospective of music videos from MTV's weekly heavy metal series, "Head Banger's Ball" offered more than 2 hours of the most popular metal videos of the 1980s. With the consent of our respondents, two microphones were arranged to allow us to record their comments and responses to our open-ended and nonjudgmental questions. While both Michael and Art appear, to us, to represent "typical" working-class male rock music fans in their early twenties, neither they nor their responses are presented here because of their "typicality." We do not offer their responses as representative. Rather, they are suggestive of some of the attitudes and conceptual relationships that our analysis has described, and further suggestive of the kind of data that must continue to be collected in an ongoing examination of the relationship of music to its fans.

Michael (whose own hair is shoulder-length and who wears a single small diamond earring) views the long hair of the male band members in the traditional 1960s terms of a sign of individuality, difference, and defiance of societal expectations ("It lets people know that I'm different."). Art, however, seemed at times more cynical, arguing that the outrageous-for-its-time, gender-bending attire of the members of Poison was designed more out of a desire to secure the band a major-label recording contract, than it was a sign of solidarity with feminists or gays. More interestingly, in his comments Art differentiated between Poison's "hairstyle as marketing ploy" and the feminist political signification of Irish singer/activist Sinead O'Connor's shaved head. These comments also point back to our earlier observations on the rigidity of male roles and constructions of masculinity in heavy metal. While women, like Sinead O'Connor, may alter various signifiers on the surface of the body and present challenges to the dominant codes of gender, men are much more restricted in their ability to disrupt these codes within the context of contemporary popular culture.

This notion was made particularly evident in comments generated by the brief appearance of singer George Michaels during a commercial break. Michael responded with revulsion to the pop star's high-pitched voice, leather outfit (both common elements in most metal bands), and stylized dance moves ("Ugh! He thinks he's a woman or something!"). While Michael balanced his own contempt for the performance with the singer's popularity with female fans ("I'll listen to him because the ladies really get off on that shit."), Art's response represented more of a critical dismissal of the performer based on the inauthenticity of his commercial-oriented pop in contrast to the previously established "authenticity" of his preferred '60s and '70s art rock. A brief argument ensued between the two participants as Michael tried to get Art to take less of an intellectual stance (based upon the perceived intent of the music to entertain rather than enlighten) and more of an affective rejection based upon the unacceptable play with masculine signifiers. Interestingly, the argument shifted in Michael's favor when he raised the further example of Boy George of the now defunct Culture Club.

Culture Club's music was a gentle melodic pop more reminiscent of Motown "girl group" performers of the mid-1960s than the angular synthesized new wave of its own era. The group's lead singer, Boy George, was unlike any of the gender-bending glitter rock performers who preceded him. With a wardrobe of unisex clothing, long hair done up with ribbons and braids, and extremely feminine applications of facial and eye makeup, Boy George presented a serious disruption of the dominant performative aspects of gender coding. And more important, these superficial feminine traits were applied to a body that was, itself, a challenge to the traditional binaries of gender coding. While all of these accessories of clothing and makeup are present, in various combination, in heavy metal performance, Boy George presented himself as softly sensual, pudgy, flabby, and markedly unmuscular, nonthreatening and unaggressive.

When located within the aggressive heterosexuality of heavy metal performance, this play with gender coding on the surface of the body seems to be read more as another sign of "outrageousness" connected to the general theme of decadence ("sex, drugs, and rock 'n' roll") prevalent to hard rock performance, rather than a serious challenge to established gender binaries.[3] In keeping with this, both respondents expressed disgust bordering on physical revulsion at the mention of Boy

George, with Art now in agreement with Michael, commenting that: "His music was good, but I couldn't *ever* get past his *look*."

Conclusions

The critical study of media audiences across the past decade has established that media receivers are capable of constructing a variety of responses to any given media text. The central question, however, remains: To what extent do these variant decodings represent liberating pleasures and social empowerment?[4] Within the specific site of contemporary heavy metal performance, we have asked: Does heavy metal's play with the codes of gender represent a potentially empowering challenge to dominant gender constructions? For all its elaborate posturing and outrageous theatrics, heavy metal's appropriation of feminine gender signs fails to offer a meaningful challenge to the socially constructed core identity of binary sex, offering instead a thinly disguised reproduction of traditional masculine roles of power and domination presented in the context of an aggressive heterosexuality.

In presenting our analysis we have tried to suggest the heuristic value of a performative theory of gender in approaching the structures of masculinity in contemporary U.S. culture. Just as this notion of the *performativity* of gender both disrupts and offers us an alternative to the more restrictive conceptualizations of gender binaries, so too may more complex theorizations of the media audience offer an alternative to the binary of resistant reader or cultural dupe. It is toward the continued interrogation of both the popular media and the popular media audience that future research in women's studies and men's studies is directed.

Notes

1. Many of these elements are hilariously satirized in Rob Reiner's pseudo-documentary parody, *This is Spinal Tap*, in particular, a scene in which one of the band members is stopped at an airport metal detector and must remove a large foil-wrapped cucumber, which he had stuffed into the front of his trousers.

2. See Denski (1992).

3. The performer most reminiscent to Boy George in the 1990s is Perry Farrell, the leader of the band Jane's Addiction. Farrell's transsexual persona, however, is located

within a much more aggressive hard rock context (the sound of Jane's Addiction is often compared to that of Led Zeppelin) and has generated less controversy among hard rock fans. These observations are also in keeping with a central component of Butler's performative theory of gender, that is, that the failure to "properly" perform one's gender will always result in punitive actions taken against the performer. This is especially true in the gender performance of gay men. The lack of serious punitive penalties for male heavy metal performers (with the exception of the occasional harassment at truck stops) lends further support to our claim that this performance never intends to seriously challenge traditional gender binaries.

4. See: Condit, 1989, p. 108.

5

Superman/Superboys/Supermen

The Comic Book Hero as Socializing Agent

NORMA PECORA

Superheroes are the stuff of little boys' fantasies and young girls' dreams and they are the heart and soul of comic books. Because of the popularity of comic books, these characters have been important symbols of "maleness" in American culture since Superman was introduced in 1939. Over the years superheroes, like Superman, have been ushered in with a wide range of powers and varying degrees of success, but, except for a notable few, they have been predominantly male and have consequently presented a particular ideal of masculinity to their readers. They have functioned in a world that is male and white, where the women are either young and buxom or old and frail—but never equals.

In this chapter we will examine the world of the comic book reader through an analysis of *Superman* comics and a survey of current popular titles and characters. Working with the assumption that the media are important sources of social rules and courtesies, comic books are considered because of the overwhelmingly young male audience (McAllister, 1990, p. 57; NEC Survey, 1990b). Over the past few years these books have had a resurgence in popularity, particularly with boys between the ages of 10 and 15, and there has been the development of new series and character lines. Where Superman was once the leading superhero, joined by Spider-Man and the Fantastic Four in the early 1960s, there are now approximately 100 superhero titles published each month (NEC Survey, 1990b).

Heroes and Superheroes

Heroes play an important part in growing up. They offer us ideals and inspiration: We recognize some as possibilities (father or brother), others as desired (rock star or baseball player), and still others as fantasies (Superman or Rambo). A recent *Newsweek* magazine article examined current role models of teenagers from diverse communities in the United States (Leerhsen, 1990). Interviews with teens revealed a list of heroes that included contemporary politicians, athletes, and historical figures, such as John F. Kennedy, Martin Luther King, James Dean, and Elvis Presley. Of "nonpersons," only Winnie the Pooh and Superman made the list—the same Superman who has had a 100% recognition factor among boys between the ages of 5 and 10 (Boehm, 1984).

We learn from these heroes, real or fantasy, the rules of life: what is acceptable, desirable, attractive, successful, and possible. But increasingly these rules are changing as gender construction becomes more complex: Women enter the public arena; men, the private world. Princess Leia saved the world in *Star Wars*, and an emotional Spider-Man talked of his victimization as an abused child. For adults the reevaluation of social roles comes from relationships, conversations, and social situations. For children, such learning comes from parents, peers, and the media.

Superboys/Supermen

Although the research on adolescence group interactions is extensive (Maccoby, 1990), much of the work on mediated models has examined television, the well-worn field of media research. There have been periodic attempts to attribute a rise in juvenile delinquency and violent crimes to the books (Wertham, 1953; and documented in Gilbert, 1986; Starker, 1989; Twitchell, 1989), but beyond these simplistic arguments of delinquency and violence, comics have generally been overlooked as agents of social change. The role of the hero is the core of the comic book medium and popular culture, yet he has been ignored by those attempting to explain social constructions of reality. Superman, Batman, and the X-Men all represent an ideal that is called "male" to an increasing audience of young boys and, as such, should be considered in any explanation of mediated messages.

The "constellation of qualities" (Brooks-Gunn & Schempp, 1979, pp. 4-6) that young boys learn are "male" centered around socially constructed characteristics that define gender. Heroes present images of goodness, power, control, confidence, success, and competence (Kostelnik, Whiren, & Stein, 1986). Through popular culture young boys learn these are the attributes to emulate. They also learn that the way to cope with such behavior is through violence and action. To be a boy in our culture is to acquire traits that, according to Kimmel (1987a, p. 13), "imply authority and mastery."

> By the time adolescence is reached [the age under discussion in this chapter], American youth clearly understand the prescriptive aspects of their role —be a success, win at any cost, be tough and strong, be aggressive, be a man . . . . By meeting these role demands successfully, success in another crucial area can be realized—one is desirable to women. (David & Brannon, 1976, p. 234)

Thus Superman is the quintessential male role model. He is a success, he has power and control—he is a man. And throughout the years it has been clear to the reader that Lois Lane is his, if only he would ask. On the other hand, his alter ego, Clark Kent, is presented as a wimp. Weak and mild-mannered, he is incapable of "winning" Lois Lane and is never around when the excitement begins. Kent is easily dismissed, but Superman is to be emulated. Such characterizations reinforce a stereotype of "maleness" represented in our culture.

In addition to the "constellation of qualities" that center around mastery and dominance in the socialization of young boys, Kaufman (1987, pp. 4-6) suggested that violence is an "institutionalized . . . acceptable means of solving conflicts," that particular forms of violence are accepted and even encouraged. According to Kaufman, "racism, sexism, and heterosexism . . . are socially regulated acts of violence" (1987, p. 5). Masculinity and its inherent sense of power is an ideology that is reinforced and replayed for the young adolescent in the family, at school, among friends—and in comic books.

But what type of world does the comic book hero present to the reader? Do these reflect changing representations of "maleness"? How do they account for the era of transition described by Kimmel: "New role models for men have not replaced older ones, but have grown alongside them, creating a dynamic tension between ambitious breadwinner and compassionate father, between macho seducer and loving companion, between Rambo and Phil Donahue" (1987a, p. 9). Between Superman and Clark Kent.

The Comic Books

There are several genre of comic books, some selling to an adult audience and others to early readers. But we are all most familiar with the comic books of superheroes that, in the past, were sold at the local drugstore or newsstand. Currently these books are the dominant category in the industry, with sales of $96 million in 1988; in recent years they have accounted for about 80% of all comic books sales (Farhi, 1988; Scholz, 1985; Sporkin, 1985; M. Thompson, 1989).

Comic books have always been a part of children's culture, but recent trends indicate that they now have an extensive following in a particular market segment: adolescent boys. Sales figures and demographic information are carefully guarded industry secrets. However, according to one of the major wholesale distributors, the basic comic-book buyer is the teenage male (M. Thompson, 1990); DC Comics claims that 91% of their audience is male (M. Thompson, 1990); and a survey conducted by a Boston-based specialty shop indicates a 92% male readership, with 52% age 16 or younger (NEC Survey, 1990a, 1990b). Any trip to a comic book rack or one of the growing number of specialty shops will reveal the primary clientele as adolescent boys or young men (or academics studying the phenomenon). These shops feature comic books, posters, T-shirts, and many of the licensed products that promote the comic-book industry and serve to establish a "culture" of collectors (McAllister, 1990). The shops also function as a meeting place to trade information.

Since their introduction in the early 1930s, comic books have been an important part of American popular culture. DC and Marvel Comics were among the first publishing companies involved in the industry and have generally controlled the comic-book market (Farhi, 1988; Sporkin, 1985; M. Thompson, 1989). These two publishing houses have brought us such characters as Superman, Batman, and Wonder Woman (DC); and Spider-Man, The Incredible Hulk, the Fantastic Four, and Captain America (Marvel). DC and Marvel still dominate sales, and the top-selling 25 books in a Boston-area survey all came out of these publishing houses (NEC Survey, 1990a, 1990b). But there have been two major changes in the comic-book industry in the past 10 years. One has been the development of specialty shops, and the second has been a proliferation of titles and characters. Where once the books featured single-story issues, there are now multiple story lines and crossovers.

No longer does a Superman story start and finish within the cover of one comic, it is more likely to be Part I of a multipart story, to be continued, or the continuation of a story from another title line. For example, *Batman, Legends of the Dark Knight* is a five-part series for older readers; *Batman, Identity Crises* is a series of the Batman character first introduced 50 years ago; and Batman is the featured character in the *Detective* titles. There is currently a Superman serial running in *Superman*, *Adventures of Superman*, and *Action* comics. New marketing approaches have encouraged these serial publications, and story lines have been quite complex. A recent edition of *X-Factor* concluded with the promotion: "Next issue . . . you must read X-Men #270 and New Mutants #95 before the surprising return of one of X-Factor's most deadly foes . . . in BROTHERHOOD—Part 3 of the X-TERMI-NATOR AGENDA" (*X-Factor #59*, 1990).

This serialization of stories has contributed to the expansion of the comic-book industry: To buy one of every comic book published in one month of 1986 would have cost $200; to buy one of every comic book published in one month in 1989 would have cost $850; for 1990 the figure would be $1,115 (M. Thompson, 1990).

The Story

Traditionally, these comics have offered stories of adventure, good versus evil, heroes doing battle against aliens or "commies," all with a little gore and some sexy costumes. This chapter sets out to examine what these stories offer the adolescent boy and the ideals of masculinity that comic-book superheroes represent. Although the number of superhero titles exceeds 100 each month (NEC Survey, 1990a, 1990b), and many have been translated to radio, television, and motion pictures, all are derivative of Superman; therefore, we will begin with a look at the text of Superman. No one character can be truly representative of the comics just as no one character can truly be representative of any genre; however, because of his overwhelming popularity and longevity, Superman offers an interesting case study (Pecora & Gateward, 1989).

Superman as Super Man

In the 1930s Superman was introduced as a champion of the "oppressed":

> Unlike his predecessors [in science fiction], Superman not only chooses a place for himself in society, he also identifies with and aids his fellows and in turn is accepted, even glorified, by them. He is the embodiment of society's noblest ideals, a "man of tomorrow" who foreshadows mankind's highest potentialities and profoundest aspirations but whose tremendous power, remarkably pose no danger to its freedom and safety. (Andrea, 1987, p. 125)

Superman of the 1930s was at base "human," incorporating the characteristics of kindness and caring. In the early episodes he:

> [S]aves an innocent woman from being electrocuted, stops a wife-beating, halts corrupt politicians . . . deals with the [issues] of the rights of accused persons to fair and impartial justice . . . crooked unions and corrupt municipal officials, and with prison brutality, slum conditions, and other pressing social issues. (Andrea, 1987, p. 130)

He brought, as Kimmel suggested, compassion and ambition together.[1]

During World War II and the 1940s, Superman presented an ideal for the young men going off to war ("Superman Slipped," 1987). Although he was classified as 4F during the war, he maintained his representation of goodness (see Uslan, 1979, pp. 43-58). He became the embodiment of patriotism and, by extension, a true American hero. However, no longer was his fight against social injustice, his struggle turned to a defense of private property (Andrea 1987, p. 131). Although he was still the personification of good versus evil, the definition of evil shifted. Later we were told by the 1953 television adaptation that Superman fought for "truth, justice, and the American way." However, racism and sexism were accepted as the norm; in the comics, as in real life, simplistic solutions were offered for cultural conditions (Skidmore & Skidmore, 1983).

With the 1960s came enlightenment to both society and the Superman comics. Issues became more topical and comic book characters more relevant. Lois Lane became a "marginal" feminist, protesting denial of a dangerous assignment with: "That's not fair, Perry. You're discriminating against me because I'm a woman! I protest" (VanGelder & VanGelder, 1970, p. 39). And, acting out another vignette from real life, the *Daily Planet* was taken over by a multinational conglomerate with broadcasting interests, and Clark Kent moved to television (VanGelder & VanGelder, 1970, p. 39).

By the 1980s many of the growing number of superhero characters became "real." Although the characters, and particularly Superman, maintained the machismo qualities of power, control, goodness, and competence, reality was beginning to be a part of the superheroes' life. For example:

> Richard and Susan Richards of the Fantastic Four, often had to find a sitter for their son before venturing out to save the Universe. (*Fantastic Four*, 1983, 1985)

> Sam Guthrie, the Cannonball, was forced to contend with school dress codes and failing grades. (*New Mutants*, 1985)

> Matt Murdock, the Daredevil—the man without fear, is blind.

> Box, a member of the Canadian team Alpha Flight, is a double-amputee.

> And Charles Xavier, mentor of the X-Men, leads his group from a wheelchair.

Contemporary comic-book heroes now confronted such concerns as the threat of nuclear war, institutionalized racism, organized crime, corrupt government, inept judicial systems, environmental protection, and teen-age prostitution.

During each decade, *Superman* comic books appeared to reflect the time: 1940s-1950s, isolationism and a quiet conservatism; 1960s, liberalization and radicalization; 1970s, humanization; 1980s, political and social conservatism of the Reagan era (Pecora & Gateward, 1989).[2]

Most of us are familiar with the story of Superman and his journey to Earth, his susceptibility to kryptonite, and his alter ego, Clark Kent. We grew up with Superman's friends, Jimmy Olsen and Lois Lane, and his archenemy, Lex Luthor (who, until recently killed, had become an evil corporate executive). Our memories are of battles of good versus evil, of kindness and chivalry. He was described, in a story line that included several heads of state, by a representation of Ronald Reagan as follows:

President of United States: Superman hasn't let [down] the good people of the United States *or the world* yet . . . and by golly he's not about to yet.

Leader of "Russian-like" country: He is going to . . . to . . .

President of the United States: . . . to show you what a true American hero can *do*, Mr. Premier. (*Superman #387*, 1983)

A careful reading of the comics demonstrates a less-than-benign text, revealing a world where violence is used to solve problems; women, if present, are victims and nuisances; and racism reinforces a world of second-class citizenry. Such a reading supports the argument by Kaufman, presented earlier, that racism and sexism are forms of institutionalized violence. The Superman of the eighties supported a fantasy world with Superman acting as a vigilante, solving problems with violence, while maintaining the status quo. A reading of the character of Superman reveals not the simple battles of good versus evil, but rather a vigilante operating without legitimate authority. Answerable to nothing except his own code of ethics, Superman utilizes violence and physical strength as his primary method of operation.

His lack of respect for civil liberties became so intense during the 1980s that in one story line, he functioned as judge, jury, and executioner: roles he previously left to the legal system. In a story titled "The Price," Superman denied three Kryptonian villains a trial. Seeing himself "forced to stop the three of them for once and for all," Superman exposed them to deadly kryptonite. Though they begged for mercy, Superman resisted their pleas and reduced them to piles of dust (*Superman #22*, 1987).

Popular culture has been described as important because it is:

[A] realm within which racial ideologies have been created, produced, and sustained . . . not that of misportrayal, but of invisibility. (Omi, 1988, pp. 114, 121)

And certainly the *Superman* comics have contributed to such ideologies. In an analysis of 8 years of *Superman* comic books (1980-1988) examined, it was found that the world of Superman excluded people of color, class, and gender (see Pecora & Gatewood, 1989). The reader was presented with a white world, where problems were solved with violence, and women were victims. In the few stories that included people of color, the representations remain negative stereotypes. If, indeed, the media present us with social rules and courtesies, the comic books offer the young reader a world where violence and exclusion are acceptable.

Virtually every issue of the *Superman* comics offers themes of violence. Terrorists bomb embassies (*Superman #399*, 1984) and national monuments like Mt. Rushmore (*Superman #396*, 1983). The earth is conquered by Vikings (*Superman #394*, 1984) and aliens too numerous to count. In a particularly violent story line, Bloodsport, a psychotic draft-dodger, is used as a lure by Lex Luthor. Bloodsport becomes a sniper, believing he is in the jungles of Vietnam and shooting at anyone he sees in the streets.

Bloodsport is one of the many black Americans portrayed as victims in the *Superman* comics. In several story lines, black women and children live in a ghetto tenement and are burned out of their homes. Unable to do anything but cower in fear, they are, of course, rescued by Superman (*Superman* #352, 1980; see also *Superman* #394, 1984). The most dominant trend in these comics was the depiction of blacks as unskilled labor. Because the characters had virtually no "speaking parts," they served no purpose other than to "color" the background. The jobs at which they were employed included security guards, cab drivers, and truck drivers. The only recurring black character was Frank, the doorman of the high-rise building in which Clark Kent/Superman lives. The only professional presented was a corporate lawyer, referred to as a "shyster" by the chief of police, who appeared only in the last few frames of one comic (*Superman* #10, 1987).

One of a few black characters representing the criminal element was a young man who served as a lackey. In a group of five, this character, in terms of spatial representation, was consistently drawn behind the other criminals and was the only member without a weapon—denying him equality even as a criminal (*Superman #346*, 1980). Baron Sunday was the major black opponent to Superman but, unlike other *Superman* villains, he did not utilize science and technology to achieve his goals, rather his sole source of power was voodoo magic (*Superman #26*, 1988).

Another group featured in the stories was Native Americans and they, too, were subject to treatment similar to that of the black characters. In one issue, as an attack was made on Superman, he exclaimed: "Now I know what Custer felt like at Little Big Horn" (*Superman #377*, 1982). Of all the issues examined, Native Americans played a prominent role in one, a story titled "The Master of Wind and Storm" (*Superman #348*,

1980). It concerned an elderly Native American who perceived of himself as a powerful individual. He was mistaken, however, because he was actually being tricked and used by an alien. Superman saved the community from a disaster caused by the old man and closed the issue with the comment: "He's just a harmless old man with dreams." Thus the writers and artists managed to simultaneously insult both the elderly and the Native Americans.

Other groups were also represented as ethnic or racial stereotypes. The Italian was in organized crime (*Superman #385*, 1983); the Hispanic was a priest (*Superman #352*, 1980); Mrs. Goldstein talked of "bubelah" (*Superman #393*, 1984), and the lesbian was an unfit mother (*Superman #15*, 1988).

Though the women of the *Superman* comics are more visible than other groups, they are no less victims. They are old ladies with cats (*Superman #390*, 1983) or silly girls (*Superman #358, #362*, 1981). And though Lois Lane and Lana Lang, the two female protagonists, are both professional journalists, their main function has been to depict the "damsel in distress syndrome," continually in need of rescue by Superman (For example: *Superman #346, #348, #350*, 1980; *#370*, 1982; *#392*, 1984; *#1*, 1987; *#21*, 1988). Lois has long pined for Superman to no avail.[3] More often than not, the women's overzealousness and aggressiveness in their careers place them in precarious positions. For these two women competition often results in fights, such as the argument over an assignment during a Middle Eastern conference (*Superman #388*, 1983). Though they are successful career women, Lana and Lois are presented as incomplete women—hence, their other function as love interests.

Quite frequently their careers were depicted as inadequate. In one issue, set in the future, Lois gives up her career as a prize-winning journalist to become a wife and mother (*Superman #423*, 1986). The most obvious example, however, was that of Lana, who continually complains about not "having a man" and she longs for Superman to "look at her the way he looks at Lois" (*Superman #350*, 1980). Lana consoles herself here by saying: "At least I have my work." Again a few years later we find her thinking of her career as a "substitute for love" (*Superman #373*, 1982). As proof she eventually offered to give up her career for an alien hero, Vartox (*Superman #374*, 1982).

Just as Lois and Lana were punished for qualities usually expected in men (zealousness and aggressiveness in the workplace), so were several other women. The most extreme case involved the creation of a horrific female villain—the Banshee. In this tale, according to family tradition, the firstborn of each generation must conduct a particular ritual. Because the old law made no reference to gender, the current firstborn, a female, claimed the right. Engagement in the ritual transformed her into a ghoul-like apparition, tortured by her curse. She was, of course, destroyed (*Superman #17*, 1988).

This brief analysis of *Superman* comics indicates that, indeed, Superman, storyteller and conscience to many of us as we were growing up, offers a picture of the world that reinforces the old models of violence and machismo. Themes of violence, sexism, and racism are repeated, overtly as well as subtly reinforcing a particular ideology to the young readers.

Though there was a liberalization or, as the VanGelders argue, a radicalization of the *Superman* comic books during the 1960s and 1970s, in the 1980s Superman represents and reinforces a particular ideology, an illusion of masculinity. More recent readings indicate that there has been the introduction and support of a lesbian character, that Superman has adopted somewhat "human" qualities (Robinson, 1988). And at long last he has proposed to Lois Lane (*Action Comics*, November 1990). But in general there have been no major ideological shifts in the character or stories of Superman.

Superman is a character with a long history and tradition; however, he no longer claims the popularity of his early years. Quite the contrary, in one survey of comic-book characters he ranked among the least-liked titles (NEC Survey, 1990b). So what about the other comics that have replaced him? A survey, conducted by a local specialty store chain, listed the following as the most popular title lines.

The top five favorite characters: Spider-Man, Batman, Wolverine, Punisher, and the X-Men were each represented in the top 10 favorite titles. Of these titles, three are published by DC and seven are published by Marvel; they represent seven different characters. Batman is the lead character in three (1, 7, 10); the Punisher in two (5, 6); and Spider-Man (3), the Wolverine (4), Excalibur (8), and Avengers (9) are each represented in one title series. But there is crossover as the X-Men star in *Excalibur* and Wolverine in the *X-Men* titles. All but the Punisher rely on superhuman qualities, advanced technology, or magic to fight their adversaries. And all depend on multiple issues to tell the story.

A reading of the most recent issues of these comics indicates that little has changed. Table 5.1 lists the titles available for the top five favorite characters; these comics were examined for the stories they tell. (Titles available on October 10, 1990; New England Comic Store, Malden,

Table 5.1   Top-Ranked Comic Books Titles: 1990

Rank	Title	Character
1.	*Batman*	BATMAN
2.	*The X-Men*	X-MEN
3.	*The Amazing Spider-Man*	SPIDER-MAN
4.	*Wolverine*	WOLVERINE
5.	*The Punisher*	PUNISHER
6.	*The Punisher War Journal*	PUNISHER
7.	*Detective Comics*	BATMAN
8.	*Excalibur*	CAPTAIN BRITAIN
9.	*Avengers, West Coast*	CAPTAIN AMERICA
10.	*Legend of the Dark Knight*	BATMAN

SOURCE: From *New England Comics Newsletter*, 1990b (September/October). Used by permission. Five most popular characters are shown in capital letters.

Massachusetts.) Superman may no longer be among the most popular characters, but the ideological representations of violence as a solution, sexism, and racism are all a part of these stories as well.

For example, in a complex tale of violence and relationships, Spider-Man gave up his powers after being defeated in a ruthless battle with the Femme Fatales because he feared for his elderly Aunt May, and he is "all the family she has left" (*The Amazing Spider-Man #340*, October). However, he soon found that he had to "turn his back" on criminals (*The Amazing Spider-Man #342*, December). He returned to his Spider-Man persona, without his previous strength and agility but with the technology he had previously relied on—and the support of his rival, Cat Woman.

In a particularly poetic turn of phrase, Spider-Man, Peter Parker, asked for his wife's advice on relinquishing his powers:

> He needs her, in every nuance of the word, and to have her here now, sharing his fears and misgivings, means more than any phrase the poets could dream. He listens to her thoughts, her offerings. They give shape to the illusive puzzle, lend light to the shadowy gray of possible solutions. (*The Amazing Spider-Man #340*, October)

Though, of course, the final decision is his. However, he is soon back fighting evil. In the next issue, he returns to his life as Spider-Man

Table 5.2 Top Characters: Fall 1990

Issue	Character	Title
456	Batman	*Batman Identity Crises Part Two*: "Without Fear of Consequences"
270	X-Men	*X-Men The X-tinction Agenda*: "First Strike"
271	X-Men	*X-Men The X-tinction Agenda:* "Flash Point"
340	Spider-Man	*The Amazing Spider-Man*: "The Hero Subtracter"
342	Spider-Man	*The Amazing Spider-Man*: "The Jonah Trade"
33	Wolverine	*Wolverine*: "Grave Undertakings"
42	The Punisher	*The Punisher*: "St. Paradines"
24	The Punisher	*The Punisher War Journal*: "Fire Power Among the Ruins: Part Two"
622	Batman	*Detective Comics*: "Dark Genesis"
623	Batman	*Detective Comics*: "Death of Innocence"
31	Captain Britain	*Excalibur*: "No Man Is An Island" (X-Men as "guests")
12	Batman	*Legends of the Dark Knight*: "Prey: Part Two, Dark Sides"

because of his powerlessness to fight young hoodlums who were robbing tourists in dark alleyways (*The Amazing Spider-Man #342*, December).

Batman appears in three of the top 10 rated titles. In each of the three, the police were evident, yet it was Batman who gave them advice (*Batman #456*, November) or acted as vigilante (*Detective Comics #622*, October; *#623*, November; *Legends of the Dark Knight #12*, November). The police chief approved of Batman's breaking the law to capture criminals because "it works" and even the criminals refer to him as the "vigilante" (*Batman #456*, November, p. 12). The *Detective* titles present a complex story line of copyright violation, mythical temples, comic-book philosophy, big-city despair, and a character based on a current prime-time television program (*Midnight Caller*). In this three-part series, there was a publisher releasing counterfeit *Batman* comics, a spurious Batman acting as vigilante, and a radio talk-show host concerned with ratings. Except for a meddlesome reporter (*Batman #456*, November), mugging victims, and crowd scenes, there were no women and no minorities (*Detective Comics #622*, October; *#623*, November). The *Dark Knight*, a comic generally marketed to a slightly older audience, 17- to 20-year-olds, featured scenes of semi-nudity (*Legend of the Dark Knight #12*, November).

The *Wolverine* comics are generally set in Asia. In the comic book discussed here, the story line included evil Asian drug lords and exotic women. It was the Wolverine's mission to destroy the drug, Thunder-bolt, "another blasted poison for the body and the soul." The drug lord, Dai-Kumo, explains that,

> Thunderbolt induces the ultimate euphoria. . . . Fortunately, it also results in the death of the user, freeing society of the burden of another useless drug addict. A wondrous symmetry is achieved. The user gets what he wants, society gets what it wants, and we all make windfall profits. (*Wolverine #33*, November)

Here the Wolverine single-handedly destroyed the evil scientist's lab, the vicious drug lord's cadre, and the supply of Thunderbolt. It was the betrayed woman who killed the drug lord. The Wolverine character appeared in several titles. In his feature titles, the setting and story line are much like that described. However, he is also a part of the X-Men team discussed later (*Wolverine "Letters," #33*, November).

In both of the top 10 rated Punisher titles, *The Punisher* and *The Punisher War Journal*, Frank Castle was a self-proclaimed vigilante: "I'm just a vigilante—a lone lunatic" (*The Punisher #42*, p. 30). And as described in the introduction: "When mobsters slew his family, Frank Castle vowed to spend the rest of his life avenging them! Trained as a soldier, and equipped with a state-of-the-art arsenal, he now wages a one-man war on crime" (*The Punisher War Journal #24*, November; *The Punisher #42*, November).

The Punisher is one of the few characters to work without super powers (Spider-Man will no doubt regain his in a future episode). He relies instead on an arsenal of weapons and high-tech equipment. In *The Punisher* he captured a gun-runner and explained, "I dropped a dime to the Feds, took a few pieces and split." He also confiscated some video-tapes in the raid, tapes that led him to a military academy and the use of young boys in pornographic movies. Single-handedly, the Punisher infiltrated the academy and rescued the "children" (*The Punisher #42*, November). In *The Punisher War Journal*, a two-part series, the Punisher fought Guatemalan rebels/drug lords and protected the elderly female archaeologist. Again, women are old and victims (*The Punisher War Journal #24*, November) or young and naive, as is the secretary in another story (*The Punisher #42*, November).

One of the most complex story lines was offered by the X-Men, a team of supermutants who "guest star" in *Excalibur* comic books and are a part of a nine-issue series, *The X-tinction Agenda,* published in three series: *X-Men*, *New Mutants*, and *X-Factor*. Relying on telekinetic powers to fight the enemy, the X-Men (and women) include Jubilee, Wolverine, Psylocke, Storm, Boom-Boom, Wolfsbane, Rictor, Gambit, Banshee, Forge, Marvel Girl, Sunspot, Cannonball, Cable, and Warlock among others. This author will make no attempt to articulate the relationships between the X-Men, the X-Factor, and the New Mutants. However, the plot of *The X-tinction Agenda* revolves around a war between the mutants and an "East African Island Republic of Genosha," where the mutants are viewed as terrorists. To make a very long and complex story short, Genosha is a country run by an evil scientist who, "Nazi-like," creates genetic robots. The mutants set out to free the robots and destroy the government of Genosha—over nine issues. This is one of the few series where women are also a part of the story, although they are usually secondary heroes (*X-Men #270*, November).

As is evident, each of the five "most favorite" characters act as vigilantes. Spider-Man, Batman, the Wolverine, the Punisher, and the X-Men all use their power to maintain order outside the law. As is the case with Superman, their battles are no longer simply good versus evil, but rather these superheroes are vigilantes operating without legitimate authority. They belong to no government; self-appointed, they act on their own to maintain order. And, like Superman, each maintains his own code of ethics. Seldom is the enemy killed, but most return to fight another day/issue.

Evil is represented by drug lords (*The Wolverine* and *The Punisher War Journal*), rebel cabals (*The Punisher War Journal*), mad scientists (*Legends of the Dark Knight* and *The Amazing Spider-Man*), psychotic army colonels (*The Punisher*) and social control (*The X-tinction Agenda*). One statement particularly representative of several stories appeared at the end of the Punisher's battle with the army colonel. The colonel, in charge of the military academy and responsible for the child pornography videos, stated: "It's fashionable to denigrate military training, after all, peace has broken out, eh? Communism is an endangered species. Don't you believe it . . . the history of mankind is written in blood" (*The Punisher #42*, p. 9). On his office wall is a portrait vaguely reminiscent of former president Ronald Reagan.

Images of racism and anti-feminism are still very much a part of the comic book culture. Again, the superheroes are predominantly white— Spider-Man, Batman, Wolverine, the Punisher, and the majority of X-Men—and male, as above. When individuals of color are present, they follow the patterns of background discussed in the analysis of

Superman. They are often villains such as Knockout, leader of the Femme Fatales (*The Amazing Spider-Man #340*, October) or they are assorted background characters as in *The X-Men.* One interesting anomaly was a sequence of panels in the middle of a *Spider-Man* book: On one full page there was a vignette that had no relevance to the story, before or after. It was a brief scene with a black medical doctor, Dr. Wirtham, who saved the life of a patient having a heart attack.

Occasionally the comic-book characters will have a female partner: The Wolverine has an Asian woman and black male as his support team, although they are only in the first and last sequences (*The Wolverine #33*, November). And Felicia, the Black Cat, supports Spider-Man when he must fight without his powers (*The Amazing Spider-Man #342*, December). Otherwise, women are left to be wives and elderly aunts (*The Amazing Spider-Man*), victims (the archaeologist in *The Punisher War Journal*, and various *Batman* episodes), or "harpies" (*The Amazing Spider-Man #340*, October) and "harridans" (*X-Men #271*, December). Of the titles discussed here, only one (*The Amazing Spider-Man #340*, October) featured female characters. Spider-Man introduced us to a new series of characters mentioned earlier, the Femme Fatales, in an issue subtitled "Female Trouble" (*The Amazing Spider-Man #340*, October). It was after a particularly grueling fight with the villains, Knockout, Mindblast, Whiplash, and Bloodlust, that Spider-Man decided to give up his powers—coincidence? The X-Men series features a number of female heroines, though they tend to be secondary characters and often juveniles. For example, in Part Four of the *X-tinction Agenda*, the Wolverine and Psylocke are compared:

> Wolverine's the natural brawler . . . fighting as integral a part of his being as breathing. But where his skills are raw and rough-edged, as fierce as his nature . . . Psylocke is the personification of power and grace. Literal poetry in motion—where he's more a berserk battering ram—but no less effective. (*X-Men #270*, November).

A cursory look at the top-rated characters makes it evident that the values and representation in the stories of Superman are indeed reinforced and reiterated in the new generation of superheroes. The new egalitarian role models are hardly those of a Phil Donahue. Like Superman, the characters are predominantly white males, and the tales are those of vigilantes. The evil "commies" of the past are replaced by evil drug lords, and women and people of color are still invisible. The women of *Spider-Man, Batman, Wolverine, The Punisher*, and the *X-Men* fare no better than Lois Lane and Lana Lang. They are sidekicks and seconds; only the Femme Fatales are presented as worthy adversaries, and yet Spider-Man loses to them because he is "distracted" (*The Amazing Spider-Man #340*, October). Spider-Man's wife is asked to help decide his fate, but becomes the jealous wife when he is seen in battle with Cat Woman (*The Amazing Spider-Man #341*, November). Although Spider-Man made a rather impassioned speech, accompanied by illustrations of tenderness, when making his decision to become "powerless," the image of a partnership was negated by later scenes of exclusion. The women in *X-Men* are presented as a part of the team, yet fight much of one battle in their bathing suits (*X-Men #270*, November). Indications of parity are offered in violent scenes of the Femme Fatales and women of *X-Men*, a parity based on a male model.

> An editorial in the *Chicago Daily News* in 1940 stated, Superman heroics, voluptuous females in scanty attire, blazing machine guns, hooded "justice" and cheap political propaganda were to be found almost every page [of the comics]. ("A national disgrace," 1940)

Young boys are still offered cultural representations that reinforce maleness as machismo. The superheroes are loners, fighting evil in their own way, a way that invokes violence. Technology is used for power and control. Women are elderly and weak or voluptuous and unimportant. And, it would appear, little has changed.

Notes

1. No analysis of superheroes over time exists. Dubbert (1979, p. 5) claims that we know little of the formation of male images in American history, and that is certainly true of images in popular culture. The historical view presented here is culled from several analyses of *Superman*. A true history of the male image in the comic book is yet to be done and is left for another time.

2. The following analysis is based on a reading of all issues of the 1980 to 1988 *Superman* series available at the Library of Congress. From the collection, only 5 months were missing from the series; 108 *Superman* comic books were analyzed. The issues are identified in the text by the issue number and the year. See the reference list for actual books included in this discussion. In 1987 John Byrne began as the author of the books, and at that point the series reverted to the number 1.

3. The November 1990 series of *Superman's Action Comics* has Superman, not Clark Kent, proposing to Lois Lane, and her accepting. In the next issue he agonizes over revealing his true identity to her. Stay tuned.

6

Beer Commercials

A Manual on Masculinity

LANCE STRATE

Jocks, rock stars, and pick-up artists; cowboys, construction workers, and comedians; these are some of the major "social types" (Klapp, 1962) found in contemporary American beer commercials. The characters may vary in occupation, race, and age, but they all exemplify traditional conceptions of the masculine role. Clearly, the beer industry relies on stereotypes of the man's man to appeal to a mainstream, predominantly male target audience. That is why alternate social types, such as sensitive men, gay men, and househusbands, scholars, poets, and political activists, are noticeably absent from beer advertising. The manifest function of beer advertising is to promote a particular brand, but collectively the commercials provide a clear and consistent image of the masculine role; in a sense, they constitute a guide for becoming a man, a rulebook for appropriate male behavior, in short, a manual on masculinity. Of course, they are not the only source of knowledge on this subject, but nowhere is so much information presented in so concentrated a form as in television's 30-second spots, and no other industry's commercials focus so exclusively and so exhaustively on images of the man's man. Most analyses of alcohol advertising acknowledge the use of masculine characters and themes, but only focus on their persuasive function (see, for example, Atkin, 1987; Finn & Strickland, 1982, 1983; Hacker, Collins, & Jacobson, 1987; Jacobson, Atkins, & Hacker, 1983). In my own research on beer commercials (Postman, Nystrom, Strate, & Weingartner, 1987; Strate, 1989, 1990), the ads are analyzed as a form of cultural communication and a carrier of social myths, in particular, the myth of masculinity. A similar approach is taken by Craig (1987) in his analysis of Super Bowl advertising, and by Wenner (1991) in his analysis of beer commercials and television sports. A major concern in my research has been the relationship between alcohol advertising and drinking and driving, a problem especially among young, unmarried men. Drawing on that research, I will discuss here the ways in which the myth of masculinity is expressed in beer commercials.

Myths, according to semioticians such as Roland Barthes (1972), are not falsehoods or fairy tales, but uncontested and generally unconscious assumptions that are so widely shared within a culture that they are considered natural, instead of recognized as products of unique historical circumstances. Biology determines whether we are male or female; culture determines what it *means* to be male or female, and what sorts of behaviors and personality attributes are appropriate for each gender role. In other words, masculinity is a social construction (Fejes, 1989; Kimmel, 1987a). The foundation may be biological, but the structure is manmade; it is also flexible, subject to change over time and differing significantly from culture to culture. Myth, as a form of cultural communication, is the material out of which such structures are built, and through myth, the role of human beings in inventing and reinventing masculinity is disguised and therefore naturalized (and "biologicized"). The myth of masculinity is manifested in myriad forms of mediated and nonmediated communication; beer commercials are only one such form, and to a large extent, the ads merely reflect preexisting cultural conceptions of the man's man. But in reflecting the myth, the commercials also reinforce it. Moreover, since each individual expression of a myth varies, beer ads also reshape the myth of masculinity, and in this sense, take part in its continuing construction.

Myths provide ready-made answers to universal human questions about ourselves, our relationships with others and with our environment. Thus, the myth of masculinity answers the question: What does it mean to be a man? This can be broken down into five separate questions: What kinds of things do men do? What kinds of settings do men prefer? How do boys become men? How do men relate to each other? How do men relate to women? Let us now consider the ways in which beer commercials answer these questions.

What kinds of things do men do? Although advertisers are prevented from actually showing an individual drinking beer in a television commercial, there is no question that drinking is presented as a central masculine activity, and beer as the beverage of choice. Drinking, however, is rarely presented as an isolated activity, but rather is associated with a variety of occupational and leisure pursuits, all of which, in one way or another, involve overcoming challenges. In the world of beer commercials, men work hard and they play hard.

Physical labor is often emphasized in these ads, both on and off the job. Busch beer features cowboys riding horses, driving cattle, and performing in rodeos. Budweiser presents a variety of blue-collar types, including construction workers, lumberjacks, and soldiers (as well as skilled laborers and a few white-collar workers). Miller Genuine Draft shows men working as farm hands and piano movers. But the key to work is the challenge it poses, whether to physical strength and endurance, to skill, patience, and craftsmanship, or to wit and competitive drive in the business world. The ads do associate hard work with the American dream of economic success (this theme is particularly strong in Budweiser's campaign), but it is also presented as its own end, reflecting the Puritan work ethic. Men do not labor primarily out of economic necessity nor for financial gain, but rather for the pride of accomplishment provided by a difficult job well done; for the respect and camaraderie of other men (few women are visible in the beer commercial workplace); for the benefit of family, community, and nation; and for the opportunity to demonstrate masculinity by triumphing over the challenges work provides. In short, work is an integral part of a man's identity.

Beer is integrated with the work world in three ways. *First*, it is represented in some commercials as the product of patient, skillful craftsmanship, thus partaking of the virtues associated with the labor that produced it; this is particularly apparent in the Miller beer commercials in which former football player Ed Marinaro takes us on a tour of the Miller brewery. In effect, an identity relationship between beer and labor is established, although this is overshadowed by the identification between beer and nature discussed below. *Second*, beer serves as a reward for a job well done, and receiving a beer from one's peers acts as a symbol of other men's respect for the worker's accomplishment— "For all you do, this Bud's for you." Beer is seen as an appropriate reward not just because drinking is pleasurable, but because it is identified with labor, and therefore can act as a substitute for labor. Thus, drinking beer at the end of the day is a symbolic reenactment of the successful completion of a day's work. And *third*, beer acts as a marker of the end of the work day, the signal of quitting time ("Miller time"), the means for making the transition from work to leisure ("If you've got the time, we've got the beer"). In the commercials, the celebration of work completed takes on a ritualistic quality, much like saying grace and breaking bread signal the beginning of meal time; opening the can represents the opening of leisure time.

The men of beer commercials fill their leisure time in two ways: in active pursuits usually conducted in outdoor settings (e.g., car and boat racing, fishing, camping, and sports; often symbolized by the presence of sports stars, especially in Miller Lite ads) and in "hanging out," usually in bars. As it is in work, the key to men's active play is the challenge it provides to physical and emotional strength, endurance, and daring. Some element of danger is usually present in the challenge, for danger magnifies the risks of failure and the significance of success. Movement and speed are often a part of the challenge, not only for the increased risk they pose, but also because they require immediate and decisive action and fine control over one's own responses. Thus, Budweiser spots feature automobile racing; Michelob's music video-like ads show cars moving in fast-motion and include lyrics like "I'm overheating, I'm ready to burn, got dirt on my wheels, they're ready to turn"; Old Milwaukee and Budweiser commercials include images of powerboat, sailboat, and canoe racing; Busch beer features cowboys on galloping horses; and Coors uses the slogan, "The Silver Bullet won't slow you down." Activities that include movement and speed, along with displays of coordination, are particularly troubling when associated with beer, in light of social problems such as drinking and driving. Moreover, beer commercials portray men as unmindful of risks, laughing off danger. For example, in two Miller Genuine Draft commercials, a group of young men are drinking and reminiscing; in one they recall the time when they worked as farm hands, loading bales of hay onto a truck, and the large stack fell over. In the other, the memory is of moving a piano, raising it up by rope on the outside of a building to get it into a third-story apartment; the rope breaks and the piano crashes to the ground. The falling bales and falling piano both appear dangerous, but in the ads the men merely joke about the incidents; this attitude is reinforced visually as, in both cases, there is a cut from the past scene to the present one just before the crash actually occurs.

When they are not engaged in physical activity, the men of beer commercials frequently seek out symbolic challenges and dangers by playing games such as poker and pool, and by watching professional sports. The games pose particular challenges to self-control, while spectator sports allow for vicarious participation in the drama of challenge, risk, and triumph. Even when they are merely hanging out together, men engage in verbal jousts that contain a strong element of challenge, either in the form of good-natured arguments (such as Miller Lite's ongoing "tastes great—less filling" conflict) or in ribbing one another, which tests self-control and the ability to "take it." A sense of proportion and humor is required to overcome such challenges, which is why jokers and comedians are a valued social type in the myth of masculinity. Women may also pose a challenge to the man's ability to attract the opposite sex and, more important, to his self-control.

The central theme of masculine leisure activity in beer commercials, then, is challenge, risk, and mastery—mastery over nature, over technology, over others in good-natured "combat," and over oneself. And beer is integrated into this theme in two ways: one obvious, the other far more subtle. At the overt level, beer functions in leisure activities as it does in work: as a reward for challenges successfully overcome (the race completed, the big fish landed, the ribbing returned). But it also serves another function, never explicitly alluded to in commercials. In several ways drinking, in itself, is a test of mastery. Because alcohol affects judgment and slows reaction time, it intensifies the risks inherent in movement and speed, and thereby increases the challenge they represent. And because it threatens self-control, drinking poses heightened opportunities for demonstrating self-mastery. Thus beer is not merely a reward for the successful meeting of a challenge in masculine work and leisure, but is itself an occasion for demonstrating mastery, and thus, masculinity. Beer is an appropriate award for overcoming challenge because it is a challenge itself, and thereby allows a man to symbolically reenact his feat. It would be all but suicidal for advertisers to present drinking as a challenge by which the masculine role can be acted out; instead, they associate beer with other forms of challenge related to the myth of masculinity.

What kinds of settings do men prefer? In beer commercials, the settings most closely associated with masculinity are the outdoors, generally the natural environment, and the self-contained world of the bar. The outdoors is featured prominently as both a workplace and a setting for leisure activity in ads for Busch beer, Old Milwaukee, Miller Genuine Draft, and Budweiser. As a workplace, the natural environment provides suitable challenge and danger for demonstrating masculinity, and the separation from civilization forces men to rely only on themselves. The height of masculinity can be attained when the natural environment and the work environment coincide, that is, when men have to overcome nature in order to survive. That is why the cowboy or frontiersman is the archetypical man's man in our culture. Other work environments, such as the farm, factory, and office, offer their own form of challenge, but physical danger is usually downplayed and the major risk is economic. Challenge and danger are also reduced, but still present, when nature is presented as a leisure environment; male bonding receives greater emphasis, and freedom from civilization becomes freedom for men to behave in a boyish manner.

In the ads, nature is closely associated with both masculinity and beer, as beer is presented as equivalent to nature. Often, beer is shown to be a product that is natural and pure, implying that its consumption is not harmful, and perhaps even healthy. Moreover, a number of beers, including Rolling Rock, Heileman's Old Style, and Molson's Golden, are identified with natural sources of water. This identification is taken even further in one Busch beer commercial: We see a cowboy on horseback, herding cattle across a river. A small calf is overcome by the current, but the cowboy is able to withstand the force of the river and come to the rescue. The voice-over says, "Sometimes a simple river crossing isn't so simple. And when you've got him back, it's your turn. Head for the beer brewed natural as a mountain stream." We then see a six-pack pulled out of clear running water, as if by magic. The raging water represents the power and danger of nature, while the mountain stream stands for nature's gentler aspect. Through the voice-over and the image of the hand pulling the six-pack from the water, beer is presented as identical with the stream, as bottled nature. Drinking beer, then, is a relatively safe way of facing the challenge of raging rivers, of symbolically reenacting the taming of the frontier.

Beer is identified with nature in a more general way in the ads for Old Milwaukee, which are usually set in wilderness environments that feature water, such as the Florida Everglades, and Snake River, Wyoming. In each ad, a group of men is engaged in recreational activities such as high-speed air-boating, flat-bottom boat racing, or fishing. Each commercial begins with a voice-over saying something like, "The Florida Everglades and Old Milwaukee both mean something great to these guys." Each ad includes a jingle, which says, "There's nothing like the flavor of a special place and Old Milwaukee beer." In other words, Old Milwaukee is equivalent to the special place. The place is special because it is untouched by civilization, allowing men to engage in forms of recreation not available elsewhere. It therefore must be fairly inaccessible, but since beer is presented as identical to the place, drinking may act as a substitute for actually going there.

Beer is also identified with nature through animals. For example, the symbol of Busch beer, found on its label and in its commercials, is a horse rearing on its hind legs, a phallic symbol that also evokes the idea of the untamed. And in another Busch ad, a young rodeo rider is quickly thrown from his mount; trying to cheer him up, an older cowboy hands him a beer and says, "Here. This one don't buck so hard." Thus, the identification of beer and nature is made via the horse. Drinking beer is like rodeo-riding, only less strenuous. It is a challenge that the rider can easily overcome, allowing him to save face and reaffirm masculinity. Budweiser beer also uses horses as a symbol: the Budweiser Clydesdales, a breed of "draft" horse. Whereas the Busch Stallion represents the frontier wilderness, the Clydesdales stand for the pastoral. Also, Colt 45 malt liquor, by its very name, invokes images of the Old West, horses, and of course guns, another phallic symbol. Another way in which beer is identified with nature and animals is through Budweiser's "Spuds McKenzie" and Stroh's "Alex," both dogs that behave like humans; both are in turn identified with masculinity as they are male characters, and canines are the animals most closely associated with masculinity.

As a setting for masculine activity, the bar runs a close second to nature, and many commercials seem to advertise bar patronage as much as they do a particular brand of beer. Of course, the drinking hall has a venerable history in Western culture as a center for male socializing and tests of skill, strength, and drinking ability. It is a setting featured prominently in the myths and legends of ancient Greece, and in Norse and Old English sagas. The pub is a popular setting in British literature, as is the saloon in the American Western genre. Like its predecessors, the bar of the beer commercial is presented as a male-dominated environment, although it sometimes serves as a setting for male-female interaction. And it is generally portrayed as a relaxed and comfortable context for male socializing, as well as a place where a man can find entertainment and excitement. The bars are immaculate and smokeless, and the waitresses and bartenders are always friendly; thus, along with nature, bars are the ideal male leisure environment. The only exception is the Bud Light bar, where men who are so uninformed as to ask for "a light" rather than a specific brand are subjected to pranks by the bartenders; still, even in this case the practical jokes are taken in stride, reaffirming the customer's masculinity.

It is worth noting that in the romanticized barroom of beer commercials, no one ever pays for his drinks, either literally or in terms of alcohol's effects. In other words, there are no consequences to the men's actions, which is consistent with the myth of masculinity's tendency to ignore or downplay risk and danger. The bar is shown as a self-contained environment, one that, like the outdoors, frees men from the constraints of civilization, allowing them to behave irresponsibly. Moreover, most settings featured as drinking-places in beer commercials are probably places that people would drive to—and drive home from. Because the action is confined to these settings, however, the question of how people arrived and how they will get home never comes up.

How do boys become men? In the world of beer commercials, boys become men by earning acceptance from those who are already full-fledged members of the community of men. Adult men are identified by their age, their size, their celebrity, and their positions of authority in the work world and/or status in a bar. To earn acceptance, the younger man must demonstrate that he can do the things that men do: take risks, meet challenges, face danger courageously, and dominate his environment. In the workplace, he demonstrates this by seizing opportunities to work, taking pride in his labor, proving his ability, persisting in the face of uncertainty, and learning to accept failure with equanimity. Having proven that he can act out the masculine role, the initiate is rewarded with beer. As a reward, beer symbolizes the overcoming of a challenge, the fulfilling of the requirements for group membership. The gift of beer also allows the adult male to show his acceptance of the initiate without becoming emotional. Beer then functions as a symbol of initiation and group membership.

For example, one of Budweiser's most frequently aired commercials during the 1980s features a young Polish immigrant and an older foreman and dispatcher. In the first scene, the dispatcher is reading names from a clipboard, giving workers their assignments. Arriving late, which earns him a look of displeasure from the foreman, the nervous young man takes a seat in the back. When he is finally called, the dispatcher stumbles over the immigrant's foreign name. The young man walks up to the front of the room, corrects the dispatcher's mispronunciation—a risky move, given his neophyte status, but one that demonstrates his pride and self-confidence. He receives his assignment, and the scene then shifts to a montage of the day's work. At the beginning, he drops a toolbox, spilling its contents, a mishap noted by the foreman; by the end of the day, however, he has demonstrated his ability and has earned the respect of his co-workers. The final scene is in a crowded tavern; the young man walks through the door, making his way to the bar, looking around nervously. He hears his name called, turns around, and the foreman, sitting at the bar, hands him a beer. In both the first and final scene, the immigrant begins at the back of the room, highlighting his outsider status, and moves to the front as he is given a chance to prove himself. The commercial's parallelism is not just an aesthetic device, but a mythic one as well. Having mastered the challenge of work, the neophyte receives the reward of a beer, which is both a symbol of that mastery and an invitation to symbolically reenact his feat. By working hard and well, he gains acceptance in the work world; by drinking the beer, he can also gain acceptance into the social world of the bar. The foreman, by virtue of his age, his position of authority, and his position sitting at the bar in the center of the tavern, holds the power of confirmation in both worlds.

The theme of initiation is also present in a subtle way in the Bud Light ads in which someone orders "a light," is given a substitute such as lamp or torch, and then corrects himself, asking for a "Bud Light." As one of the commercials revealed, the bartenders play these pranks because they are fed up with uninformed customers. The bizarre substitutions are a form of hazing, an initiation into proper barroom etiquette. The mature male is familiar with brands of beer, knows what he wants, and shows decisiveness in ordering it. Clearly, the individuals who ask for "a light" are inexperienced drinkers, and it is important to keep in mind that, to the barroom novice (and especially to the underage drinker), bars and bartenders can seem very threatening. While the substitute "lights" come as a surprise to the patrons, and thus threaten their composure, they are a relatively mild threat. The customers are able to overcome this challenge to their self-control, correct their order, and thereby gain entry into barroom society.

The biological transition from childhood to adulthood is a gradual one, but in traditional cultures, it is symbolized by formal rituals of initiation, rites of passage which mark the boundary between childhood and adulthood, clearly separating these two social positions. In our own culture, there are no initiation rites, and therefore the adolescent's social position is an ambiguous one. A number of events and activities do serve as symbols of adulthood, however. The commercials emphasize entry into the work world as one such step; financial independence brings the freedom of adulthood, while work is an integral part of the adult male's identity. As a symbol of initiation into the work world, beer also functions as a symbol of adulthood. And although this is never dealt with in the commercials, drinking in and of itself is a symbol of adulthood in our culture, as is driving, particularly in the eyes of underage males. Bars are seen as exclusively adult environments, and so acceptance in bars is a further sign of manhood. In the commercials, bars and work-places complement each other as environments in which initiation into adulthood can be consummated.

How do men relate to each other? In beer commercials, men are rarely found in solitary pursuits (and never drink alone), and only occasionally in one-to-one relationships, usually involving father-son or mentor-protegé transactions. The dominant social context for male interaction is the group, and teamwork and group loyalty rank high in the list of masculine values. Individualism and competition, by contrast, are downplayed, and are acceptable only as long as they foster the co-hesiveness of the group as a whole. Although differences in status may exist between members of the group and outsiders, within the group eq-uality is the rule, and elitism and intellectualism are disdained. This re-flects the American value of egalitarianism and solidifies the impor-tance of the group over individual members. The concept of group loyalty is extended to community and to country, so that patriotism is also pre-sented as an important value for men.

The emotional tenor of relationships among men in beer commercials is characterized by self-restraint. Generally, strong emotions are es-chewed, especially overt displays of affection. In the workplace, mutual respect is exhibited, but respect must be earned through ability and attitude. In leisure situations, humor is a major element in male inter-actions. Conversations among men emphasize joking, bragging, story-telling, and good-natured insults. The insults are a form of symbolic challenge; taking a ribbing in good spirit is a demonstration of emo-tional strength and self-mastery. By providing a controlled social con-text for the exchange of challenges and demonstrations of ego strength and self-control, the group provides continuous reinforcement of the members' masculinity. Moreover, gathering in groups provides men with the freedom to act irresponsibly; that is, it allows men to act like boys. This is particularly the case in the Miller Lite ads that feature retired sports stars, comedians, and other celebrities.

In beer commercials, drinking serves several important functions in promoting group solidarity. Beer is frequently the shared activity that brings the group together, and in the ads for Miller Genuine Draft, sharing beer acts as a reminder of the group's identity and history. Thus, beer becomes a symbol of group membership. It also serves as a means for demonstrating the group's egalitarian values. When one man gives a beer to another, it is a sign of acceptance, friendship, or gratitude. In this role, beer is also a substitute for overt display of affection. Although the commercials never deal with why beer takes on this role, the answer lies in the effects of alcohol. Certainly, its function as mood enhancer can have a positive influence on group interaction. And, as previously discussed, alcohol itself constitutes a challenge, so that drinking allows each member of the group to publicly demonstrate his masculinity. Alcohol also lowers inhibitions, making it easier for men to show their affection for one another. The well-known saying that you cannot trust a man who does not drink reflects the popular conception that under the influence of alcohol, men become more open and honest. Moreover, the effects of drinking on physical coordination make a man less of an immediate threat. All these properties contribute to beer's role as a medium of male bonding and a facilitator of group solidarity.

In general, men are not portrayed as loners in beer commercials, and in this respect the ads differ markedly from other expressions of the myth of masculinity. There are no isolated Marlboro men in the Busch frontier, for example. When he saves the calf from being swept away by the river, the Busch cowboy appears to be on his own, but by the time he is ready for his reward, another cowboy has appeared out of nowhere to share his beer. In another Busch ad, a jingle with the following lyrics is heard: "There's no place on earth that I'd rather be, than out in the open where it's all plain to see, if it's going to get done it's up to you and me." In this way, the ideal of individual self-reliance that is so central to the American myth of the frontier is transformed into group self-reliance. In the world of beer commercials, demonstrating one's masculinity requires an audience to judge one's performance and confirm one's status. Moreover, the emphasis the ads place on beer drinking as a group activity undermines the idea that it is in any way problematic. One of the most widespread stereotypes of problem drinkers is that they are solitary and secretive loners. The emphasis on the group in beer commercials plays on the common misconception that drinking, when it is done socially and publicly, cannot be harmful.

How do men relate to women? Although the world of beer commercials is often monopolized by men, some of the ads do feature male-female interaction in the form of courtship, as well as in more established relationships. When courtship is the focus, the image of the man's man gives way to that of the ladies' man, for whom seduction is the

ighest form of challenge. And while the obvious risk in courtship is
ejection by the opposite sex, the more significant danger in beer ads is
oss of emotional self-control. The ladies' man must remain cool,
onfidant, and detached when faced with the object of his desires. This
ocial type is exemplified by Billy Dee Williams, who plays on his ro-
nantic image in Colt 45 commercials. Strangely enough, Spuds McKenzie,
Budweiser's "party animal," also fits into this category, insofar as he,
ike Alex, is treated like a human being. In his ads, Spuds is surrounded
y the Spudettes, three beautiful young women who dance with him,
erve him, even bathe him. The women are attractive enough to make
nost males salivate like Pavlov's dogs, but Spuds receives their atten-
ons with casual indifference (and never betrays the insecurities that
aunt his cousin Snoopy when the *Peanuts* dog assumes his "Joe Cool"
ersona). While the commercials do not go so far as to suggest bestial-
ty, there is no question that Spuds is a stud.

Emotional control is also demonstrated by the male's ability to divide
is attention. For example, in one Michelob commercial, a young woman
s shown leaning over a jukebox and selecting a song; her expression
s one of pure pleasure, and she seems lost in thought. Other scenes,
resumably her memories, show her dancing in the arms of a handsome
oung man. His arms are around her neck, and he is holding in one hand,
ehind her back, a bottle of beer. This image emphasizes the difference
etween the myths of masculinity and femininity; her attention is
ocused entirely on him, while his interests extend to the beer as well
s the woman. According to the myth of masculinity, the man who loses
ontrol of his emotions in a relationship is a man who loses his inde-
endence, and ultimately, his masculinity; dividing attention is one way
o demonstrate self-control. Michelob also presents images of ladies'
nen in the form of popular musicians, such as the rock group Genesis,
ock star Eric Clapton, and popular vocalist Frank Sinatra. Many male
op stars have reputations as sexual athletes surrounded by groupies;
n the ads, however, they function as modern troubadours, providing a
omantic backdrop for lovers and facilitating social interaction. Acting,
ke Spuds McKenzie, as mascots for the beer companies, they imply
hat the beer they are identified with serves the same functions.

By far the most sexist of beer commercials, almost to the point of
arce, are the Colt 45 ads featuring Billy Dee Williams. One of these,
which is divided into three segments, begins with Williams saying:
There are two rules to remember if you want to have a good time: Rule
number one, never run out of Colt 45. Rule number two, never forget

rule number one." In the next segment, Williams continues: "You war to know why you should keep plenty of Colt 45 on hand? You neve know when friends might show up." As he says this, he opens a can an a woman's hand reaches out and takes it. In the third segment, h concludes, "I don't claim you can have a better time with Colt 45 tha without it, but why take chances?" As he says this, the camera pull back to reveal Williams standing, and an attractive woman sitting nex to him. The ad ends with a picture of a Colt 45 can and the slogan, "Th power of Colt 45: It works every time." There are a number of ways t interpret this pitch. First, malt liquor has a higher alcohol content tha beer or ale, and therefore is a more *powerful* beverage. Second, the a alludes to alcohol's image as an aphrodisiac, despite the fact that actually reduces male potency. As noted, the Colt 45 pistol is a phalli symbol, while the slogan can be read as a guarantee against impc tency—"it works every time." Third, it can be seen as referring t alcohol's ability to make men feel more confident about themselves an more interested in the opposite sex. And fourth, it plays on the popula notion that getting a woman drunk increases her desire for and willing ness to engage in sex. Williams keeps Colt 45 on hand not just fc himself, but for "friends," meaning "women." His secret of seductio is getting women to drink. In the ad, the woman is eager to drink Co 45, implying that she will be just as eager to make love. The idea tha a woman who drinks is "looking for it" is even clearer in a second ad

This commercial begins with the title "Billy Dee Williams on Bod Language." Moving through an outdoor party, Williams says, "Yo know, body language tells you a lot about what a person is thinking. Fc instance, that means she has an interest in the finer things in life." A he says this, the camera pans to show an attractive women sitting at bar alone, holding her necklace. She shifts her position and strokes he hair, and Williams says, "That means she also wants a little fun in he life, but only with the right man." At this point, the woman fills her glas with Colt 45, as Williams says, "And now she's pouring Colt 45 and w all know what that means." He then goes over to her and asks if sh would mind if he joined her, and she replies, "You must have read m mind." Williams responds, "Something like that," and the ad ends wit the same slogan as the first. What is implied in this commercial is tha any woman who would sit by herself and drink must be looking to ge picked up; she is sending out signals and preparing herself to be se duced. And although she is making herself approachable, she must wa for Williams to make the first move. At the same time, the woma appears to be vain, fondling her jewelry and hair. And in both ads, the women are seated while Williams stands. This portrayal of the woman's woman, based on the myth of femininity, is the perfect counterpart to Williams' image as a ladies' man.

When the commercials depict more established relationships, the emphasis shifts from romance and seduction to male activities in which women are reduced largely to the role of admiring onlookers. Men appear to value their group of friends over their female partners, and the women accept this. Women tend to be passive, not participating but merely watching as men perform physical tasks. In other words, they become the audience for whom men perform. For the most part, women know their place and do not interfere with male bonding. They may, however, act as emotional catalysts for male interaction, bringing men together. Occasionally, a woman may be found together with a group of men, presumably as the girlfriend or wife of one of the group members. Here, the presence of women, and their noninterference, indicates their approval of masculine activity and male bonding, and their approval of the role of beer in these situations. Even when a group of men acts irresponsibly and/ or boyishly, the presence of a woman shows that this behavior is socially sanctioned.

Alternate images of femininity can be found in beer commercials, but they are generally relegated to the background; for the most part, the traditional roles of masculinity and femininity are upheld. One exception is a Michelob Light ad that features Madeline Kahn. Introduced by a male voice-over, "Madeline Kahn on having it all," she is lying on her side on a couch, wearing an expensive-looking gown and necklace, and holding a bottle of beer. Kahn does a short humorous monologue in which she acknowledges her wealth and glamour, and the scene shifts to a shot of the beer, as the male voice-over says, "Michelob Light. You *can* have it all." While this represents something of a concession to changing conceptions of femininity, the advertisers hedge their bets. The male voice-over frames, and in a sense controls, Kahn's monologue, while Kahn position, lying on her side, is a passive and seductive one. To male viewers, the commercial can easily imply that "having it all" includes having a woman like her.

Conclusion

In the world of beer commercials, masculinity revolves around the theme of challenge, an association that is particularly alarming, given the social problems stemming from alcohol abuse. For the most part beer commercials present traditional, stereotypical images of men, and uphold the myths of masculinity and femininity. Thus, in promoting beer, advertisers also promote and perpetuate these images and myths. Although targeted at an adult audience, beer commercials are highly accessible to children; between the ages of 2 and 18, American children may see as many as 100,000 of these ads (Postman et al., 1987). They are also extremely attractive to children: humorous, exciting, and offering answers to questions about gender and adulthood. And they do have an impact, playing a role in social learning and attitude formation (Wallack, Cassady, & Grube, 1990). As Postman (1979) argues, television constitutes a curriculum, one that children spend more time with than in schoolrooms. Beer commercials are a prominent subject in television's curriculum, a subject that is ultimately hazardous to the intellectual as well as the physical health of the young. The myth of masculinity *does* have a number of redeeming features (facing challenges and taking risks are valuable activities in many contexts), but the unrelenting one-dimensionality of masculinity as presented by beer commercials is clearly anachronistic, possibly laughable, but without a doubt sobering.

7

Buddies and Pals

A History of Male Friendships on Prime-Time Television

LYNN C. SPANGLER

The reputation of male friendships has changed throughout history. Many would agree today that men bond in war zones, on playing fields, and in bars; however, most research indicates that men are not emotionally intimate with each other, an aspect of friendship that is characteristic among women friends. According to L. Rubin (1985), the current lack of closeness in most male friendships is quite a change from the past, when men's relationships were supposedly models of support and love.

While a variety of written documents has been used to enhance our understanding of friendships in the distant past, O'Connor (1983) says now "historians can find in television a rich mine of sources for studying social and cultural history" (p. xxvii). Television is renowned as a business that sells audiences to advertisers yet, as Kimmel (1987d) has pointed out, "images of gender in the media become texts on normative behavior, one of many cultural shards we use to construct notions of masculinity" (p. 20).

The cultural history and interpretations of gender seen on television, however, are very likely to be skewed. After a 10-year study of the production of television drama, Cantor (1980) concluded that profit is the major determinant of program content, although other factors, such as government and citizens' groups, also contribute. Gitlin (1983) found, in his interviews with more than 200 television industry people, that the business was a closed society, with relatively few companies creating most of the programming. Meehan (1983) concluded, in her study of female characters in prime time between 1950 and 1980, that the "presentation of women always in relation to men, cheerleaders to the male players, is a male vision, the product of a medium in which male creators have predominated" (p. 113). Furthermore, several researchers report how producers/writers of popular programs receive little network interference in their creation of stories and characters by virtue of their ratings successes (e.g., Broughton, 1986; Newcomb & Alley, 1983; R. Thompson, 1990). Whatever visions of male friendships have been on television, then, primarily have been created by a relatively few men in powerful, lucrative positions.

Target audiences, however, are often primarily women, the major purchasers of most advertised products. In his discussion of "gendered television," Fiske (1987d) describes the types of programming created to appeal separately to men and women. *The A-Team* is an example of "masculine television," along with other action/adventure series, which is created for a primarily male audience. Unlike feminine genres, such as soap operas, which show men as "caring, nurturing and verbal" (p. 186), programs targeted toward men not only exclude women, but they reinforce a capitalistic patriarchy by making men constantly prove their worth through work. While programs targeted toward women in prime time would also certainly reinforce the dominant ideology, male characters, according to Fiske, would be more loving and expressive.

Homosexuality, however, still is not accepted in patriarchal society and is rarely seen in fictional network broadcast television. For example, in the late 1970s ABC was picketed and received thousands of letters of protest before it even aired its satire of soap operas, *Soap*, because of the open sexuality, including homosexuality, of its characters. In the early 1980s public pressure on NBC resulted in the homosexuality of the title character in the movie pilot *Sidney Shorr* to be unspoken in the resultant series, *Love, Sidney*. In 1990, *TV Guide* alleged that ABC succumbed to pressure from sponsors not to repeat an episode of *thirtysomething* that showed two gay lovers in bed. Viewers are primarily heterosexual and, evidently, intolerant of homosexuality. As target audiences and the power structure of the television production industry change, representations of gender are expected to change.

Previous studies on gender portrayals in television have often been content analyses, which have found both men and women heavily stereotyped according to the traditional sex-role paradigm. While both researchers and audiences frequently have evaluated characters on their level of realism, a structural approach (Fiske, 1987a, pp. 151-154) explores portrayals as social representations of ideology. While research-ers of interpersonal behavior have been reporting the repressed nature of male friendships, television has been sending its own messages about them. People spend more time with television than any other medium. Conse-quently, the images it presents of men and their friendships have the po- tential to influence millions of people. This essay will compare research on real friendships to the representations of male friendships in more than 40 years of prime-time television programming. While me-diated images of cross-gender relationships and female friendships are also important (Spangler, 1989), it is the lament of the decline of intimate, nonsexual male friendships that is of immediate concern.

Same-Sex Friendships

Friends give us a sense of belonging and provide emotional support. People without such relationships are more vulnerable to a variety of problems. According to Duck (1983):

> Researchers have now established that friendship problems go hand in hand with many different social problems such as alcoholism, violence and sui-cide. It is also found that unpopularity in childhood foreshadows many diffi-culties in later life, such as delinquency and career misadventures. (p. 7)

Studies have shown, however, that male friends interact quite differ-ently from female friends. Most research confirms L. Rubin's (1985) summary that women's friendships with each other rest on shared in-timacies, self-revelation, nurturance, and emotional support (p. 66). In contrast, men's friendships are marked by shared activities. Their talk usually centers around work, sports, and sharing expertise. Men also trade complaints and concerns about women, along with talk of exploits, but most of the time their interactions are emotionally contained and controlled.

The key difference between men's and women's friendships seems to center on the higher level of emotional intimacy among women. Sherrod (1987), however, questioned comparing the verbal intimacy of women with the more unspoken commitments found with male friends, suggest-ing different standards of evaluation may be more appropriate. L. Rubin (1985) wrote about how men could become deeply bonded to one another without becoming intimate, just as parents and children can become bonded. Bonding can come from an intuitive understanding of one another as men or, on a more personal level, from shared life-and-death experiences, such as in war. Intimacy, according to Rubin, however, is "only possible between equals who have both the emotional development and verbal skills to share their inner life with each other" (p. 68). She and many other researchers suggest that while men may feel connected or bonded to each other, they are not intimate; they do not share problems and emotions. Sherrod (1987) explained how men might perceive themselves as close friends and discover they are not, arguing that:

> [M]en infer intimacy simply because they are friends. . . . Inferred intimacy seems to work well until a disturbing problem demands more from the relationship than unquestioned acceptance. At that point, many men find themselves without the kind of friend on whom they can rely. (p. 222)

Why aren't men as emotionally intimate with each other as women are? In his search for a close male friend, Miller (1983, p. 129) found that most men expressed a fear of appearing homosexual. He found that a more important inhibition to closeness, however, is the competition among males learned in school, sports, and business. Chodorow (1978) offers a psychoanalytic explanation based on the psychological separation boys make from their mothers in order to develop their male identity. As Messner (1987) points out, however, men still need closeness, so they seek the rule-bound structure of activities such as games and sports as a psychologically safe way to connect to one another.

Garfinkel (1985) offers another influence on how men should relate to one another and how they should behave: images of men in the media. Looking at films, advertisements, books, and magazines, he found an emphasis on winning at all costs. Aggressive behavior, including violence, was one means of winning often used in the media. The "strong, silent type" is often found in the media, particularly in films, because men hide their pain on the way to winning and maintaining an independent stance. Garfinkel summarized male friendships interpersonally and in print and film media when he said, "Our bonds come through *doing* together; we have not learned about *being* together" (p. 3).

As the roles of men and women have been created, stereotyped, and dichotomized, so have their friendships. Television plays a role in our notions of what it is like, or what it should be like, to be male and female, including how each gender behaves in relationships. In the following analysis of four decades of fictional television programming, trends will be noted and specific series highlighted that are particularly illustrative of mediated male friendships. Comparisons to research on real friendships will be made throughout, with the recognition that their mediated counterparts are, to a large extent determined by television economics.

Male Friendships on Television

The 1950s

During the 1950s situation comedies, anthology dramas, variety shows, quiz shows, and Westerns were the most popular genres during prime time. Of the regular series, Westerns were the ones to obviously demonstrate male bonding. MacDonald (1987, p. 2) writes that the Western was truly the all-American genre, no other being associated so completely with American civilization. Originating on radio, *The Lone Ranger* was one of the first Westerns on television. On ABC from 1949 until 1957, the Lone Ranger was in constant company of Tonto, an American Indian, who addressed him as *kemo sabe*—faithful friend (Brooks & Marsh, 1981, p. 430). Tonto had nursed John Reid (the Lone Ranger) back to health after a deadly ambush, and vowed to stay with him as the Ranger avenged the deaths of his other comrades. MacDonald writes that, "more than a friendship, the bond between Tonto and the Ranger was an alliance between mature men who recognized their interdependency and innate equality" (p. 31). Primarily targeted toward children, as most early television Westerns were, the program's emphasis was on action, not character development or intimacy. Avenging the death of friends, however, is a common theme in Westerns. Another example is found in *The Life & Legend of Wyatt Earp*, on ABC from 1955 until 1961. Earp became marshal of Ellsworth, Kansas, to avenge the death of his friend and formal marshal of the town (Brooks & Marsh, 1981, pp. 428-429).

MacDonald (1987) writes that "self-flattering and reinforcing, the mythic West depicted in the adult Western was at base a metaphor for the United States in the 1950s and 1960s" (p. 72). While cowboys fought easily identifiable villains (renowned as the guys in the black hats), communism and an international Cold War were the clear enemies of the audience. *Gunsmoke*, considered to be the first "adult" Western, began in 1955 and ran for 20 years. Adult Westerns were targeted for an older audience and contained more character development. The creators of *Gunsmoke* attempted a realistic program, based on "the revolutionary but entirely valid principle that in the early West the most hated man in town was usually the marshal" (Whitney, 1980, p. 43). Co-creator Norman Macdonnel said in 1958 that "If you look closely you will see that there are only three in the world who care at all whether Matt lives or dies. One is Doc, who digs the bullets out of him; another is Chester, who admires him and called him Muster Dellon; and the other is Kitty, the dance-hall girl, who loves him" (p. 43).

Although sidekicks and admirers such as Chester were common in Westerns, many men, particularly in the earlier Westerns, were loners. Even men who were bonded by virtue of needing to save one another's lives could hardly be called intimate friends; rarely, if ever, did the men in television Westerns discuss their feelings and fears with one another. Their bonds, however, could be quite powerful and also exclusive of women. MacDonald (1987) gives an example of this from a 1965 episode of *Laredo*, where one of the closely knit trio of Texas Rangers has resigned his job to leave town with his fiancée. Just before the engaged Ranger leaves, his buddies need him in a fight against warring Comanches, "and rather than renounce the ties of male bonding, Cooper abandoned his sweetheart at the stagecoach, ended his engagement, and explained that 'there are certain things a man's got to do' " (p. 76). MacDonald attributes the later demise of the television Western to sociopolitical changes, including an increasing disillusionment and skepticism on the part of audiences in their own political environment (e.g., Vietnam).

While the friendships in Westerns are usually implied by the necessary bonding of the men in dangerous environments, the idea of friendship is verbalized and tested more often in situation comedies of the 1950s. Perhaps the most tested friendship between two men is the relationship of Ralph Kramden and Ed Norton on *The Honeymooners*, which started as sketches on Jackie Gleason's variety show in 1952. Of the 39 episodes originally released in syndication from the 1955-1956 season, Ralph threw Norton out of his apartment 21 times (Crescenti & Columbe, 1985, p. 293). Despite Ralph's threats to Norton and his constant insinuations that Ed is crazy: "You been comin' up through too many manholes where they forgot to take off the cover!" (p. 267), the men are almost constant companions.

Episodes of *The Honeymooners* frequently revolve around Ralph's getting jealous or angry at Ed; however, their fights always end with the two making up, often after Alice has convinced Ralph he was wrong. Ralph and Ed also express their affection for each other. In "A Matter of Life-and-Death," Ed thinks Ralph is dying and he cries. Ed also confesses to crying when he heard an apology Ralph recorded for Alice: "Ya got me right here . . . and when ya came to that part about 'come back to your Poopsie' it was all I could do to keep from rushin' into your arms!" (p. 124). In "Pardon My Glove," Ed consoles Ralph when he thinks Alice is cheating on him. Perhaps the most telling episode of their friendship is "Pal O' Mine," when Ralph gets jealous over a ring Ed bought for his boss. Thinking it is for him, Ralph tries the ring on and it gets stuck. At the end of the episode, Ralph rushes to the hospital, thinking Ed has been seriously injured, and he offers to donate blood. Finding this out, Ed says Ralph is the "finest human being of all time" and tells the nurse to tell Ralph to keep the ring (p. 74). Ed was usually the more sentimental of the two, particularly in comparison to Ralph's penchant for physical threats. Regardless of Ralph's awkwardness in expressing himself occasionally, the two were intimate. They were not bonded together because they faced life-and-death situations; they shared their normal, working-class problems and helped each other get through them.

There were other male friendships in situation comedies in the 1950s, often part of "couple" friendships, as was found with the Kramdens and Nortons in *The Honeymooners*. Perhaps the only other significant male friendship in television comedy in the 1950s, however, was that between Dobie Gillis and Maynard G. Krebs on *The Many Loves of Dobie Gillis* (1959-1963). While Maynard referred to Dobie as his "best buddy" and the two frequently schemed together, even went to college and into the army together, one gets the feeling Dobie would rather spend his time with girls. As a matter of fact, one episode begins with a lament by Dobie about how his preoccupation with girls led him to ignore Maynard, who had a problem that Dobie should have helped with. Maynard is open in his expression of affection for Dobie; Dobie does not hide his affection for Maynard, but it is clear girls come first.

While comedies in the early 1950s included working-class and ethnic families, Taylor (1989) writes how they were phased out and replaced with the upper-middle-class coziness of programs such as *Ozzie and Harriet*. Taylor says that the television industry may have been trying to reproduce the typical American family, the people advertisers wanted to reach; however, what they actually reproduced in these programs was "less the experience of most family lives than a postwar ideology breezily forecasting steady rates of economic growth that would produce sufficient abundance to eliminate the basis for class and ethnic conflict" (p. 40). What also seemed to disappear in these later family comedies was close male friends like Ralph Kramden and Ed Norton, suggesting that the family would supply all the companionship and emotional needs of its members, an idea perhaps television industry executives thought would appeal to women. In their appeal to men, Westerns are a good example of Fiske's notion of masculine television, where men are bonded in activity and women play a secondary, if any, role.

The 1960s

While Westerns were still very popular at the beginning of the 1960s, the genre increasingly became replaced by more situation comedies, variety shows, and even spy thrillers. As MacDonald (1987) writes, the Western lost its popularity as American attitudes and values changed; other genres made more radical adaptations to maintain audiences and specifically, in the late 1960s, to attract younger and more affluent people. Until the end of the decade, it was primarily only on the news that television admitted to assassinations, civil unrest, riots, and an escalating, controversial war.

One of the most intimate male friendships in the 1960s, like that in the 1950s between Ralph Kramden and Ed Norton, was to be found on a comedy involving two working-class men. *The Andy Griffith Show* began in 1960 on CBS and ran through 1968, focusing on life for a sheriff and his friends in a small Southern town. The relationship between Sheriff Andy Taylor and his deputy Barney Fife was explained by Andy Griffith who played the sheriff:

> The characters were very fond of each other. Whenever there was any little joke between them, it was always based on that fondness—that was always in the background. And Andy was always very protective of Barney. He might laugh, have a lot of fun, and know Barney would get madder than hell, but you knew that in a little while it would be worked out. He was always by his side, just in case. (Kelly, 1981, p. 43)

While police work rarely got dangerous enough in Mayberry for Andy and Barney to be bonded in the traditional sense, they were constant companions, working together, often double-dating, and Barney had many meals with Andy, his son, and his aunt. Some of the most endearing moments of the series were the segments of realistic small talk between Barney and Andy. Their conversations could be considered intimate; while feelings were more often "understood" than verbalized, the two men knew things about each other that perhaps their families did not even know. Andy Griffith recalled an example:

> One time we did a show where we were at Barney's house looking through a box full of stuff from our old high school annuals. . . . And Barney came up with a rock, and he looked at it a long time in silence, and he said, "You know what this is?" And I said, "What?" "My dad's rock." And we both looked at this stupid rock—and then he explained that his dad used to strike matches on it when he was a little boy, and he would watch him. (p. 43)

There were several series in the 1960s that included teams of men working together (e.g., *Combat, Twelve O'Clock High, Adam 12, Wild Wild West, Man from U.N.C.L.E., Hawaii Five-O, Batman*) and even living or traveling together (*The Monkees, Route 66*), but one of the most interesting relationships was that of Bill Cosby's and Robert Culp's characters on *I Spy*. The first dramatic series to have a black star, *I Spy* was an espionage thriller on NBC from 1965 through 1968. The men traveled around the world as American spies; Kelly Robinson's (Culp) cover was as a tennis player, and Alexander Scott (Cosby) was his trainer and traveling companion. These men were, of course, bonded; they saved each other's lives on many occasions. They also had an easy relationship with each other, sparked by touches of humor. They occasionally double-dated and spent free time with each other; their racial difference was never a problem. Robinson knew Scott's mother well enough to receive letters from her, and evidently spent time at Scott's family home. Occasionally Robinson even threatened to write Scott's mother if he misbehaved. Although the series was filled with action, there were usually at least two short scenes in each episode where the two men were seen casually chatting and enjoying each other's company. While they occasionally had trouble expressing emotions, they shared many intimate times. For example, in an episode called "Tashia," Kelly had fallen in love with a woman who turned out to be working with enemies. Instead of expressing his feelings, Kelly took Scott's offer of punching at him; then the two walked silently away together. They obviously cared for each other and understood each other's feelings; the gentle teasing and use of nicknames ("Kel" and "Scotty") gave way to more serious conversations when it was warranted.

The characters on *Star Trek* (NBC, 1966-1969) could represent a number of ways males relate to each other. The international and interplanetary crew was bonded with fierce loyalty to their captain, but it was a running joke about the lack of emotion in Captain Kirk's first officer and possibly best friend, Spock. Spock, because he was half human and half unemotional Vulcan, often struggled with intense feelings. Episodes that dealt either with Spock's parents or with returning to his home planet were particularly difficult for Spock, and it was the captain ("Jim," in more intimate moments) to whom he would speak. "Bones," the ship's doctor, who was quite expressive himself, would get particularly frustrated at Spock. Perhaps Spock's struggle with expressing emotions was more symbolic of modern American males, who were struggling with their traditional sex role, than Vulcans. In a particularly touching episode, Spock and Captain Kirk were forced to fight each other, because of Vulcan customs, for the woman to whom Spock was betrothed in childhood.

In many ways, relationships in television drama and comedy in the 1960s were like their counterparts in the 1950s. Westerns were replaced by other types of action/adventure programs, but, except for *I Spy* and perhaps *Star Trek*, the emphasis was on bonding through activity, not intimacy. Andy and Barney in *The Andy Griffith Show* continued the same closeness found between working-class men, as demonstrated by Ed and Ralph in *The Honeymooners*, but in other comedies most men were rooted in middle-class families. It was not until the end of the 1960s, when advertisers wanted to pursue a younger target audience, that network programming would reflect the turbulence of that decade. While most previous entertainment programming promoted the nuclear middle-class family, unquestioned patriotism, and hegemonic masculinity, some programming of the early 1970s would question almost everything.

The 1970s

Taylor (1989) discusses *The Mary Tyler Moore Show*, *All in the Family*, and *M*A*S*H* as the first programs to question the status quo and reflect the confusion of American culture. Although many situation comedies in the past were set in the military, sometimes during wartime, none achieved either the character development or the longevity of *M*A*S*H* (CBS, 1972-1983) and none were as critical of war. The friendship between Hawkeye and Trapper John, and later with B.J., is evident. As characters developed over the 11 years of the series, so did relationships. While the emphasis was on comedy, occasionally the mood got serious and the friends would help each other get through tough times. Intimate talk did not come easily, however, even among friends who daily faced the threat of death together, but it did come. When B.J. cheated on his wife for the first and only time, he had trouble talking to Hawkeye about it, perhaps because he was afraid womanizer Hawkeye would not think it was a "big deal." He did tell Hawkeye, however, and Hawkeye clearly understood B. J.'s feelings. And it was Hawkeye's trouble with expressing his fear and horror of war that led to his spending time in a ward with a psychiatrist. Hawkeye and B.J. (and earlier, Trapper John) expressed their affection more in what they did. In the final episode, Hawkeye is seen rushing back to camp to say goodbye to B.J. Although he is too late, B.J. had left a "goodbye" spelled out in a field.

Like *M*A*S*H*, several other comedies in the 1970s involved people working together who were like families, including *The Mary Tyler Moore Show* (known as the first "character," as opposed to "situation," comedy), *Barney Miller*, and *WKRP in Cincinnati*. As real-life families were becoming less stable, Taylor (1989) writes, the workplace represented an idealized construction of family: "a workplace utopia whose most fulfilling attributes are vested not in work activity but in close emotional ties between co-workers" (p. 111). In *Taxi*, Alex was the co-worker to whom all the other characters went with their problems, including Bobby, Jim, Tony, and even Louie. Sometimes the problems were personal and Alex might be somewhat embarrassed about it, but he always helped. These co-workers knew each other intimately.

A comedy that dealt with best friends growing up was *Happy Days* (ABC, 1974-1984). Although the characters rarely spoke of their friendship, in a particularly poignant episode where Richie had been seriously injured in an accident, Fonzie was seen praying out loud, finally expressing his feelings for Richie, although Richie could not hear. The "tough guy" image of Fonzie increasingly softened throughout the series, making it easier for him and Richie to communicate on a more intimate level.

There is one comedy from the 1970s that, similar to *The Honeymooners*, constantly tested and reaffirmed the friendship of two men. The opening sequence of *The Odd Couple* established the premise of the series: "Can two divorced men live together without driving each other crazy?" Oscar and Felix were complete opposites: Oscar was the slob, and Felix was the "neat-freak" who was always trying to improve Oscar and was more in touch with his feelings. Some episodes revolved around one's explaining a significant past event of the other (e.g., Felix discussing Oscar's marriage while in the army reserve, Felix destroying his own marriage while trying to save Oscar's during a Caribbean vacation, and how they met on jury duty). Their frequent fights, however, led the men to go to a therapist in one episode. The therapist suggested role reversal, but it only ended in more fighting. In the last episode of the series, Felix remarried, and Oscar was so delighted that he vowed to turn neat (Eisner & Krinsky, 1984, p. 630). Despite the fighting and contrasting characters, though, it is unlikely the two would have stayed together if they did not care for each other. While Felix was often willing to express his feelings, it was not in Oscar's nature to do so. Oscar cared for Felix; he just could not or would not often express emotions other than anger.

Several dramas in the 1970s involved men who were bonded in various degrees because of their work or other circumstances. Examples include the detectives on *The Streets of San Francisco* (ABC, 1972-1977), the paramedics on *Emergency* (NBC, 1972-1977), and the young policemen on *The Rookies*. The friendship of Charles and Jonathan on *Little House on the Prairie* was a little more intimate occasionally, but it was obviously secondary to their families. *Starsky and Hutch* was perhaps the closest male friendship portrayed in drama in the 1970s. Obviously bonded because of their jobs, the men also spent time together outside of their police work. Fiske (1987a) wrote that:

> Starsky and Hutch exhibited many signs of a homosexual relationship, but their physical and emotional intimacy was not, in itself, a source of satisfaction and pleasure to them. Their fulfillment came from the goals that their relationship enabled them to achieve, not from the relationship itself. (p. 213)

The men seemed more physically, rather than emotionally, intimate. The opening credits, for example, showed them frequently touching, even falling in each other's arms. Regardless of whether one sees signs of homosexuality in their relationship, however, the emphasis in the series was on action, and the men got emotional only when the other was in jeopardy. It is interesting that Fiske reads the physical and emotional intimacy of Starsky and Hutch as homosexual when the same kind of relationship between women probably would not be suspect. It is doubtful that the series would have been as popular if many people had read their relationship this way; perhaps the characters were portrayed as more intimate to appeal to women in a genre (action/adventure) that normally appeals more to men.

Prime-time programming in the 1970s generally was targeted toward a younger audience, capitalizing on a cultural "youth movement" felt by many. Comedy became based on character rather than situation, beginning with *The Mary Tyler Moore Show* and also exemplified by the growth of characters on *M*A*S*H* throughout the run of the series. Action/adventure series seemed to try to appeal to more women by emphasizing caring relationships, such as on *Starsky and Hutch*, or by starring women, such as on *Charlie's Angels*. It is interesting to contemplate the rising role of women and feminism in the television industry during this time. Many male characters were becoming more sensitive and expressive, even if it was difficult and rarely shared with other men. Lou Grant on *The Mary Tyler Moore Show* learned some hard lessons through his divorce, and Hawkeye on *M*A*S*H* did some soul-searching about his attitudes toward women. Hawkeye's attitudes toward a woman doctor, for example, were explored in the Emmy Award-winning episode, "Inga," written by Alan Alda, a self-proclaimed feminist (Reiss, 1983).

The 1980s

The 1980s were the "Reagan Years" and a return to more conservative values. This decade saw a resurgence of nuclear family comedy and action dramas. Of the two, the latter has seemed to stress the bonding of men, as did Westerns in the late 1950s, but emotional disclosure is not necessarily a part of their relationships. Both *The A-Team* and *Magnum, P.I.* began in 1980 and featured Vietnam veterans as their main characters. Both also have characters with a noticeable lack of serious permanent relationships with women. Fiske (1987a) writes, basing his criticism on Chodorow's psychoanalytic explanation of the development of the male role:

> The exscription of women leads to a male bonding which is a close relationship protected from the threat of intimacy. The bond of the A-Team, of Magnum and his co-heroes, is goal-oriented, not relationship-oriented. The relationship is there to serve a common goal, not the needs of the relationship itself; it depends on action not on feeling. (p. 212)

It is not until the final episode of the *Magnum, P.I.* series that the three bonded Vietnam veterans have the promise of permanent female relationships. In "Resolutions," Rick got married, T.C. was reunited with his wife, and Magnum found his daughter. Magnum's reenlistment with the Navy could also change the nature of the men's friendship; their lack of goal-centered activities together could even dissipate their friendship.

The use of the Vietnam war is different in *Magnum, P.I.* than in *The A-Team*. The A-Team veterans were wrongly accused of a war crime, so their experience in Vietnam made them fugitives from the law and committed to helping others. The Vietnam War was often seen in flashbacks on *Magnum*, and people often came back to haunt the characters in some way. Anderson (1987) writes that:

> Thomas Magnum himself is more generally concerned with sorting out his own past than with solving cases; in fact, he is an inept detective through the series. The overwhelming burden of his memory, combined with his struggle to master the past, make Magnum the first tragic character on prime-time television. (pp. 124-125)

Part of Magnum's tragic character is certainly his inability to share his emotional problems with his closest friends, Rick and T.C. As Fiske has pointed out, however, their relationship was goal-oriented; Magnum frequently enlisted the help of Rick and T.C. in his detective work, often against their will. While their bonding was evident, both from their Vietnam experiences together and their frequent endangerment in Hawaii, their intimacy was not. Like almost all the other male friends on television, they *do* together; expressing feeling was not part of their relationship. Their doing together, however, could be an excuse for *being* together. The final episode of the series in 1988 was typical of the friendship of Magnum with Rick and T.C. and even Higgins. In stereotypical fashion, the men have a bachelor party for Rick at a strip joint and happily get into a brawl; however, when it comes to Magnum's serious concern over his future and the death of his daughter, he ventures off by himself, barely hinting to his male friends what has been going on in his mind, the lone cowboy riding off to face the enemy by himself.

Many action/adventure series in the 1980s contained characters who were Vietnam veterans, such as *Riptide*, created by Stephen J. Cannell, producer of *The A-Team*. R. Thompson (1990) says several of Cannell's "male bonding" series contain "fistfights-cum-love" scenes (p. 130) between main characters who compete to have the most injuries. The Vietnam drama begun in 1987, *Tour of Duty*, demonstrates the problems many men have in dealing with intimacy while they can be strongly bonded. In one episode, Sergeant Anderson received a letter from his ex-wife, asking him to write to his 3-year-old daughter. Not able to write the letter himself, he asked the camp chaplain to do it for him. Usually a brave man, Anderson appeared visibly nervous about going on a mission to rescue a couple of parachutists. Nevertheless, the group rescues a severely wounded man. Anderson had encouraged the others to leave the wounded man behind, however, because they were surrounded by North Vietnamese. The wounded man (a captain) also ordered them to leave him, and requested Anderson to write to his daughter for him. As the Vietnamese got closer to the wounded man, Anderson turned around in a desperate attempt to rescue him. The others followed, severely outnumbered, but were miraculously able to rescue the captain and all get out alive. Anderson is seen writing to the man's daughter at the end of the episode. The idea of intimacy with his daughter evidently made Anderson weak and afraid of dying, but the bond with the other man made them all strong enough to beat down three times their number in enemies. It seems they could only express their feelings for each other by risking their lives, and any other expressions of affection or fear would make them weak.

Other dramatic series in the 1980s depicted men bonded in life-and-death situations, including *Miami Vice* and *Hill Street Blues*. The 1980s also saw an increase in vulnerable men, although the macho type were still to be found. Whether as an appeal to reach more women, or out of a recognition that men are also human, even ex-football player Alex Karras (1985) wrote in an article in *TV Guide* that he appreciated the change and considered the "real men" on television to be sensitive, expressive of feelings, and not intimidated by independent women. Examples Karras gave of such males were Cliff Huxtable of *The Cosby Show* and the title character in *Remington Steele*, men whose best friends seemed to be women, as is often the case with men in real life. He also found Thomas Magnum, Captain Furillo of *Hill Street Blues*, and the men on *Barney Miller* to be three-dimensional. All three programs contained life-and-death situations in which the male characters bonded. Karras wrote about the police on *Barney Miller*:

They talked to each other. You could feel the growth in them week after week. And they were all vulnerable, in tune with life. . . . I liked the fact that they never were sent out—or wanted to be sent out—alone to capture someone. It was always: take so-and-so with you and go take care of that. Two guys facing reality. Not one guy riding solo into the sunset. (pp. 7-8)

At least two more of these vulnerable "real men" of the 1980s are to be found on the highly acclaimed *thirtysomething*. Of particular interest is the relationship between Elliott and Michael, who shared not only a business, but also feelings about dating, cheating on their wives, and other personal things. When the two must close down their advertising agency, they decide to continue working together elsewhere. It is to Michael that Elliott turns when he is agonizing over his separation and reconciliation with his wife. Michael confides to Elliott when he is distressed that he wants a child and his wife, Hope, does not. Toward the end of the 1989 season, Michael risks his job partially to ensure that Elliott will still be able to work there after a failed takeover attempt. The two men are undoubtedly emotionally intimate as well as bonded in their everyday lives.

As noted above, comedy in the 1980s tended to stress family, and not necessarily friendship outside the home. A particularly poignant episode of *Family Ties* ("A, My Name Is Alex") demonstrated not only the guilt Alex had at the news of a friend's death, but also the difficulty he had, and will continue to have, in expressing his feelings. A comedy that did focus on two friends, *Bosom Buddies* (1980-1984), had the premise of two men who dressed as women in order to be able to live in an all-women residence. Henry and Kip had gone to public school together and worked in the same advertising agency. Despite the silly premise, the series demonstrated a close relationship between two men who helped each other in their various schemes and dreams, and they discussed their feelings. In one particular episode Henry gets jealous of a new friend of Kip's and explains his feelings to him. Kip understands and apologizes for taking Henry for granted.

The 1980s continued the trend of more sensitive men in both comedy and drama. A return to 1950s conservatism, however, found most men happily married with their wives as their best friends. With the public finally able to talk about Vietnam, television drama depicted friendships between men as bonds developed during the Vietnam war, such as in *Magnum, P.I.* Men able to discuss intimate subjects with each other were found mostly on programs such as *thirtysomething*, targeted at more upscale, educated men and women or yuppies—those young, urban professionals whom advertisers craved to reach.

Conclusion

Male friendships on television throughout the years have occasionally depicted intimate relationships, although most programs have demonstrated bonding rather than emotional disclosure. Both Westerns and action/adventure series are typical of the "masculine" programs Fiske describes, where male relationships are goal-oriented, depicting men doing together, rather than being together. Intimate relationships between males are more likely to be found on comedies, where, interestingly enough, women and children make up the majority of the audience. While producers of comedies may depict men as more vulnerable and self-disclosing to attract women viewers, comedies also seem to have enjoyed more creative freedom to take chances (such as with *All in the Family* and other 1970s character comedies). Male characters in comedies generally were more intimate than males in other genres; however, one male friend was usually more self-disclosing than the other, possibly symbolizing difficulty with the rigid boundaries of the male role.

On television in the 1950s and 1960s, the nuclear family and hegemonic masculinity dominated. Two working-class comedies depicted the most intimate male friends: *The Honeymooners* and *The Andy Griffith Show*. While Westerns and most action/adventure series depicted bonding and goal-oriented relationships, *I Spy* was a landmark in depicting a truly intimate friendship between men. Interestingly, both *I Spy* and *Star Trek* portrayed friendships among men of different races and cultures. When television of the 1970s caught up with the turbulence of the 1960s, comedies continued to depict the most intimate relationships in shows such as *The Odd Couple* and *M*A*S*H*. *Starsky and Hutch* depicted two men bonded and physically intimate in their line of work, but their intimacy could not rival that between the main characters in *I Spy*. The conservatism of the 1980s saw a return to the nuclear family and a proliferation of action/adventure series portraying Vietnam veterans. In programs such as *Magnum, P.I.*, buddies from Vietnam continued their relationship in a series of goal-oriented activities. Feelings were not expressed, and women were excluded. Again in comedies, such as *Bosom Buddies* and *Taxi*, are found the most emotionally expressive male friendships. When men self-disclose in drama, it is usually with women. The friendship between Elliott and Michael on *thirtysomething* is the exception that may someday prove to be the rule. Significantly, unlike many male buddies in comedies, neither has trouble expressing his feelings to the other. As network television seeks the more upscale demographics of "quality" programs such as *thirtysomething*, male friendships may be characterized as more intimate to attract more women and educated, "liberal" male viewers.

There have been intimate male friendships depicted on television for more than four decades, but never in abundance. The majority of men on TV are seen doing together, not being together, as is reported to happen in real life. The failure of *Men*, a short-lived network series in 1989 that focused on the intimate friendship of several males, may be an indication that American culture is not ready for such depictions except, perhaps, in comedy. The portrayal of male friendships on television will change as the representation of masculinity changes and large audiences find it acceptable. The influence of women and feminists in the industry may also create some changes, as indicated by Alan Alda's influence on *M*A*S*H*. A more recent example may be found in *American Dreamer*, an NBC comedy introduced in the fall of 1990 and produced by Susan Seeger and Gary David Goldberg, creator of *Family Ties* and husband of feminist Diana Meehan. An early episode, starring Robert Urich and written by Goldberg, explored the problems male friends have in sharing intimate details of their lives; it was almost as if Goldberg based the story on research on male friendships. The direct contribution of women in the television industry, such as Diane English, co-creator of *Murphy Brown*, and Linda Bloodworth-Thomason, co-creator of *Designing Women*, on the portrayals of men are yet to be explored, but the economic influence of women as target audience is quite evident. Meanwhile, syndication keeps the intimate male friendships on *The Honeymooners* and *I Spy* alive.

8

From Good Times to The Cosby Show

Perceptions of Changing Televised Images Among Black Fathers and Sons

VENISE T. BERRY

Young black men run the highest risk of losing their life to violent crimes (64.6%); 41% of black youth are raised in fatherless homes; and black males account for 42% of all men in American prisons

Matney & Johnson, 1984; Hare & Hare, 1984

Introduction

With statistics like these, it is no wonder that the image of low-income black males in our society is often a dismal and confusing one, both on television and in reality. Many studies have examined televised male sex roles that evolve from stereotypical ideologies of gender. They indicate that images usually center around the male as a role model in the work force, and the female in domestic environments (Farrell, 1974; McGhee & Frueh, 1980; O'Donnell & O'Donnell, 1978).

Women tend to portray more emotion and sensitivity, while men are prone to violence, dominance, and a more serious nature (Gunter, 1986; Morgan, 1982; Pleck, 1982). Stereotypical sex roles have been identified in much of today's television programming. Available research suggests that heavy television viewing contributes to sex-role development and/or reinforcement among youth (Cobb, Stevens-Long, & Goldstein, 1982; Drabman, Robertson, Patterson, Jarvie, Hammer, & Cordua, 1981).

Studies involving the ability to change stereotypical ideas through counter-stereotypical images yield conflicting results. Several have realized little success in efforts to change job stereotyping through televised roles (Durkin & Hutchins, 1984; O'Bryant & Corder-Bolz, 1978a, 1978b). On the other hand, the potential for change has been a primary component in other areas, such as message adoption and modeling behaviors (Eisenstock, 1984; Johnston & Ettema, 1982; Williams, La Rose, & Frost, 1981).

An examination of the relationship between black youth and television suggests that black youth, particularly low-income black youth, tend to be influenced to some degree by television. They watch more often, identify with it to a greater extent, and perceive it as reality more readily than other youth (Dates, 1980; Donohue, 1975; Donohue & Donohue, 1977; Lee & Browne, 1981).

The images of black characters on television have improved slightly, yet many are still found to be stereotypical and negative (Bowser & Hunt, 1981; Comstock & Cobbey, 1979; Gray, 1986; Greenberg & Neuendorf, 1980; Lemon, 1977; Poindexter and Stroman, 1981; Reid, 1979; Roberts, 1975). Finally, available data also show that black audiences tend to prefer black shows and characters (Allen & Bielby, 1979; Berry, 1982; Greenberg & Atkin, 1978).

Any examination of the televised black male image must also take into account the powerful historical experience of black males in this country. During slavery, black bucks were admired and exploited for their strength and endurance. The era of civil rights found many black men standing tall and speaking loud, only to be stifled by limited employment opportunities and a welfare system that made it easier for their women and children to survive without them (Meier & Rudwick, 1970).

Many of today's black male youth find themselves in what Jesse Jackson called, "a cycle of poverty." Black male youth lack many of the opportunities and motivations through education, contacts, knowledge, and money to rise within the system. Often frustrated and angry, they overcompensate physically and project an exaggerated manliness, assessing other avenues of power and control (Rainwater, 1970).

This chapter presents the perceptions and interpretations of a specific group of low-income black adolescents as they perceive the male images of two distinctly different black, family-oriented comedy shows: *Good Times* and *The Cosby Show*. It examines these three specific areas:

(a) the assessment of the extent to which the environment of each show is considered a representation of real life by these youth; (b) the interpretations of black male teen images through the oldest sons on each show, J.J. Evans (*Good Times*) and Theo Huxtable (*The Cosby Show*); and (c) the exploration of attitudes and values among these young people, as they relate to the father figures and their methods of discipline (James Evans' physical approach on *Good Times* and Heathcliff Huxtable's interactive approach on *The Cosby Show*).

Sample and Methodology

The sample for this project consisted of 54 black youths participating in the 1987 Upward Bound/JTPA Summer Program at Huston-Tillotson College in Austin, Texas. The Upward Bound/JTPA Program serves as a source of educational, cultural, and social enrichment for low-income black adolescents. The participants are considered low-income because the family's income falls within the specific federal guidelines for the program.

All of the sample were black (100%). Twenty-eight (51.9%) were female and 26 (48.1%) were male. The age of the sample ranged from 14 to 18; and they were in the 8th through 12th grades in school. Single-parent households were the norm as 45 (83.3%) reported living with their mother only, 5 (9.3%) lived with both mother and father, 3 (5.6%) lived with their father only, and 1 (1.8%) was living with a grandparent.

In an in-depth structural analysis of *The Cosby Show*, Blue (1989) identifies within the program what she calls "codes of ethnicity." According to Blue, in response to changes in today's society, *The Cosby Show* has invented new definitions of the black male and black family for television. She describes the character of Heathcliff Huxtable as loving, caring, responsible, perceptive, and good-humored. She acknowledges Cliff both as a parent who gets involved with his children and as a husband who shares decisions with his wife.

In contrast, James Evans of *Good Times* is not nearly as involved with his children's upbringing. He represents the typical (or stereotypical) image of black manhood. There is no doubt that James is in control and has the final say. While his character can also be seen as loving and caring, his circumstances often dictate the nature of his understanding and good humor. James Evans is often unemployed. His family lives in a Chicago housing project and his wife, Florida, primarily plays a domestic role within the home. In the Evans family, J. J. is the oldest son. He is portrayed as a buffoon, a modern-day Stepin Fetchit. Michael, the younger son, is very intelligent and rebellious.

In Blue's analysis, the Huxtable family, which lives in New York City, is promoted as stable and upwardly mobile across generations. Heathcliff Huxtable, the father, is a doctor, and Claire Huxtable, the mother, is a lawyer. In the Huxtable family, Theo is the only son. He is portrayed as ambitious with average intelligence.

The group viewed an episode of *Good Times* and an episode of *The Cosby Show* in a media criticism class. Everyone in the group had seen episodes of these shows before, and 41 (75.9%) had previously seen the two specific episodes shown that day.

The episode of *Good Times* involved Michael's not completing a standardized test because of the biased questions on it. James gets very upset, reaches for his belt, and threatens to beat Michael. Florida has to hold him back. J.J. plays instigator throughout the show, contrasting himself very obviously with Michael's more serious character.

In *The Cosby Show* episode, Cliff and Claire Huxtable find a joint in Theo's book and verbally confront him about it. He denies that the joint is his and is so upset about the situation that he finds the owner of the joint and forces him to admit his guilt.

After watching both shows, the participants filled out a one-page survey consisting of both closed- and open-ended questions. The consensual coding of consistent themes in the open-ended questions was completed by the researcher and an assistant. An independent evaluator assessed the reliability of selected themes from 10% of the sample. The intercoder agreement level was 94% (Atwood & Mclean, 1983).

Results

Class Status/Environment

The images of low-income status in *Good Times* and upper-income status in *The Cosby Show* were both considered valid pictures of real life by this group of adolescents. Table 8.1 presents the four thematic categories coded from their responses to *Good Times*. Table 8.2 shows the similar categories that emerged from their explanations of *The Cosby Show*. Examples of responses from each show are also included.

Table 8.1   In your opinion, was the *Good Times* program we watched a real picture of life for a poor family in America?

Perception	*Yes 49 responses (90.74%)* No.	%	Example
Discussed how the show related to their own reality	30	61.2%	In the projects people are poor. Poor people do live like that.
Discussed the lack of money and material objects	7	14.3%	They don't have things rich people have. A lot of poor families don't have houses.
Discussed white society's role in the situation	5	10.2%	The white man criticizes minorities. White people don't think black people can make it in life.
Discussed attitudes and abilities of family members	2	4.1%	Poor families have children who are smart. Most poor people really don't try.
NR	5	10.2%	
Total	49	100%	

Perception	*No 5 responses (9.26%)* No.	%	Example
Relate to their own reality	1	20%	I know families like that and they're not happy.
lack of money	4	80%	They don't have as much money in real life.
Total	5	100%	

When the youths explained why they believed the shows were a reflection of real life, the primary category that emerged involved how each show related to their own knowledge and experience in real life (*Good Times*, 61.2%; *The Cosby Show*, 52.9%).

Black Male/Teen Images

The participants were asked to assess the images of the oldest son on each show. Table 8.3 reflects their evaluations of J.J. Evans (*Good Times*). Surprisingly, J.J. was considered a negative image by only 20.4%, while a large number of participants reported mixed feelings when assessing J.J.'s image (57.4%).

As Table 8.4 indicates, Theo Huxtable (*The Cosby Show*) was selected as a positive image by most (66.7%). However, 27.8% of the

Table 8.2   In your opinion, was *The Cosby Show* we watched a real picture of life for a well-off family in America?

Perceptions	Yes 51 responses (94.4%)		Example
	No.	%	
Related the show to their own reality	27	52.9%	My family and other families are the same. They have the same problems that we have.
Discussed availability of money and material objects	11	21.6%	They have money and are funny. They have nice things.
Discussed the actions, attitudes, and abilities of family members	6	11.8%	The children have good stuff, but want more. Because they were tripping.
Discuss white society's role in their situation	1	1.9%	Whites know most black people can make it. Some blacks can progress in this country.
NR	6	11.9%	
Total	51	100%	

Perceptions	No 3 responses (5.6%)		Example
	No.	%	
Related to the reality	2	66.7%	Even with money people are sometimes unhappy.
NR	1	33.3%	
Total	3	100%	

respondents, a larger number than anticipated, reported mixed feelings about his character.

Father Figures

Most of these respondents (87%) saw the father image of James Evans in *Good Times* as a strong and manly one. A majority (61.1%) also said that his image was a stronger and more manly one than that of Heathcliff Huxtable in *The Cosby Show*.

Table 8.5 shows the categories that emerged from their explanations. The reasons cited for choosing James Evans as a stronger and more manly image fell into three categories. First, his dominance and control over his family, as well as his harsh disciplinary approach, were cited as characteristics of a strong and manly father (72.7%). Second, the sensitive, soft-hearted nature of Heathcliff Huxtable was seen as weak

Table 8.3 Does the J.J. Evans character in *Good Times* give us a positive or negative image of black male teens?

	No.	%	Example
Mixed	31	57.3%	He does good and bad things. He's a good artist, but jokes too much.
Positive	11	20.4%	He's proud to be himself. He's very talented, a good artist.
Negative	11	20.4%	He's illiterate and always after girls. He shows that black people don't know how to respect others.
NR	1	1.9%	
Total	54	100%	

Table 8.4 Does the Theo Huxtable character in *The Cosby Show* give us a negative or positive image of black male teens?

	No.	%	Example
Positive	36	66.6%	He's chill, a good example. He's smart and rich, shows a black man can make it.
Mixed	15	27.8%	He's good-looking, but doesn't make good grades. He shows both sides.
Negative	2	3.7%	The way he acts sometimes. His grades are not real good.
NR	1	1.9%	
Total	54	100%	

and unmanly by some (18.5%). Third, a few of the students described both father figures as strong and manly (20.4%).

When asked specifically about Heathcliff Huxtable's image as a weak one, the group split in half. While 51.8% disagreed with that idea, another 42.6% agreed. Those participants who disagreed either praised Heathcliff's positive interactive approach to discipline (30%) or criticized James Evans' negative physical approach (30%). Of those who believed that both characters represented strong and manly father images (20.4%), the primary attributes they cited as important were love, pride, and concern for their families.

Table 8.5 Is James Evans a stronger, more manly father image than Heathcliff Huxtable?

Perceptions	Yes: 61.1% (33) No.	%	Examples
James' strength and control/ his approach to discipline	24	72.7%	Evans has more authority. Evans will beat his kids before Cosby will.
Relates Evans image to real life	4	12.1%	Evans shows how it really is in black families. That's how parents act.
Cosby's soft heart/his approach to discipline	2	6.1%	He's too soft-hearted. He's afraid to to correct his kids.
NR	3	9.1%	
Total	33	100%	

Perceptions	No: 18.5% (10)		Examples
Cosby's positive approach to discipline and punishment	3	30%	Bill has more respect for his children. Being physically strict doesn't make a real man.
Evans' physical approach to discipline and punishment	3	30%	Evans hollers, you can't get anywhere hollering. It doesn't take a man to threaten his kids.
No Response	4	40%	
Total	10	100%	

Perceptions	Same: 20.4% (11)		Examples
Both protect, love, have pride in their families	6	54.5%	Both have pride in their family/ culture.
Each has his own way of dealing with his family	4	36.4%	Each has his own way of being a a father. Each has his own way.
No Response	1	9.1%	
Total	11	100%	

Both father images can be found in real-life experiences, according to these youth. As a matter of fact, most (53.7%) said many of the fathers they know are representative of these two characters. Only 16.7% felt that most of the fathers they know are like James Evans' character, and 14.8% cited the Heathcliff Huxtable character as the typical father figure in their experience. Another 14.8% explained that neither image is dominant; most of the fathers they know are both characters encompassed in one.

An unexpected and interesting finding involved only a slight difference between genders in relation to strong and manly father figures and black male teen images. As Table 8.6 shows, several females (32.2%) disagreed that Heathcliff Huxtable was a weak father figure. At the same time, more females than expected (57.1%) cited James as a stronger and more manly father figure, along with a majority of the male respondents (65.4%). A large number of both males (73.1%) and females (42.9%) saw J.J. Evans' character as both a negative and positive one.

Discussion

This study explored the power of real-life experience in relation to televised gender images. When explaining why they believed the shows were a reflection of real life, the majority of these respondents discussed how each show related to their own knowledge and experience. Among these youth, the image of a strong and manly father figure is still one who uses physical punishment, takes control of a situation, and dominates the family environment.

In the lower socioeconomic household, men tend to be authoritarian fathers (Baumrind, 1973). They believe they are expected to provide punishment that includes both physical and verbal confrontation. They see themselves as the head of the household, therefore obligated to maintain a sense of control (Staples, 1978). In working-class families, manhood also means authority. The working-class father often comes home tired and irritated. He spends very little time with his children and also maintains a physically disciplined control (Stearns, 1979).

Many participants cited the James Evans character as a stronger image of manhood than Heathcliff Huxtable because he exhibited such characteristics. While it may be true that *The Cosby Show* is presenting new definitions of black manhood and the black family, the failure of the show to address class status differences may be affecting the show's ability to actually deliver those images to the lower-class audience as anything more than entertainment.

Blue admits that *The Cosby Show* fails to directly address class/group status in any depth and also projects the mainstream image of manhood and family as the norm. She considers the show a compromise because the transition of dissident values into ruling-class ideology can result

Table 8.6 Male/Female Differences

Is the father image of James Evans stronger and more manly than Heathcliff Huxtable?

	Male		Female	
	No .	*%*	*No.*	*%*
Yes	17	65.4%	16	57.1%
No	3	11.5%	7	25%
Same	6	23.1%	5	17.9%
Total	26	100%	28	100%

Is the father image of Heathcliff Huxtable a weak or less manly one than James Evans?

	Male		Female	
	No.	*%*	*No.*	*%*
Agree	13	50%	10	55.7%
Disagree	12	46.2%	16	57.2%
NR	1	3.8%	2	7.1%
Total	26	100%	28	100%

Is the image of J.J. Evans a positive or negative one?

	Male		Female	
	No.	*%*	*No.*	*%*
Mixed	19	73.1%	12	42.9%
Positive	3	11.5%	8	28.5%
Negative	4	15.4%	7	25%
No Response			1	3.6%
Total	26	100%	28	100%

Is the image of Theo Huxtable a positive or negative one?

	Male		Female	
	No.	*%*	*No.*	*%*
Positive	18	69.2%	18	64.3%
Mixed	7	26.9%	8	28.5%
Negative	7	3.9%	1	3.6%
No response			1	3.6%
Total	26	100%	28	100%

in message modification. The recent addition to the Huxtable household of a poor cousin from inner-city New York may change this outcome.

The primary concern with many content analysis studies is the assertion that what the researcher *sees* is what the audience *receives*. Blue makes this same mistake in her assertion that the new definitions presented by *The Cosby Show* can be effective in moving all of black society into this new realm of thinking.

Heathcliff Huxtable is an example of the new modern male sex role, characterized by greater family involvement and maintenance of a viable employment status (Farrell, 1974). Although some research shows that this egalitarian, nurturing image of manhood may be catching on in black middle-class families (McAdoo, 1988; Willie & Greenblatt, 1978), Heathcliff Huxtable, the character that Bill Cosby has frequently said is an attempt to show the audience another approach (Johnson, 1988), is apparently not taking hold among these low-income viewers.

The sex-role stereotype of the male as provider and protector is an important component of conflict for these low-income black youth. McAdoo (1988) discusses the need for black men to legitimize their authority. Yet, among low-income families, unemployment is a common experience. In their experience, failure and disappointment are regular occurrences. They learn to expect very little and have a hard time trusting (Willie, 1981).

According to Hatchett (1986), the street image is an all-encompassing one, stressing a macho, cool attitude in relation to women and authority figures. This street image of a macho, cool individual represents a kind of power and control, which translate into a certain walk, style of dress, dance, and other verbal abilities, like signifying and rapping.

The assessment of the J.J. Evans character proved relevant to this image because J.J. was seen by many as having both good and bad qualities. For example, his artistic abilities were often contrasted with his lust for women. Theo Huxtable, of course, was seen as a positive black male image by most, but a higher number than expected also reported mixed feelings about his character. His general attitude about life and actions toward school were cited as problematic.

Theo Huxtable, as the male child of a middle-upper class black family with a positive father figure, is in a precarious situation, according to Stearns (1979). He suggests that this kind of environment, along with our current school system, contributes to the gap found between fathers and sons, because a child in an environment such as Theo's is expected to display not only the traditional excellence in physical abilities but also intellectual potential. For example, in one episode of *The Cosby Show*, Theo is diagnosed as having a learning disorder called dyslexia. Cliff and Claire actually cheer when they learn that his academic deficiencies are justified as a legitimate disability.

Differences between the perceptions of females and males in the sample also proved interesting. As expected, a majority of the male participants saw the James Evans character as a stronger and more manly father figure than that of Heathcliff Huxtable, but a large number of females also leaned toward James Evans. And even though the number of females who viewed Heathcliff Huxtable as a strong, manly father was higher than the number of males who did, that number was much smaller than expected.

As early as 1967 Liebow found that the wives and lovers of the street-corner men he studied wanted the man to be head of the family. They wanted him to take control, make financial and emotional decisions. They needed him to be someone they could lean on. According to Hare (1986), that attitude has not changed much. In his discussions with black feminists across the country, Hare has found that their number-one complaint involves a lack of competitiveness in the marketplace among black males.

In *The Cosby Show*, however, Claire Huxtable is the reflection of a successful, educated black woman. While she can be seen as nurturing and supportive at times, she is nevertheless closer to an equal relationship with Cliff and she often has the final say in the Huxtable home. The confusing nature of the relationship between males and females has been explored by Pleck (1982).

In his work, Pleck discusses the three following identity theories concerning hypermasculinity and men's attitudes toward women: (a) maternal domination—an early psychological relationship with mom resulting in female dominant experiences of power and control; (b) maternal identification—the ability of the male child to identify with the mother, leading to a contradictory sex-role identity; and (c) maternal socialization—boys are socialized by their mothers concerning viable male activity by way of negative responses for typical female-type behavior.

The majority of this sample (83.3%) reported living without a father figure in the home. In such homes, male gender roles are confused. The image of the black male as provider and protector is replaced by a strong mother figure who must fill in the gaps.

This study, therefore, suggests that television is an important element of gender awareness. However, it doesn't seem to be as powerful a predictor as the reality of the social, cultural, and environmental experience of the audience. The influence of television appears to be restricted when the projected message is different from the real-world experience of the viewer.

Conclusion

A more comprehensive analysis of gender role acquisition as a component of social, cultural, and environmental influences presents several important results. First, such findings tend to suggest that traditional stereotypical roles are very difficult to change, despite the contrasting images presented on popular television. Second, that difficulty illuminates the limited power of television in creating change.

Third, this group of low-income black youth indicates a strong link between televised images and real life. These two shows were considered representatives of real life. The respondents related program ideas and values, such as status, pride, unity, and love, to their own personal situations.

So while life may be changing for middle-class black youth, according to some researchers, many of those who remain part of a lower socioeconomic lifestyle realize that opportunity and knowledge do not necessarily equal manhood and/or success. The traditional image of the man as the breadwinner is not always possible in their real world. Their definitions of manhood are often adapted and redefined to better accommodate the situation. Television as a mirror of changing and contrasting definitions of black manhood remains a significant, yet limited component of black male gender image and style.

9

Masculinity and Machismo in Hollywood's War Films

RALPH R. DONALD

In *Sands of Iwo Jima* (1949), John Agar bitterly recalls his Marine colonel father's disapproval of his sensitive, intellectual son, revealing his own jealousy over the colonel's admiration of macho Sergeant Stryker (John Wayne):

> I embarrassed my father. I wasn't tough enough for him—too soft. "No guts" was the phrase he used. Now Stryker: He's the type of man my father wanted me to be . . . yeah. I bet [my father and Stryker] got along just fine together. Both of them with ramrods strapped on their backs.

As American boys become socialized, parents, relatives, and peers assail them with hundreds of admonitions describing what they must *not* become. Unfortunately, most of these caveats, delivered by well-meaning relatives and friends, amount to simplistic, anxiety-arousing prohibitions against any behavior deemed vaguely stereotypical of the female or the homosexual male (Hacker, 1957; Hartley, 1976; Sabo & Runfola, 1980). Also, because maleness is a difficult concept to define in positive terms, and because men themselves are often closed-mouthed regarding it, youngsters are mostly left to their own devices to learn manly behaviors.

Increasingly in our television-centered culture, boys find that male heroes in our popular media are among the most accessible, frequently encountered, and publicly approved models for manly socialization. It is a sad but true commentary on our society that often these youngsters spend more time per week with these mediated men than with their own fathers (Barcus, 1983).

There are many kinds of simplistic examples of stereotypical manhood readily available to children and young adults on television: They range from older, basic types, such as the heroes found in Westerns and war pictures, to the newest permutations of the warrior, as found in *G.I. Joe* and the *Teenage Mutant Ninja Turtles*. It is in these portrayals of the warrior that the aggressive qualities of the male of the species are the least inhibited by the moderating influences of civilization.

For males over the age of 35, the cowboy was one of their earliest images: "the rugged 'he-man,' strong, resilient, resourceful, capable of coping with overwhelming odds" (Balswick & Peek, 1976). Thus, many of these boys' first male-role-play simulations consisted of imitating this six-gun-toting symbol of understated masculinity. It is no wonder, then, that this first generation of young men to display the results of television's conditioning power (those raised on Hopalong Cassidy and the Lone Ranger) would dream dreams of frontier life similar to Phillip Caputo in his book and TV miniseries, *A Rumor of War* (1978):

> I would dream of that savage, heroic time [the old West] and wish I had lived then, before America became a land of salesmen and shopping centers. This is what I wanted, to find in a commonplace world a chance to live heroically. Having known nothing but security, comfort and peace, I hungered for danger, challenges and violence.

Also consider Komisar's observation (1976):

> Little boys learn the connection between violence and manhood very early in life. Fathers indulge in mock prize fights and wrestling matches with eight-year-olds. Boys play cowboys and Indians with guns and bows and arrows proffered by their elders. They are gangsters or soldiers interchangeably—the lack of difference between the two is more evident to them than to their parents. They are encouraged to "fight back," and bloodied noses and black eyes become trophies of their pint-sized virility.

As both Carpenter (1990) and J. Smith (1975) suggest, in many ways war films are Westerns taking place in locations other than the West. After all, in addition to their many specific similarities, both are essentially melodramatic portrayals of men performing virile, courageous deeds designed to protect helpless civilians from some sort of aggressor. Whether these villains are land-hungry cattle barons, rampaging Indians, or rapacious Nazis, Japanese, and Viet Cong, the outcomes (good triumphs over evil) are the same. Thus, regardless of the passage of time and the popularity of genres, sooner or later, most young boys' playacting evolves in sophistication into the twentieth-century equivalent, the soldier in modern warfare.

Jeffords (1989), Leed (1989), and others maintain that war itself is a gendering activity, one of the few remaining true male experiences in our society. Even the increasingly androgynous American armed forces' most recent liberalizing of regulations regarding sexual equality stops short of parity in combat assignments. Our paternalistic culture seems always to stop short of ordering women into harm's way. When women do fight in American war pictures, Hollywood usually shows it to be an aberration. For example, in *A Guy Named Joe* (1943), Irene Dunne flies a dangerous bombing mission, but does so without permission, and with guardian angel Spencer Tracy to assist her with the tactical aspects. In *The Edge of Darkness* (1943) and *This Land is Mine* (1943), Ann Sheridan and Maureen O'Hara end up fighting back against the Nazis, but only as civilians attempting to resist an occupying force, not as soldiers. In *Aliens* (1986), Sigourney Weaver finds herself in deadly personal combat with an army of monsters, but only after all of the platoon of Marines sent for that purpose have been killed or wounded.

In short, whenever the powers that rule can help it, combat is reserved exclusively for males, for whom the quality of belligerent performance is also clearly prescribed:

> Be a man. Conceptions of masculinity vary among different American groups, but there is a core which is common to most: courage, endurance and toughness, lack of squeamishness when confronted with shocking or distasteful stimuli, avoidance of display of weakness in general, reticence about emotional or idealistic matters, and sexual competency. (Stouffer, Lumsdaine, Lumsdaine, Williams, Smith, Janis, Star, & Cottrell, 1976)

If one accepts the preceding as both a culturally sanctioned definition of maleness and a blueprint for male role models in war, then the specifics that follow will serve as a more detailed explanation of this socializing influence.

Initiation Rites

In most human cultures, there exists some rite of passage from the relatively sexless existence of a child into the adult community of their sex. In this transition, each sex possesses its own set of rituals. In many human cultures, becoming a warrior goes hand in hand with becoming a male adult. In examining the ceremonial rubrics of several native cultures, vanGennep (1960) describes a process that bears close resemblance to the basic training regimen practiced by the American armed forces: Candidates for male adulthood are first separated from their families, most specifically from the world of women, which has been their childhood milieu. More often than not, initiates are also stripped of the clothing they previously wore, their hair is shaved and/or rearranged in the fashion of adult males. Then they undergo a period of instruction in the behaviors and responsibilities of adult males/warriors. Frayser (1985) notes that in these rituals initiates must passively and submissively obey all orders given them by their male elders, as befits their status as neophytes. Tiger (1970) also points out that this process often includes ordeals and tests of manly endurance. These range from the American Indian practice of hanging a would-be brave by thongs pierced through his pectoral muscles, to "depilation, head-biting, evulsion of teeth, sprinkling with human blood, drinking human blood, immersion in dust or filth, heavy flogging, scarification, smoking and burning, circumcision and subincision." Finally, properly reconditioned and educated, the initiates "graduate" and take their place as full-fledged adult males.

So there is great similarity between this process and armed forces basic training, as portrayed in such films as *Full Metal Jacket* (1987), *Take the High Ground* (1953), and *The D.I.* (1959). Recruits are separated from their families and local subcultures, and removed to training depots that are usually located in some other part of the country. For the majority of their training, they are deprived of all female contact. In *Full Metal Jacket* the drill instructor even insists that the recruits substitute their rifles for their high school sweethearts. To reinforce this point, the men are ordered to sleep with their weapons.

In all three films, the men are deprived of their former hairstyles and are given the standard G.I. butch haircut (the practical equivalent of primitive head-shaving). As well, their clothes are exchanged for uniforms and a set of Marine/Army gear.

Routinely, recruits are not given the status of soldiers at the outset. They are "boots," "trainees," or "young people," but never Marines or soldiers. Sometimes, in these films, recruits are not even allowed the status of males. Often derisively called "girls" or "ladies" by their D.I.s, recruits must earn manhood by achieving success in their training. In

The D.I., when Jack Webb reports to his company commander that a certain recruit continuously "fouls up" in his training, the captain offers to assist Webb in "cutting the lace off his panties." In *Full Metal Jacket*, when a recruit says that he hails from Texas, the D.I. retorts with this verbal assault:

D.I.:   Holy dog shit! Texas! Only steers and queers come from Texas, Private "Cowboy," and you don't much look like a steer to me, so that kinda narrows it down. Do you suck dicks?

Cowboy: Sir, no sir!

D.I.:   Are you a peter pumper?

Cowboy: Sir, no sir!

D.I.:   I bet you're the kinda guy who would fuck a person in the ass and not even have the goddamn common courtesy to give him a reach-around! I'll be watchin' you.

Despite all these indignities, recruits are required to passively submit to all orders, no matter how disgusting, demeaning, or physically taxing they are. For example, also in *Full Metal Jacket*, a feeble-minded recruit whom the D.I. has used as the platoon scapegoat is punished for failure to properly respond to drill commands. He must march behind the others with his thumb in his mouth, his trousers around his ankles, his hat turned backward, and his rifle carried on his shoulder upside down.

But finally, suitably reconditioned and instructed in proper soldierly behavior, the initiates, now full-fledged Marines or soldiers, graduate and are transferred to advanced training.

The Men's Club

Of all of these initiatory customs and practices, probably the most significant is the physical and symbolic separation of candidates from the world of women. But unlike Tiger's native tribesman, Americans begin to establish this separation long before a boy reaches puberty. Kimmel (1987d) states that gender is a relational construct, providing males with the opposite sex as a basis of comparison and a clearly drawn negative role model. Practically from the time an American boy-child is old enough to understand English, he hears that "Big boys don't cry

—only girls do," or "Don't play with dolls; dolls are for girls," or "That scraped knee doesn't really hurt a little man like you, does it?" In various ways, boys are shown multiple examples of the allegedly lesser, more flawed kind of human being they must avoid becoming: a female. By the time most boys reach manhood, many have become firmly convinced that females must be grossly inferior to males—at least with respect to traditionally male activities. And by systematically excluding females from sports teams, clubs, the "old boy network" in business, from top government positions, and from combat roles in the military through the years, a self-fulfilling set of male role definitions becomes firmly embedded in our history and culture. And needless to say, in Hollywood, a patriarchy if there every was one, virtually every picture is written and produced from the paternalistic perspective, as if there is no other possible point of view on the planet.

This attitude is most clearly seen in the motion pictures of director/producer Howard Hawks. In virtually all the genre films Hawks made, there is one overriding misogynist theme: The fraternity of men and the jobs men must perform only function efficiently when women are excluded. Plus, many of the problems that inhibit Hawks' heroes from professionally completing their tasks are caused by women. For example, in *Air Force* (1943), the officers of the bomber "Mary Ann" become momentarily distracted from fighting the Japanese due to a misunderstanding over a woman.

In most war films, men relegate women to three basic roles: mothers to revere and respect, chattel to acquire and use legally in marriage or illegally via rape and pillage, or whores to provide temporary satisfaction while the men are away from home. In each case, women are clearly the "out-group," a separate entity men find distracting to the task at hand, but a commodity to think, dream, and make plans about (Komisar, 1976).

Basinger (1986) reminds us that countless combat films contain "mail call" scenes, in which young soldiers write and receive letters from their revered mothers (p. 62). In *Guadalcanal Diary* (1943), Richard Jaeckel, the "kid" of the platoon, even attempts to appear more manly by pretending that a letter from his mother is a love note from a sexually submissive girlfriend. In *The War Lover* (1962), pilot Steve McQueen considers co-pilot Robert Wagner's English girlfriend simply a prize to capture and use. In *Platoon* (1987) and *Casualties of War* (1989), soldiers consider young Vietnamese girls the spoils of war and can even rationalize away their rape and murder.

This separation of the "men's club" from the world of women is seen clearly in *Navy Seals* (1990), described by one reviewer as having the highest testosterone count since *Rambo*. These highly trained super-commandos exist in a world in which only three basic things occur: (a) their team goes out on suicidally dangerous missions; (b) they train and plan more suicidally dangerous missions; and (c) they drink, womanize, and carry on like Vikings celebrating the sacking of a town.

In one sequence, "The Chief," a member of this tightly knit team, has made what his buddies consider a serious error in judgment: He's getting married in the morning. Too taken aback by this situation to continue the drive to the church where the ceremony is about to begin, one Seal leaps from a moving auto, plunging off a bridge into a river. Later, as the bride walks down the aisle, the Seal team's electronic pagers begin beeping, which means that they have been summoned back to their base for a mission. Without blinking an eye, "The Chief" leaves his bride at the altar, and he and the other Seals make a run for their cars. "Saved by the beeper," one of them remarks. Later, "The Chief" and his fiancée discuss rescheduling the wedding. But throughout the conversation there is one thing that is virtually implicit: When she married him, she must accept "the whole package," which means that her husband's fraternity of warriors comes first: Before all, he is a Seal, a member of the male fraternity. She must resign herself to the role of "the little woman," someone to whom her man will return when naval duties and other unofficial male-bonding rituals (drinking, partying, pranks, and so on) permit.

The Quiet Man

There are many subtle characteristics to war films' stereotype of the American male warrior. Key among them is that he should be a man of few words but mighty deeds, capable of stoically enduring privations and pain, and be able to pass the stress test that war imposes on these qualities.

Farrell (1976) explains that since showing emotion is considered a feminine characteristic (and therefore should be avoided), men cultivate the image of quiet dignity. The fewer words said, the better. John Wayne typifies the foolish extremes to which this philosophy can be extended in *She Wore A Yellow Ribbon* (1949), when he gives his admonition to young officer Harry Carey, Jr.: "Never apologize, mister: It's a sign of weakness."

The ability to watch one's comrades die and yet appear to suffer no emotional trauma is shown to be a valued commodity in most war pictures. In the 1958 film *The Hunters*, fighter group commander Richard Egan proudly calls Robert Mitchum "the iceman," because of Mitchum's ability to perform his lethal tasks in an emotionless manner, oblivious to the deaths of his comrades. Showing that wars and warriors adjust to the times while fundamental maleness criteria remain intact, in *Top Gun* (1986), Val Kilmer, the most coolly efficient, emotionless pilot attending the fighter weapons school, also adopts the nickname "iceman."

Fear is also an emotion that men in war must hide. Also in *The Hunters*, pilot Lee Philips becomes a drunk because he cannot meet his own expectations of fearlessness. Especially when he compares himself to "iceman" Robert Mitchum, Philips considers himself a coward—this despite the other pilots' assessment of Philips as the "bravest man in the squadron." They consider him brave because despite his fear, despite his mediocre flying ability, and despite the fact that he can turn in his wings to the flight surgeon at any time and take a desk job, Philips still willingly goes in harm's way.

Actually, when a war movie hero does admit fear, it is usually to punctuate the fact that fear is intentionally hidden. For example, in *Sands of Iwo Jima* and *Destination Tokyo* (1943), young troops about to face death for the first time confess to John Wayne and Cary Grant that they are frightened. Much to the amazement of these youngsters, Wayne and Grant admit to being afraid themselves before a battle, and to steer clear of men who say that they are not. Implicitly, both heroes show by example that one routinely hides any emotions counterproductive to the belligerent objective.

If a warrior gives in to this fear and commits some act of cowardice, the usual war film plot "conversion convention" calls for him to pay some price for this offense (Donald, 1990). The most common expiative act follows this scenario: After the character decides to reject the coward's role, he attempts some heroic act, during which he is killed or seriously wounded. For example, in *The Fighting 69th*, James Cagney's cowardice causes the death of some of his comrades. He is jailed prior to a court-martial for his sins, but fate intervenes and he escapes. Faced with a choice of flight or a return to the trenches, Cagney chooses the latter, and is killed while fighting bravely. Again the point is made: Even if a soldier is guilty of as grave an offense as "showing the white feather," there is a manly option and a formula for redemption.

Although it is acceptable for G.I.s to gripe about the lack of warm food and decent lodging, an almost invisible line is drawn between acceptable and taboo complaints. In *Platoon*, only in his letters to his grandmother does Charlie Sheen admit that the physical and emotional stress of "humping the boonies" (fighting the jungle war in Vietnam) may be too much for him to bear; to his comrades-in-arms, Sheen just quietly does his job.

Not even painful wounds are an acceptable reason for movie soldiers to resort to emotionalism. Early in *Platoon*, a sergeant confronts a soldier screaming in pain from a gunshot wound: "Shut up, shut up!—take the pain," he orders. The compliant soldier obeys. Leed (1989) characterizes this self-destructive self-delusion this way: "Men become what they are, realizing a masculine character and a strength through what they lose rather than what they gain." In *The Longest Day* (1962), John Wayne suffers a compound fracture of the lower leg in a parachute drop—but does he complain? No. It does not even slow him up much. Wayne orders the medical corpsman examining his injury to re-lace his combat boot tightly, so he can continue hiking along with his men. In *They Were Expendable* (1945), Wayne becomes extremely indignant when he is ordered to stand down from a mission because of an injury to his arm. Despite being told that if he does not rest and submit to antibiotic therapy he may lose his arm to gangrene, Wayne tells the doctor to "slap a little iodine on it and let me get outta here."

The Immortal Legion

Shatan (1989) writes that military trainers "fear that the death of a beloved buddy will render a soldier useless for combat. Instead, training fosters 'antigrief'—soldiers are absorbed into the corporate entity of the 'immortal legion.'" Countless war films reinforce this, showing how unprofessional and unsoldierly it is to unduly fret over the death of a comrade. For example, in *Top Gun*, the death of "Goose," Tom Cruise's electronic warfare officer, co-pilot, and best friend, causes him to lose his courage and become unable to engage the enemy. Only when he is willing to "let Goose go" can Cruise fight again.

In war, succinctly described by ship's captain Richard Crenna in *The Sand Pebbles* (1966) as "the give and take of death," there must be some kind of carrot dangled in front of warriors to compensate for the possibility of having to give up one's life. Immortality is the key, allowing the finality of death to be denied and the grief suffered by a deceased warrior's friends to be assuaged. On graduation day in *Full Metal Jacket*, the D.I. explains it this way:

> Today you people are no longer maggots. Today you are Marines. You're part of a brotherhood. From now on until the day you die, wherever you are, every Marine is your brother. Most of you will go to Vietnam; some of you will not come back. But always remember this: Marines die, that's what we're here for. But the Marines Corps lives forever, and that means *you* live forever.

To reinforce this concept in some World War II combat films, a crescendo of patriotic music would rise at the end of the picture, appropriate narration would reinforce the gratitude of a nation for those who gave their lives, and then the smiling faces of the men who died during the film would be superimposed, ghost-like, over the picture on the screen. Thus, as members of the immortal legion, the dead live on in glory.

However, there still must be some manly outlet for emotion over lost buddies. Shatan describes the "authorized" manly alternative for grief and remorse at the death of a comrade as "militarized grief and ceremonial vengeance" (pp. 137-138). These behaviors can take the form of either dedicating the next enemy kill to the deceased comrade, or by generally raising the level of mayhem. Examples of both are found in *Destination Tokyo*. An older, much-revered submarine crew member named Mike is stabbed in the back by a downed Japanese pilot whom he was attempting to rescue. His shipmates cease attempting to rescue the pilot and instead repeatedly and redundantly pound him into the water with slugs from a 50-millimeter machine gun. Later the crew paints the dedication, "For Mike, torpedoman first class, R.I.P." on the next torpedo the sub fires at a Japanese ship. In the 1940s skillful screenwriters routinely sanitized and thereby legitimized such vengeful enthusiasm. However, in recent years, Vietnam war films have provided audiences with more starkly realistic portrayals of soldierly revenge. In films such as *Platoon* and the 1980 television miniseries *A Rumor of War*, soldiers and Marines commit atrocities like that at My Lai as a way of extracting vengeance for the loss of their buddies.

Following the manly credo, Hollywood's contemporary soldiers prefer committing war crimes to sitting down and having a good cry over a lost friend.

Risking one's life daily with buddies on whom one grows to depend for survival often leads to natural feelings of affection and to lifelong

friendships. But there is a strict homophobic code to follow in expressing this amity. When the protagonists of both *Platoon* and *Casualties
of War* protest the rape of young Vietnamese girls, the would-be rapists
accuse these protagonists of being homosexuals. As previously mentioned about *Full Metal Jacket*, the D.I. threatens a recruit with the label
of homosexual to achieve dominance. In another basic training film,
Biloxi Blues (1989), a recruit is discovered to be homosexual. He is
immediately arrested, handcuffed, and whisked away from the platoon
as if he were a dangerous criminal suffering from leprosy. Under certain
circumstances, namely combat, men may partake in activities that
would be sexually taboo in civilian life. Mellen (1977) reminds us that
in *Wings* (1927) and in *Beau Geste* (1938), what amounts to tender love
scenes between two men are allowed to occur. Of course, this overflow
of emotion and affection is only permitted because one of the two men
is either dying or already dead. Only then is a man allowed to cradle
another man in his arms, or to plant a chaste kiss on his forehead.
Easthope (1986) puts a near-masochistic spin on this scenario:

> In the dominant versions of men at war, men are permitted to behave towards
> each other in ways that would not be allowed elsewhere, caressing and hold-
> ing each other, comforting and weeping together, admitting their love. The
> pain of war is the price paid for the way it expresses the male bond. War's
> suffering is a kind of punishment for the release of homosexual desire and
> male femininity that only war allows.

On other selected occasions, the buddies of less-than-mortally wounded men are allowed similar "unmanly" liberties. In *Platoon Leader*
(1988), a lieutenant tenderly cradles his badly wounded sergeant in his
arms. But later, when the sergeant's wounds have healed and the non-
com is sent back to the platoon, all he can expect from the lieutenant is
a brotherly pat on the back. Once again, friendship verging on love reverts
to the manly rules of personal contact that govern relationships between
teammates in sports.

Sports Metaphors

General George Patton is credited with saying that the problem with
wars is that they aren't always there when you need them. Between armed
conflicts, American males participate in alternative rites of passage that

simulate warlike behavior. In our culture, among the closest substitutes for war are contact sports such as football or boxing. Fiddick (1989) reminds us that "the use of helmets [as opposed to 'caps'] and such terms as 'the bomb' and the 'blitz' make football ideal as a central metaphor of war." Hoch's (1980) observations at a football game are similarly enlightening:

> The movements of the cheerleaders are plugged into what amounts to a set of stereotyped military drill routines. Watching the drum majorettes and girls' drill teams prancing about in their mini-skirted mock uniforms, in precision goose steps, it is hard to miss the symbolism of sexuality subordinated to militarism, sexuality used as an advertisement for militarism, and frustrated sexuality used as a spur to militarism and machismo generally.

It will also not come as a surprise that war films also make use of sports metaphors. For example, in *Air Force*, there are countless allusions to baseball, such as Harry Carey's statement that the Japanese mounted their sneak attack on Pearl Harbor "before Uncle Sam had a chance to come to bat." Throughout the first portion of the picture, Carey and John Ridgely try to preach sports teamwork to malcontent John Garfield. Finally, Garfield agrees to "play ball" with the rest of the bomber's crew.

Boxing is also a sport that is frequently alluded to in war films. In *Thirty Seconds Over Tokyo* (1944), the Doolittle raid is described as "Uncle Sam's first counterpunch in this war." Countless motion pictures describe their particular war mission as the one that will provide the "knockout punch" against the enemy.

A Conclusion: Warning About "Winning"

An integral part of sport in America is the paramount importance of *winning*. Shatan (1989) says, "In the United States, winning is the central theme in the making of a boy's self-image. Boys learn early that 'any boy can win.' Corporations love Coach Lombardi's motto, 'Winning isn't everything. It's the only thing.'" But the male fixation with winning has its dangers: Fear of showing weakness by backing down from a schoolyard fight can result in, at worst, a bloody nose. When Presidents Johnson and Nixon refused to back down from the debacle of Vietnam, 57,000 Americans were killed (Fasteau, 1976; Komisar,

1976). Consider Mellen's (1977) statement concerning film heroes she describes as "indomitable males":

> The stereotype of the self-controlled, invulnerable, stoical hero who justifies the image of unfeeling masculinity as a means of winning in a world that pounces on any sign of weakness. . . . Male heroes pontificate platitudes such as that invoked by an elderly John Wayne in *The Shootist*: "I won't be wronged, I won't be insulted, I won't be laid a hand on. I don't do these things to others, and I require the same of them."

Winning has become much too important in our culture. In *Heart-break Ridge* (1986), Clint Eastwood's Marine gunnery sergeant characterized his entire career as if it were a won-lost statistic on the sports page: When the film ended, he was satisfied, and finally ready to retire, now that his war record was evened out at "1-1-1," one win (Grenada), one loss (Vietnam), and one tie (Korea).

Perhaps this obsession with winning is the most serious and most potentially dangerous of all the absurd notions that Americans and their war films stuff into the psyches of their male young. But it is the most outmoded and the least helpful value in a contemporary world in which everyone must adapt, change, and compromise. If half-century-old governments and political philosophies can give way, if all the world is changing and adapting, perhaps the macho, uncommunicative, un-emotional, pseudo-athletic misogynists America seems intent on turning out should also consider some fundamental alterations.

10

When Men Put on Appearances

Advertising and the Social Construction of Masculinity

DIANE BARTHEL

Advertising invites us into a privileged, exciting world of appearances. Advertising conveys information, but that is just the beginning. Some critics, in fact, believe it embeds its limited information in a whirlpool of disinformation. The more claims are made for a product, the more this seems to be the case. Simple bits of hardware, for example, are advertised with brand name, small illustration, and price. But other products aim at a more abstract form of construction, namely self-construction. This chapter examines how visual and verbal symbols are used to construct images of masculinity and to associate these images with specific products.

Advertising is big business. A large corporation like Philip Morris or General Motors will spend $200 million to $300 million on magazine advertising alone. The top 15 companies who advertised in magazines in 1989 spent a total of $1.7 billion on magazine advertising—in addition to the $3.9 billion they spent on television advertising. What they are buying is the chance of catching our attention, or of slipping the product into our minds while we are in a state of relative inattention and relaxation. One recent study showed that the typical reader spends an average of 25 to 35 minutes daily looking at magazines, during which time he or she would be exposed to 65 to 70 advertisements. About 35 of these will be seriously scanned. In addition, the average television viewer see 95 to 100 commercials daily, seriously watching about 60 of them. Yet polls suggest that people respond more favorably to magazine advertising than to television advertisements (Christenson & Redmond, 1990). Is this response a form of art appreciation or social enculturation? Is it the medium or the message that turns people on? And what do both medium and message have to do with masculinity?

As Georg Simmel recognized (1978), we use goods not simply to do a job—to clothe us, shelter us, get us from point A to point B. We also use goods as extensions of ourselves. They extend our power. They communicate our sense of ourselves to others. And they give that sense back to us again. Sometimes, however, instead of extending our power, they become the locus of power. By finding our identities in and through products, we actually hand over our identities. Marx (1976) saw how people empower goods, treating them like magical fetishes to be worshipped. When such *commodity fetishism* occurs, we no longer have power over goods. Rather, they have power over us. They rule our lives and determine our actions.

We use consumer goods to define and reinforce definitions of what is masculine and what is feminine. The idea that these definitions are not *natural* but rather are *socially constructed* is given weight and credibility when we look at how such definitions have changed over time.

In earlier centuries, fashionable gentlemen wore ruffles of lace, colorful tights, and pantaloons. Eighteenth-century gentlemen favored colorful silks and considered it only proper to appear in public heavily powdered and bewigged. By the nineteenth century, the Industrial Revolution imposed stricter standards of serious masculine behavior and appearance. The Doctrine of Separate Spheres encouraged a strict divide between the man's world and the woman's world, and this divide was symbolically communicated by appearance. As other gentlemen increasingly retreated into a dark and somber standard, from black top hat and coat down to conservative suit and shoes, the "dandy" was singled out for derision, due to what was seen as his extravagant attention to the details of dress. For most status-conscious middle-class men, competitive dressing focused on the cut and the fabric and the quality of the tailoring.

In the twentieth century, young men rebelled against this standard either by wearing sports clothes as street clothes or playing with innovations such as the zoot suit. But the standard of serious dress for serious men remained, susceptible only to relatively minor changes, compared with earlier transformations. Recent history has seen a movement from the 1950s "man in the gray flannel suit" to the 1960s psychedelic breakout, complete with beads, bellbottoms, and Indian motifs. Men in the 1970s continued to explore their feelings, enjoying some new freedoms and communicating their sentiments through their appearance. But corporate conformity never totally disappeared. In the 1980s, it was back with a vengeance, updated to serve the times. The new male role model was the young man on the make: neither a stoic, inner-directed achiever (Riesman, 1950) nor a dull, outer-directed organiza-tion man (Whyte, 1957). The new achiever was out to win, out for power and the perks that go with it. He knew that, in the end, "whoever has the most toys wins." Merchandisers, advertisers, and retailers loved him. This new achiever was a challenge, at times difficult, but he could be sold. As we enter the nineties he is still out there, a little chastened by eco-nomic reverses but still raring to go, struggling and shopping his way the top. He is one of capitalism's most successful products: a consumer and a gentleman. Let us examine what he is sold, and of what stuff he is made.

The Corporate Game

"Clothes make the man" is an adage with some truth to it. Dressing for success took the point to the extreme as the acquisition of the "power look" came to precede the acquisition of power itself. Yet this new achiever, this yuppie hell-bent-for-corporate-glory, was he not merely a hard-living, free-spending version of the earliest corporate conformist?

For all their glamour, it certainly seemed so from the advertisements in men's magazines such as *GQ, M,* and *Esquire,* and more general interest magazines, ranging from *Fortune* and *Forbes* to *Sports Illus-trated.* In page after page the solitary male figure appears handsomely turned out in a three-piece suit and top coat. He is the existential executive. He either stares out confidently at the camera or seems lost in his own deep, important thoughts. Sometimes he is on his way to a power lunch. Sometimes he stands scrutinizing the business pages; some-times he makes a call on a cordless phone. The backdrop to his activities is a panoramic view through a skyscraper window of other corporate towers. This is a common advertising technique, which tells us that the man modeling the suit is a high-powered executive able to buy and sell those who are below him, both literally and figuratively (Marchand, 1985). If there is furniture, it is either expensively modern, sleek and avant-garde, or more often polished old-worldly, solid oak or mahogany com-plemented by leather sofa and armchairs.

The executive pictured may be above the riffraff, but even at these exalted heights he is not above the competition. A hotel advertisement depicts a late-night work session in an upper-story office. Discussion comes to a full stop when a male executive turns in amazement to address a commanding-looking female executive, who is holding a credit card and a phone: "You're checking into your hotel over the phone? Who do *you* know?" She answers confidently: "Hyatt."

It is the very real threat of women invading such centers of power that makes the social construction, and perpetual *re-construction*, of masculinity so important. Men must show that they have the right stuff, that they have what it takes. In the 1950s, C. Wright Mills described what it took to become part of the power elite:

> The fit survive, and fitness means, not formal competence . . . but conformity with the criteria of those who have already succeeded. To be compatible with the top men is to act like them, to look like them, to think like them: to be of and for them—or at least to display oneself to them in such a way as to create that impression. This is, in fact, what is meant by "creating"—a well-chosen word—"a good impression." This is what is meant—and nothing else—by being a "sound man," as sound as a dollar. (1956)

To create a good impression in today's highly competitive world, a man must know how to recognize, as Bally of Switzerland puts it, "the difference between dressed, and well dressed." Casual T-shirts and jeans are fine for college students and economic dropouts. But the man looking to climb the corporate ladder has to learn both how to read the messages given off by other men's appearances (polished and confidant or cheap and sleazy) *and* how to send the right messages himself. As a shoe advertisement says, "Powerful men leave strong impressions"— and not just on thick carpets. A man's clothes speak for him before he opens his mouth. It is up to him to make sure they say the right things. It is a tough world out there. This message is reinforced by the lawyer role model in a clothing advertisement, who says, "Sometimes the right suit is the best defense." In this case, the right suit is a double-breasted charcoal wool with a discreet pin-stripe, set off by a patterned red silk tie (just a touch assertive) and a muted silk handkerchief (not to overdo the effect). Even the right wallet can be seen as a "high interest investment." Plastic or bright colors just won't do.

America has no traditional aristocracy. Its self-made men have to create their own place in time, assert their own importance. One way they do this is by linking themselves to status symbols that legitimate their recent upward mobility. For American millionaires, this once meant castles in Wales or property in the South of France. To the upwardly mobile men of today, advertisements promise that, even if they do not own a castle in Wales, they can look as if they do. Barbour jackets and Burberry raincoats have become easily recognized status symbols. Suits and jackets are advertised as having "the perfection of tradition," transcending "time and trend."

These and similar advertisements for status clothes emphasize fine craftsmanship, natural fibers, and traditional styling. Key words are value, quality, and sophistication. "Distinguished by an air of traditional refinement, today's classic sportscoat suggests a most suitable alternative." The square-jawed model with the tortoiseshell glasses sits in the soft light of an expensive lamp, as though he were relaxing in his private library. This impression is reinforced by the thick volume he holds in his hand. The "gentleman in his library" is a common advertising image of the gentleman at home. This is man the thinker, surrounded by his treasures: his leather-bound volumes, his old photographs, his private collection of Renaissance bronzes, his Parker Duofold Roller ball pen. It is this sort of image that is promoted by Ralph Lauren, the boy from Brooklyn who encourages others to act out their fantasies through his brands marketed with such prestigious names as Chaps and Polo University Club.

Such advertisements are appealing in part because they show the gentleman at leisure: relaxed, cosseted, choosing how to dispose of his time. But men on the make have a far different relationship to time. Life in the fast lane does not allow time for quiet contemplation. Advertisements promise commodities that will help men beat time, winning their way to the finish line. A brand of personal organizers puts it simply: "Either you run your life or it runs you." A deodorant imagines a high-pressure situation likely to affect the business traveler: "You're at gate 3. Your plane leaves from gate 33 in two minutes. Only one deodorant will turn on extra protection for the last hundred yard dash." A shoe brand reminds corporate climbers that the clock never stops ticking. "Tuesday 10 AM . . . Clock in. Another day at the firm begins as time flies in the fast track . . ." The confident young man shown looks as though he can handle time, insofar as he has put his foot on the base of the standing clock, the sole prop pictured to drive the point home.

With all this pressure, why bother striving for success unless, of course, one gets a kick out of wearing three-piece suits? This question has been around a long time. Once men were motivated to achieve by advertisements that linked the individual's desire for more goods with the nation's prosperity and growth. As in Mandeville's eighteenth-century "Fable of the Bees," individual vices (such as envy and greed) added up to public virtues when they expanded markets and promoted production. Now, however, the capitalist realism (Schudson, 1984) of advertising images is so well accommodated in the public mind that advertising seldom needs to appeal to patriotism. Private self-interest is good and goal enough, and it does not even need to pretend to be enlightened self-interest at that. Like popular inspirational speakers, advertisements reinforce self-indulgence and self-promotion with buzz phrases like "Enjoy" and "You're worth it."

Advertisements provide a whole panoply of seductive goods and glittering prizes not only for fast-track finishers but also as encouragement along the way. The consumer goals are meant to justify the means: spending one's time and energies chasing after the gold ring. Consumerism becomes an end in itself—more definitive, more physical, more real than any abstract (love, patriotism, fulfillment) can ever be. As the advertisement for Wild Turkey puts it, "It's okay to pay the price for success. Just make sure you're reimbursed."

Back to Nature

All work makes a dull boy; there has to be time for play. That is why weekends were invented. Time off allows for psychic and physical batteries to be re-charged. It allows man to come to terms with nature and with himself. But this is not an unmediated encounter. Rather, judging by advertisements, a whole set of consumer goods are necessary to accomplish the transition from work style to weekend style. And a consumer and a gentleman does everything with style. As the successful executive in the sports jacket says, "I take my weekends very seriously."

Man at leisure needs the right pair of shoes. Rugged shoes. Hardworking shoes. Shoes that are worn by men who do a real man's job: that is, who don't sit in an office shuffling paper and making phone calls. Advertisements wax poetic about rugged shoes that are "as comfortable on the forest floor as on the shoe store carpet," that allow man to "go toe to toe with Mother Nature and keep dry every step of the way," shoes that "cover a lot of territory." Unlike dress shoes, perpetually polished to perfection to make the right impression, even if it is the wrong impression, these are honest shoes for honest guys:

> You knew exactly what you wanted . . .
> an honest pair of waterproof handsewns.
> They had to be great looking, comfortable and keep
> your feet dry. No splashy colors, nothing rubber,
> you trashed the gummys years ago . . .

In other words, real men are not dumb kids. They know quality and they will settle for nothing less, nothing flashy, nothing ineffectual. Such advertisements are accompanied by images of trees, rocks, and cool moss, of sunbeams breaking through clouds to shine on a solitary walker. Man in nature. Protected by Gore-Tex.

Honest shoes demand honest clothes. Thoreau warned that one should be careful of any activity that demanded the buying of new clothes. New clothes always suggest some measure of dishonesty, some impression-management going on. The most honest clothes are old clothes, clothes that have grown on you and literally "become you." But not everyone has old clothes. Some people have to buy new clothes that are deliberately made to look old. Since "everyone agrees that a denim shirt ought to look as though years of wearing and washing went into that perfect, faded shade of blue," Banana Republic promises that all its shirts are "washed and finished to a weathered shade of indigo." These shirts are pre-laundered, if not pre-lived in: They save their owners years of life experience. Other brands promise more layers of life experience than most people can crowd or even care to crowd into their holidays and weekends. Ralph Lauren's advertisements are heavily symbolic of the good life lived elsewhere, which can become yours here and now: the country retreat, the faithful dog, the fishin' 'n' huntin' gear, the piles of *National Geographic*, and stacks of cozy wool blankets. Such images are for men who never have to mow the lawn on weekends—or who wish they never had to.

When the gentleman-consumer goes back to nature, he confronts his own nature. From underneath the modern-day corporate conformist there emerges the Great American Individualist. But even an individualist needs the right goods to express his autonomy. He needs Oshkosh sportswear, "Because life becomes clearer when you don't watch it through a window." He drinks Suntory Japanese beer, "for those who drink to the beat of a different drummer," And he wears Timberland boots, like the outdoorsman in the advertisement, sitting pensive in front of a waterfront shack with his trusty hound. He is "an individualist who has two good reasons to abandon the comforts of civilization. One, his passion for the outdoors. Two, his trust in Timberland gear."

Advertisers call this "mass-marketing individuality." Each consumer fancies himself an individual wearing and using the same goods as millions of other men. The original and still-present image of the rugged individualist is the Marlboro Man, riding through the Big Country, doing a man's job in a man's way. Men who do jobs that women can do must find other ways of being masculine. One way is to distill the essence of masculinity. If they can't join in the activity, they can at least have the attitude. For Jean Baudrillard, this attitude is one of *exigence*: the masculine attitude of demanding the best and achieving perfection.

Power and Perfection

> All of masculine advertising insists on rule, on choice, in terms of rigor and inflexible minutiae. He does not neglect a detail . . . It is not a question of just letting things go, or of taking pleasure in something, but rather of distinguishing himself. To know how to choose, and not to fail at it, is here the equivalent of the military and puritanical virtues: intransigence, decision, *virtus*. (Baudrillard, 1970, p. 147)

The male mode of exigence is found in advertisements ranging from cigarettes: "Buck the System," to group insurance: "Accept no substitutes." It is most in evidence in car advertisements, where the keywords are masculine: power, precision, performance.

Sometimes the car is a woman. It responds to the touch and the will of the male driver more directly and pliantly than any real woman with a mind of her own. The car's sexy, streamlined body attracts him: "Pure shape, pure power, pure Z. It turns you on." As the juxtaposition of shape and power suggests, the car is not simply the Other. It is also an extension of the owner. As he turns it on, he turns himself on. Its power is his power. Through it, he overpowers other men and seduces women. "How well does it perform? How well can you drive?"

The car, like the driver, has to have the right attitude, a masculine attitude. The slick monochromatic skin, like a Bond Street suit, makes a good first impression. But the car, like the driver, must have what it takes underneath. It must be able to go the distance faster and better than the competition. Both car and driver "pass the entrance exam" that others fail: "Going from zero to traffic speed in the length of an on-ramp can be a real test of nerve for the average sedan owner." But then Toyota's V-6 engine "is not at all average." Other advertisements refer to competition in the world of business. "To move ahead fast in this world, you've got to have connections." Ferrari says, simply, "We are the competition."

In this competition between products, owners are almost superfluous. The cars fight it out among themselves. The advertisements suggest the power of the automobile to bestow its qualities on the owner. Pontiac's sport couple has "the motivation to match its looks" and "a level of refinement" to complement its "formidable performance potential." It is a car to live up to. BMW gets back to basics in its stark black-and-white "anti-advertising" advertisement, which reads, simply: "Deeds, not words." That is the serious attitude, a manly attitude, an attitude of *exigence* appropriate to a car "engineered like no other car in the world."

As Todd Gitlin points out, most of the drivers in these advertisements are young white males, loners empowered by the car that makes their escape possible, that allows them to transcend everyday reality into some higher realm of experience and existence. Gitlin stresses the advertisements' "emphasis on surface, the blankness of the protagonist; his striving toward self-sufficiency to the point of displacement from the recognizable world." Even the Chrysler advertisements that co-opt Bruce Springsteen's "Born in the USA" for their "Born in America" campaign lose the original political message, "ripping off Springsteen's angry anthem, smoothing it into a Chamber of Commerce ditty as shots of just plain productive-looking folks, black and white . . . whiz by in a montage-made community." As Gitlin comments, "None of Springsteen's losers need apply—or rather, if only they would roll up their sleeves and see what good company they're in, they wouldn't feel like losers any longer" (1986, p. 140).

This is a world of patriarchal order in which the individual male can and must challenge the father. He achieves identity by breaking loose of the family structure and breaking free of the pack. At a certain point, though, he grows up. He comes to value his father. Maybe he becomes a father himself. The father-son relationship is translated into advertising's glowing stereotypes and put in the service of a new role model: the New Man.

The New Man

Men's liberation has emphasized the need for men to invest themselves emotionally in relationships. This need was frustrated by the straitjacket of traditional expectations regarding the strong, silent male. The old stereotype meant that men grew up never really knowing their fathers, never hearing them say they loved their sons. The old stereotype meant that men had a hard time expressing deep emotion, whether with friends or with lovers. The emergence of the New Man was meant to change all that.

It has changed appearances in some advertisements. Dad has broken his silence. In women's magazines, it is mother who gives advice. In men's magazines, by contrast, mother is almost always absent, out-of-sight, outgrown. When she is present, it is as someone the young man must *still* distance himself from, as in the Nike advertisement depicting a lone runner on the Golden Gate Bridge at sunset, with the accompanying copy: "Mothers, there's a mad man running in the streets. And he's snarling at dogs. And he still has four more miles to go." Nike says, "Just do it." Do it regardless of what mother and all mother-substitutes say or think.

While the young man must still maintain distance between himself and his mother, he proves his New Man status by breaking down the distance between himself and his father. There's a newly discovered warmth to the relationship. "You used to hate it when he told you what to do. Now sometimes you wish he would." How to celebrate the *rapprochement*? "What are you saving the Chivas for?"

Alcohol used to be an honorific product used predominantly by males. As Veblen (1919) recognized, it was a status good used to strengthen bonds and confirm the privileges of masculine identity. Ladies were meant to stay off the stuff. It is still used to impress and strengthen male ties. "How to choose a Scotch to impress your dad:"

Maturity. Sophistication. Taste. All characteristics much admired in fathers, and, coincidentally, in fine Scotch . . .

There are also family traditions in style and manner. In a Brooks Brothers advertisement, a white-haired figure in a tuxedo, identified as "grandfather," smiles beneficently down on "grandson" in his spiffy navy blazer: "Who says charm isn't hereditary?"

Madison Avenue did not oppose the New Woman, but instead welcomed her. She was a new type, and she needed new products. So too with the New Man. The New Father wants to spend "quality time" with his children. He soon appeared in their company in advertisements for products ranging from watches to underpants. In one advertisement, a young executive carries his baby on his back in a pouch, and smiles broadly at the camera: "Success is knowing which appointments to keep." This suggests one can be both a high-powered executive *and* a responsible, caring, sharing father. But will he really bring the baby into the board meeting? A man and a boy appear on horseback to sell Levi's shoes; another pair snuggles in loving embrace, if uncertain relationship, selling Calvin Klein's Eternity.

Besides being free to love his children, the New Man is also free to express himself emotionally. Clothing offers one of the most immediate forms of self-expression. He can be like the man in the Ermenegildo Zegna soft suit, "relaxed, carefree, easy as he wants to be." He can wear Fathom cologne, even if few others can fathom his emotional depths. "For men of motion whose feelings run deep." The idea of men in motion is visually, if tritely, communicated by a male runner in swim trunks. The deep emotions are similarly communicated by a man and a woman silhouetted against a sunset, and by another inset of a solitary male. The depth of feeling is also communicated by a large pair of eyes that stares out uncomprehendingly over the whole blue-toned double-page spread.

The New Man may be artistic, and still be a Real Man, as long as he has inner strength, and as long as that inner strength sells. The model with the trendy eyeglasses is posed in front of his own (ghastly) oil painting. "Even when he's by himself, he's never alone. Creativity is his constant companion. Public or private he makes statements, and the world echoes." Artists can be envied when they pull off the trick of both doing what they want *and* getting rich at it. Artists, presumably, have no bosses breathing down their necks. A real-life artist poses in front of his sizable painting. "My dream was to be a fine artist. So the fact that I can paint every day and I have an audience out there . . . For me, that's it. I have reached the point of Delirium" (brand name).

The New Man is a gift to advertisers. He continues a trend that, according to Barbara Ehrenreich (1983), started in the fifties. The old masculine definition of the serious, uptight male stoically shouldering family responsibilities was challenged by a new philosophy. The *Playboy* philosophy said that boys just want to have fun, and *should* have fun. The hippies of the sixties had their own philosophy: "Make love, not war." "If it feels good, do it." Men of the nineties continue to feel they have the right to self-expression and self-indulgence, to love and be loved, or, at least, to fool around a bit. Advertisements suggest ways to facilitate the process.

Wives and Lovers

Wives are seldom seen in advertisements for men's status goods. When seen, they are usually selling "comfortable," products such as sweat clothes, rather than the more glamorous products, such as fine liquors or automobiles. Pregnant wives are particularly useful for selling insurance and airbags: products meant to appeal to a man's sense of responsibility. An insurance company advertisement shows a pair of expectant parents, the husband placing a protective arm around his pregnant wife. He has made "A promise to dig the seat belts out from under the seats . . . A promise to reserve comment on the latest additions to your wardrobe . . . A promise that a safe world will mean more than night lights and teddy bears." The advertisement goes on to warn about broken promises, thus calling up not just masculine responsibility but masculine guilt. Has the reader purchased enough insurance? Has he had airbags installed in *his* automobile?

By contrast, the beautiful young women in provocative clothes who drape themselves over the male models in clothing advertisements look like anything but wives. They are lovers devoted to the men in their trendy outfits and their flash automobiles. The real prizes are the gorgeous Guess girls falling over the guys in the Guess men clothes. Where do they find them?

Advertising has encouraged a "feminization" of culture, as it puts all potential consumers in the classic role of the female: manipulable, submissive, seeing themselves as objects. The feminization of culture is evident in men's advertisements, where many of the promises made to women are now being made to men. If women's advertisements cry, "Buy this product and he will notice you," men's advertisements similarly promise that female attention will follow immediately upon purchase, or shortly thereafter. "They can't stay away from Mr. J." Much as in the advertisements directed at women, the advertisements for men's products promise that these products will do the talking for you:

"For the look that says come closer." "All the French you'll ever need to know."

Along with this process, men have been encouraged to use a whole range of beauty care products that have been primarily associated with women. Precisely because these products are so similar to women's products, advertisers rely heavily on language and visual symbolism to convey the impression that these are men's products. The need to legitimate such products is captured in a men's magazine cover that asked, in large letters: "Are you man enough for mousse?"

Men's fragrances need masculine-sounding names: Brut, Boss, English Leather, or Hero ("Everyone needs a hero"). They must convince the suspicious male that he can be both "romantico" and "virile." One strategy is to focus the camera on muscular male bodies in perfect physical condition: the male body as symbolic of sex and power. Personal products marketed for men must also have masculine scents: musky, woodsy, seashore, or citrus. In fact, they can smell of virtually anything except flowers. It is not simply because flowers are colorful and delicate that they are equated with femininity. It is also because their one purpose in life, botanically speaking, is to attract fertilization. Given the possible confusion, men are told to head for the woods, wearing Aspen: "As compelling as the land that inspired it. As natural as the man who wears it."

Packaging for men's products avoids pastels and emphasizes instead rich golds, browns, and blacks. Names are changed to protect the ego, if not the innocent: Cosmetics become "skin supplies" and "grooming gear." Hair permanents are sold to promote the "Manly Look," and it required a sportscaster's personal assurance that it really is okay before men would use hair spray: "Years ago, if someone had said to me, 'Hey Al, do you use hair spray?' I would have said, 'No way, baby!' "

"That was before I tried Consort Pump." Having tried the hair spray, the sportscaster vouches for the fact that his hair looked neither stiff nor phony, nor, presumably, feminine. It really is "Grooming Gear for Real Guys."

The New Man lowers his resistance to formerly feminine products, but in service of a traditional masculine goal. The payoff is still good sex, and lots of it. Not surprisingly, sex is most consistently and insistently used to sell alcohol. Sometimes the magic formula for getting good sex is quite explicit: "Always pamper her with Martell cognac. And always, always, be a tiger in bed." Sometimes it is more subtle and implicit. A man and a woman on a waterfront deck look out over the sunset. The brandy is close at hand. The copy reads, "There are some occasions when Courvoisier does mix with water." Similarly, the Hennessy cognac advertisement shows an attractive woman smiling beguilingly at the reader and holding up her brandy snifter. "You're a wanted man." Clearly, the brandy has something to do with her positive attitude.

Masculine Nostalgia

There are other games in town, and other memories to be made and treasured. Sports serves as a metaphor for the male: a special arena free of life's contradictions and contaminations, where a man can test himself and be tested. Sports terms and icons are used to sell a remarkable range of goods, from jackets to tires, from shoes to savings bonds. Once again, we find the qualities of the product transferred to the consumer. TAG-Heuer watches possess endurance and precision, qualities found among "those who thrive on pressure." Dial soap provides "extra inning relief." Sports stars, such as Orel Hershiser and Jim Palmer, transfer their magic to the product, allowing the consumer to share vicariously in their achievements.

The world of sports is colorful and challenging. It is, above all, a man's world. By comparison, the real world seems dull and banal. While there is a certain amount of macho posturing in the presence of high technology, in the computer rooms and at desktop terminals, it is not the same thing as being physically tested by a physically demanding job.

Not surprisingly, a number of advertisements take the consumer back to his past. For it is only there that a secure sense of manhood can be recaptured, in however mythic a form. The highly successful movie, *Field of Dreams*, resurrected long-dead baseball players, who looked like the strong, simple, mostly silent heroes of yesteryear. It is an image directly simulated in an American Express advertisement featuring Tom Seaver, clad in rolled-up white pants and a white singlet, standing as if contemplating a pitch, baseball behind his back, against the eerie light of evening. His trusty dog is at his side.

There are many different boyhood dreams, not all having to do with baseball or dogs, although there are lots of dogs in advertisements directed at men: Men also dream of cars. Beautiful cars.

Cars to kill for. One brand of men's clothes is advertised as being "as classic as a '55 Thunderbird," with most of the two-page spread taken up by the Thunderbird. The clothes only turn the reader on by association. Corvette relies upon its classic dream-car status to condescend to criticize the "rag-tag collection of pseudo 'sports cars' that, over the years, have challenged Corvette's supremacy." Mazda evokes the street-scapes of small-town America, when the bright red convertible in the showroom was every boy's dream. "We stood in the glow of a street-light, our faces pressed against the glass, hypnotized by visions of Route 66, road racing, and rock and roll."

Other dreams have to do with the romance of flight: The Ralph Lauren model in his sportsman's sweater stands confidently on the pontoon of his seaplane in the rugged lake country, the "bombardier watch" adver-tises "rugged precision for land, sea, or air." Sometimes a man has to travel far for adventure, leaving behind the girl foolish enough to prefer "rum you could see through." He prefers rum you can't see through, and other mysterious satisfactions of the tropics: "the club with no name, the curious but delicious daiquiri, and the waiter with the bamboo cane."

These are dreams of escape. Back home, in everyday adulthood, the man finds himself weighed down by the pressures of competition, achievement, and conformity. These pressures, ironically, are rein-forced by the mass of advertising he encounters—even when he doesn't think he's paying attention to it. Is there really any way he can succeed on his own terms? Is there really any way he can be his own man, rather than, in fact, just another walking advertisement for the capitalist system and its attendant dreams of individual success at whatever cost?

The New Role Models

There are still plenty of sports stars selling hair cream and dirt bikes. Lately, however, a new role model has been added: the ordinary person who has done, or is doing, extraordinary things. As in advertisements for the Gap, the models are interesting people with interesting faces, if not household names. In a glossy, four-page spread, Timex presents three such heroes, one woman and two men:

> The most remarkable people in this world don't appear on movie screens or in sports arenas or on television tubes. They drive cabs and work in offices and operate machinery. They're just ordinary people like us who happened to have experienced something extraordinary. And survived.

The woman in her early fifties skied to the magnetic North Pole, surviving polar bear confrontations, blizzards, and near starvation. The older man survived being sucked into an offshore water-intake pipe for a nuclear power plant, traveling 1,650 feet at 50 miles per hour. He was finally spat out into a canal at the power station. The younger man walked around the world alone. The 21,000-mile trek took him 4 years, and included a wild boar attack and being arrested as a spy (four times). The fact that some of these adventures were undertaken voluntarily, whereas others just happened, suggests to us that any of us can be extraordinary. The ordinary—our everyday selves, the inexpensive Timex watch—can be transformed into the extraordinary.

A second example. A clothing company proposes "Heroes for Today":

> The old heroes were often but a chimera. Men like Coop and the Duke, who saved the day before heading off into a technicolored sunset. Paladins of our imagination. But, today's heroes are those men and women who are guided by principles based on real and lasting values. Those who help to mend the torn fabric of the earth. And those who still seek the adventurous life. Before they head off, they don't call wardrobe. They call us. Eddie Bauer.

This is the new anti-advertising. But it is still advertising. It tells us that we are too knowing and wise to be taken in by the old advertising and its old-fashioned heroes, who were, after all, a bit obvious. So it offers us new heroes to whom we can relate in a way we no longer can to John Wayne or Gary Cooper. All that shooting was bad for the environment.

Conclusion

It has been argued, persuasively, that at some level the media reflect society. It is also argued that the media actively shape society, though it is very difficult to prove direct relationships of causes and effects (cf. Tuchman, Daniels, & Benet, 1978). Much of the power of advertising is indirect. Sometimes it directly influences us to rush out and buy a product. Advertisers wish it could and would do this more often. What it often does do is to plant an image in our minds—an image of the good life, of how the product can help facilitate its achievement, and an appealing, if flattering, picture of the people we would like to be.

Such new role models suggest new options, a new choice of heroes. It is their connection with their sponsors that remains problematic. These people are not distinctive or admirable because they wear Timex watches or Eddie Bauer sports clothes. As Simmel (1978) recognized, true distinction does not come from money but from character and applications, from people creating worthy selves in and through society. Material goods are necessary, but they are not sufficient. As Weber (1905) said of materialism in general, it should be worn lightly, like a cloak. But material goods have become more like a security blanket in an uncertain world. Social status and financial success are used to compensate for either devaluation or loss of other goals and possible achievements.

Righting the balance depends not on the actions of advertisers, but of consumers. We must unravel the cultural meanings in the messages to see how their images of masculinity exist to promote not individual identity but corporate profits. The meaning of masculinity is neither predetermined nor hidden from view: It is out there *in* society, because it is *of* society. It can be altered, shaped, and molded. Ultimately, it is ours, to do with as we will. This chapter represents one step in this process of reclamation.

11

Men and the News Media

The Male Presence and Its Effect

DAVID CROTEAU
WILLIAM HOYNES

During the past two decades, scholars in sociology, women's studies, and communications have made a priority of studying the media's depiction of contemporary gender roles. This research has generally had two central features. First, most of the work has focused on advertising images, film, entertainment television, and popular magazines (Kalisch & Kalisch, 1984; Lysonski, 1985; Rak & McMullen, 1987; Rugfiero & Weston, 1985; Skelly & Lundstrom, 1981). Very little research has focused on gender roles in the news media. Second, with good reason, the depiction of women has been the primary focus of the little research that has looked at gender and the news media. For example, feminist scholarship has pointed to the woefully inadequate coverage of women by the U.S. news media (Davis, 1982; Johnson & Christ, 1988; Miller, 1975). But there has been virtually nothing written about men in the news media, either as the primary sources and subjects of news or as the producers of the news. In fact, Fejes' (1989) overview of the recent research on men in the media does not even mention news media. This chapter begins to examine the male presence in the news media and its effect on the news product. We use our research on the guest list of ABC News *Nightline* to illustrate several points about men as both sources and subjects of the news. We then go on to discuss some of the consequences resulting from male domination of the process of news production.

The Male Presence: Men as Sources and Subjects

Male domination of the news media begins, very simply, with numerical superiority. The male presence in the news industry is immense and far-reaching. Male dominance is perhaps most conspicuous at the higher levels of media organizations. Lee and Soloman (1990) report that 94% of top management positions in U.S. news media are occupied by men. Duckworth and his associates (Duckworth, Lodder, Moore, Overton, & Rubin, 1990) report that the upper levels of major corporate media organizations are almost entirely male. For example, the top five executives at Capital Cities ABC, Times Mirror, CBS, Knight-Ridder, *The New York Times*, and the Turner Broadcasting System are all men. The boards of directors of these same corporate media outlets are also virtually all male.

As for journalists, Lee and Soloman (1990) report that more than three-quarters of network news reports are filed by men. And only 27% of front-page bylines in 10 major newspapers were women's. Furthermore, a study of *The New York Times* op-ed page (Goldin, 1990) found that 87% of the 309 opinion pieces by outside contributors during the first half of 1989 (excluding Sundays) were written by men.

Male numerical domination of the industry is accompanied by similar domination in the roles of both sources and subjects. To illustrate this point we draw upon our study of ABC News *Nightline*. In this study, we paid particular attention to who appeared as guests on the program. These guests play the mixed role of source and commentator—telling viewers both what the news is and how to understand it. We suggest that analysis of who appears in the news can tell us a great deal about the news product that viewers ultimately receive.

We analyzed the transcripts from 40 months of ABC News *Nightline* (January 1985 through April 1988), which included a total of 865 programs and 2,498 guests. We coded each program by topic, and each guest on a variety of dimensions, including gender. We also qualitatively analyzed coverage of seven issues that were the subjects of frequent *Nightline* stories during this 40-month period: terrorism, U.S.-Soviet relations, Central America, South Africa, the economy, religion, and media politics. Our general findings have been reported elsewhere (Hoynes & Croteau, 1989). For the purposes of this chapter, we focus on our data about the gender of *Nightline* guests, and its relationship to other variables. In particular, we are interested in the context in which

Table 11.1 Program Topic by Gender of Guest

	Count Row % Col %		
	Men	*Women*	*Row Total*
International Affairs	914	57	971
	94.1	5.9	38.9
	40.8	22.1	
Domestic Politics	413	51	464
	89.0	11.0	18.6
	18.4	19.8	
Economics	189	19	208
	90.9	9.1	8.3
	8.4	7.4	
Social	437	105	542
	80.6	19.4	21.7
	19.5	40.7	
Culture	174	14	188
	92.6	7.4	7.5
	7.8	5.4	
Other	112	12	124
	90.3	9.7	5.0
	5.0	4.7	
Column	2,239	258	2,497
Total	89.7	10.3	100.0

male and female guests appear, the kinds of men who appear regularly, and the effect this has on the journalistic enterprise.

The results of our study indicate that the news is interpreted almost entirely by men. All 19 of the guests who appeared more than five times in the 40-month period of our study were men. And 68 of the 74 guests who appeared alone on *Nightline* were men. Of the 2,498 guests in the 40-month period, 2,239, or 90%, were men. As Table 11.1 illustrates, 9 out of 10 guests who discussed international affairs, domestic politics, or the economy were men. The only time this figure dropped substantially was on programs about social issues (e.g., health, education, religion, family). Still, on these programs 80% of the guests were men. These figures indicate that *Nightline*'s bookers turn to men much more often than women for the "hard" political and economic news of the day.

On the other hand, 41% of all women appearing on *Nightline* over this 40-month period did so on programs about social issues, while only 22% appeared on programs about international issues. The figures for men are roughly the opposite: 41% of the male guests were on programs about international issues, while 20% were on programs about social issues. These figures are particularly significant because of *Nightline*'s reputation in journalistic circles as the television news program with the most in-depth international coverage. Analysis of international issues is almost the exclusive property of men, while women are relegated to discussions of traditionally "female" social issues.

The overwhelming numerical overrepresentation of men is only one part of how men dominate the *Nightline* guest list. They also appear earlier in the program, and are afforded more opportunity to speak. The early appearance rate of men is .12, while that of women is only .09.[1] In the rare instances when women did appear on *Nightline*, they were likely to be responding to agendas that had been framed by the male guests who appeared earlier. And men, on the average, speak 16% more (as measured in transcript lines) than women. In sum, men dominate virtually every aspect of *Nightline*. Regular viewers see the world interpreted from a perspective that is almost exclusively male.

It would be misleading, however, to suggest that *Nightline*—or other news media—is dominated by all kinds of men. *Nightline*'s guest list is not simply stratified by gender. On the contrary, our research suggests that only certain types of men have regular access to the major news media. In fact, by excluding certain types of men, news media may help to signal "appropriate" or "sanctioned" gender and political roles for men. The news, by taking some perspectives seriously and largely ignoring others, can help to constitute an "ideal" male identity. Our study of *Nightline* suggests some of the characteristics of this ideal man.

First the ideal man is an elite, white man. More than 92% of the American guests were white,[2] and, as Figure 11.1 illustrates, 80% of the guests were government officials, professionals, or corporate representatives. People of color and non-elites rarely appeared on the program. Furthermore, Table 11.2 indicates that those representatives of labor and public interest organizations who did appear on *Nightline* were twice as likely as government officials, professionals, or corporate representatives to be women. What this suggests is that access to *Nightline* and other media is structured by the intersection of gender, race, and class. While women and people of color are rarely seen, the

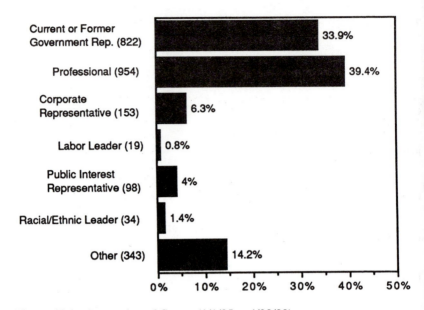

Figure 11.1. Occupation of Guests (1/1/85 to 4/30/88)

voices of white working-class or poor men, or their representatives, are also rarely heard.

Second, this ideal male displays a high degree of respect for government policymakers. *Nightline* only rarely featured appearances by potential dissenters. Only 6% of the guests represented labor, public interest organizations, or racial/ethnic organizations. On programs about the economy, for example, corporate representatives outnumbered labor representatives by seven to one. And more than half of the 68 guests on programs about Central America were current or former U.S. government officials, while only two represented independent organizations that opposed U.S. policy.

Furthermore, even those white men with elite credentials who hold strongly critical positions may have little access to programs like *Nightline*. While white, male, former government officials make for prime *Nightline* guests, critics who fit this profile, like former Attorney General Ramsey Clark, former CIA station chief John Stockwell, former Ambassador Robert White, and former Pentagon Planner Daniel Ellsberg, were absent from the guest list. Ultimately, what programs like *Nightline* bring viewers are interpretations of the world largely from

Table 11.2 Occupation of Guest by Gender of Guest

	Count Row % Col % *Men*	*Women*	*Row Total*
Government Official	782 95.2 35.6	39 4.8 17.3	821 33.9
Professional	859 90.0 39.1	95 10.0 42.2	954 39.4
Corporate	142 92.8 6.5	11 7.2 4.9	153 6.3
Labor Rep	16 84.2 .7	3 15.8 1.3	19 0.8
Public Interest Rep	81 82.7 3.7	17 17.3 7.6	98 4.0
Racial/Ethnic Leader	33 97.1 1.5	1 2.9 .4	34 1.4
Other	284 82.8 12.9	59 17.2 26.2	343 14.2
Column	2197	225	2422
Total	90.7	9.3	100.0

elite, white men who do not challenge the fundamental tenets of the status quo.

Furthermore, the ideal male exhibits a high degree of machismo or toughness when interpreting the events of the day. The four most frequent U.S. guests in this 40-month period were former Secretaries of State Henry Kissinger and Alexander Haig, then Assistant Secretary of State Elliott Abrams, and Moral Majority founder Jerry Falwell. All of these men are staunch cold warriors who espouse tough foreign policy rhetoric. Among the 19 U.S. men who appeared more than five times in the 40 months (see Table 11.3), at least 13 of them fit this general mold.

On programs about terrorism, the single-mindedness of the male commentators is readily apparent. The six most frequent U.S. commen-

Table 11.3 *Nightline* Guests Who Appeared More Than Five Times
(1/1/85 to 4/30/88)

	U.S. Guests	
Henry Kissinger	Former Secretary of State *	(14)
Alexander Haig	Former Secretary of State	(14)
Elliott Abrams	Former Assistant Secretary of State	(12)
Jerry Falwell	Moral Majority	(12)
Lawrence Eagleburger	Former Undersecretary of State	(12)
Jesse Jackson	Former Presidential Candidate	(10)
Arthur Miller	Harvard Law School	(9)
William Hyland	Former Deputy National Secretary Advisor	(8)
Patrick Buchanan	Former White House Communications Director	(7)
William Cohen	Senator (R) Maine	(7)
Arthur Laffer	Economist, Pepperdine University	(7)
William Safire	*The New York Times*	(7)
Christopher Dodd	Senator (D) Connecticut	(6)
Harry Edwards	Sociologist, University of California	(6)
Bobby Inman	Former Deputy Director, CIA	(6)
Noel Koch	Former Assistant Secretary of Defense	(6)
Michael Ledeen	Former Advisor to Secretary to State (Haig)	(6)
Alan Simpson	Senator (R) Wyoming	(6)
Marvin Zonis	University of Chicago	(6)
	Foreign Guests	
Alejandro Bendana	Sec. General, Nicaraguan Foreign Ministry	(11)
Said Rajie-Khorassani	Iranian Ambassador to the United Nations	(8)
Benjamin Netanyahu	Israeli Ambassador to the United Nations	(7)
Ferdinand Marcos	Former President of the Philippines	(6)

* Titles used here are for identification purposes only.

tators on terrorist coverage were Kissinger, Haig, and four counterterrorism experts: State Department consultant Michael Ledeen, Brian Jenkins of the RAND Corporation, Robert Kuperman of the Center for Strategic and International Studies, and former Assistant Secretary of State Noel Koch. Again, all of these men talk "tough" about the need to respond to terrorism. Their views are so similar that there was no substantive discussion about how to define the terms of the debate. In fact, the basic assumptions of U.S. policy were rarely, if ever, challenged. Discussions of terrorism were not linked to a broader discussion of political violence. Nor did analysis explain the differentiation, if any, between counterterrorism and terrorism. In short, analysis of terrorism was remarkably uniform, coming from a small cadre of men who view the world through the lenses of strategic interest, national security, and power politics.

Nightline's coverage of Central America depicted men in a similar light. All of the commentators on this hotly contested terrain were men, and debates of U.S. policy did not provide room for fundamental disagreement about the right of the United States to intervene in the affairs of Central American nations. Those who advocated different approaches, ones that rejected the military option or even questioned the just nature of U.S. goals, were rarely seen. In fact, it would be hard to tell from *Nightline*'s coverage of Central America that there were many Americans—both male and female—articulating alternative, albeit less "tough," perspectives throughout the 1980s.

Nightline's coverage of U.S.-Soviet relations followed a similar pattern. Leaders of the U.S. peace movement were virtually absent. So-called alternatives were largely represented by officials of the Soviet government, certainly a central part of the discussion, but little different in many ways from the U.S. officials. Both were almost exclusively tough-talking men. Emblematic of *Nightline*'s approach was host Ted Koppel's introduction of his three guests on January 8, 1985:

> Tonight, live from Geneva, the two Richards, Perle and Burt—Perle, the Pentagon hardliner, Burt, the State Department moderate. They will tell us how and why the U.S. and the Soviets have agreed to resume arms talks. And another view of the arms control talks and the latest White House realignment from a man who knows the ins and outs of both, former White House Chief of Staff and former Secretary of State Alexander Haig.

This kind of debate left virtually every U.S. government assumption about foreign policy intact. Any substantive critique of U.S. policy was missing, as Richard Burt, a conservative Cruise Missile proponent, served as *Nightline*'s moderate.

Finally, the ideal man is a patriotic American. While U.S. critics of U.S. policy were generally excluded, *Nightline* was more likely to include the dissenting views of foreigners, often from "enemy" states. In fact, Alejandro Bendana, of the Nicaraguan Foreign Ministry, was a regular guest on *Nightline* in the 1980s. However, these dissenting views are foreign by definition, and often anti-American by implication. This clearly diminishes their applicability to political discourse in the United States, where the audience is more receptive to the views expressed by U.S. officials pitted against officials of "enemy" states. When debates are (not-so-subtly) framed as the "American" position versus the foreign position, the virtues of patriotic behavior take on special significance.

Certainly other men do appear on *Nightline*, and not all of the men are tough-talking patriots. But there is such a preponderance of the same types of men that the terms of the debate are firmly set, even when alternative voices do make appearances. These terms assume that we understand the realities of power politics and do not suggest policies that are utopian. We do not see, for example, pacifists questioning the morality of violence. Nor do we see frank discussions about business ethics. More generally, moral questions are rarely discussed in this world of power politics. Even those who try to articulate different perspectives often must conform to the standard language and present their analyses as equally hard-nosed.

Furthermore, *Nightline* does not often probe the diversity of American society or the range of conflicts and contradictions that exist in contemporary America. For example, of the 865 programs in this study, one focused on class conflict, two focused on gender conflicts, and 11 focused on domestic racial conflicts. This left little room for viewers to see a wide range of either male or female commentators analyzing the day-to-day struggles of American men and women. And since expertise is so highly regarded on programs like *Nightline*, a traditionally male brand of detached, dispassionate analysis is the norm. Men who deviate from this form of analysis were virtually invisible. Furthermore, neither the guest list nor the topics covered gave viewers the opportunity to see men struggling with issues of male privilege—or for that matter, elite, white men dealing with issues of race or class. And given the narrow range of guests, many may have had little interest in raising such issues. *Nightline*'s "top story of the day" rarely included analyses of how men cope with relationships, with family, or with the stresses of their workplace. One exception was the large amount of coverage of AIDS. However, even here, panels were usually limited, as they rarely included people with AIDS, gay men, or AIDS activists.

In essence, *Nightline* does not provide viewers with images of or perspectives from a wide variety of men. The result is news and analysis by and about a narrow range of men with similar attitudes and similar interests.

The Effect of the Male Presence: Objectivity and Journalism

The fact that men dominate the news media through sheer numbers is extremely significant in and of itself. Liberal critics, who tend to have an individualistic approach to social problems, often see the elimination of employment and promotion barriers based on sex as the solution to male dominance of such social institutions as the media. However, male quantitative dominance also contributes to a form of qualitative dominance. This qualitative dominance is likely to be felt long after the relative numbers of male and female journalists have equalized.

One qualitative effect of the male presence in the news media has been the promotion of professional values and news-gathering techniques that draw upon a male-centered positivist tradition that has been criticized by radical feminist theories.[3] One of the most prominent of these critiques has been leveled against the notion of objectivity in the search for knowledge.

Objectivity has long been a central pillar of the positivist research tradition in the natural and social sciences. As Jagger (1983, p. 356) notes, within the positivist tradition, "good scientists are detached observers and manipulators of nature who follow strict methodological rules, which enable them to separate themselves from the special values, interests and emotions generated by their class, race, sex or unique situation." Thus, the ability to remain detached and objective has been central to the notion of positivist science. Gregg (1987, p. 8) argues that, in fact, "The control of knowledge and exercise of power that are the privilege of science and scientists derive in part from natural science's claim to this neutrality." But science is not the only field to carry the banner of objectivity. While science has its methodological approaches to ensure objectivity, journalism has its own professional values and practices, which are geared toward achieving, as completely as possible, objective reports. Thus, both fields largely share a similar belief in the positivist notion of objectivity. In fact, as Gans (1979, p. 184) puts it, "Although journalists may not be aware of it, they are perhaps the strongest remaining bastion of logical positivism in America."

Although often tempered with the realization that true objectivity may never be completely obtainable, journalists usually do see objectivity as a value for which they should strive. Yet the positivist notion of objectivity is one that has been associated with a distinctly male view of the world. This masculine view includes, among other things, a belief in monolithic notions of reality and truth. Faith in objectivity implies that an investigator, whether scientist or journalist, can obtain a clear understanding of a monolithic external truth or reality by adhering to methodological principles, regardless of the investigator's status in gender, race, class, or other hierarchies. This distinctly masculine notion of reality favors the abstract ideas of investigators and experts over the concrete and differing experiences of various individuals or groups. People with diverse opinions or views need not be active participants in the delineation of reality under the scheme of objectivity since the single (usually male) investigator can determine the truth for himself.

Such notions have had profound impact on how journalistic inquiry is conducted. First, journalists have seen themselves as the center of the information-gathering process. Interview program hosts, for example, see no need to invite policy critics on their programs since the hosts see it as being their role to ask government officials and corporate representatives tough questions—a role laden with machismo overtones. In his response to our study of *Nightline*, the program's executive producer, Richard Kaplan, argued that *Nightline* tries "to get the players, the people who really are the decision makers, to hold their feet to the fire" (Michaelson, 1989, p. 10).

Second, journalists rely upon assorted experts and informed players and they are generally treated as if they have no agenda of their own. Thus both journalists and these so-called experts portray themselves as objective reporters of events. Yet, as Gregg (1987, p. 9) points out, "objectivity, when elevated to the status of sole criterion of truth, masks interests in its claim to neutrality, devalues people's experiences and perceptions of reality, constitutes an invitation to domination, and claims for science [*and, we would add, journalism*] an authority which disguises power as truth."

Given that positions of power in our society are largely held by men, it is no surprise the notion of truth presented in the media is one based on a male view of reality. As a radical feminist critique of the notion of total objectivity would argue, "the very claim to disinterest and detachment expresses a kind of interest: it reflects the values embedded in our cultural ideal of masculinity" (Keller, 1983, p. 51). Male power has promoted male notions of truth and, simultaneously, male notions of truth have supported male power. As Gregg (1987) puts it, "Objectivity, detachment, disinterest, and neutrality have become reified, in part because the uses to which science has been put are so successful in confirming the male perspective of reality, satisfying the needs of capital, and maintaining social order" (p. 10).

The news media have, in many ways, served similar ends. As the example of *Nightline* has suggested, news program viewers are constantly bombarded with the male perspective of reality. The exclusion of dissenting voices on such programs helps to legitimize the status quo while undermining the efforts of critics. This is extremely significant when we recognize that, as Gregg says, "reality has authors." She continues:

> The question for critical communication research has been one of identifying those authors: who or what decides how we know what we know, who or what determines the legitimacy of one interpretation over another, or facts over beliefs and the difference between the two? The task for feminist communication research is the identification and legitimation of new authors of many different realities. (1987, p. 13)

But as we have seen, the news media have offered little or no room for alternative interpretations of reality. Instead, it is elite white males who are continuously given the opportunity to interpret reality for the American public.

How has the male-centered notion of objectivity affected what and how news is reported? There are at least four parts to that answer. First, an objective report does not include the journalist's own views. Detachment and separation, which are hallmark of masculine approach to knowledge, are highly prized values in journalism. Of course, actual detachment and separation are rarely, if ever, achieved. The result, then, is that the agendas of those who hide behind the shield of objectivity are often effectively obfuscated.

Second, an objective report is fair in its representation of the two sides to a story. As Tuchman (1974) has suggested, this usually entails soliciting views from two of the powerful players associated with a story. By relying on the official voices of those in power, the media, in effect, relies on male voices that support the status quo, though they may differ on specific policy details. This approach is also a result of the high value journalists place on dramatic conflict. Conflict, not consensus, makes for interesting stories, and the most interesting are those with two clearly demarcated antagonists. Such simplistic depictions often leave little room for the exploration of the complexities that underlie most major news events. Objective reporting of the two sides of a story, therefore, is reductionist, and it usually excludes a wide range of dissenting parties and perspectives.

Third, an objective report is based on facts—external and verifiable. The way journalists, who are perpetually under the threat of deadline, verify facts is to turn to powerful institutions with large public relations departments whose primary function is to provide just such information. Confirmation from an authority—from someone already in power—is enough to certify a fact. In some cases, the statements of powerful people are facts to be reported in and of themselves, regardless of the veracity of the statement's contents. For example, the President's statements are always news. The accuracy of his statements, as the Reagan years made clear, is often of little concern. Such criteria obviously do not apply to people who are outside the circles of power. Their statements are not automatically news, and organizations representing such constituencies as labor or women usually do not have the funds to staff slick public relations agencies to feed information to reporters.

In addition, abstract knowledge of expertise on an issue is usually valued by the news media over direct experience and participation. Consequently, as we have seen, news analysis and commentary is dominated by powerful white males at the expense of women, people of color, and representatives of public interest groups and social movements. Elite experts—in the world of the news media—are somehow supposed to have transcended any kind of personal interest that is thought to taint people who advocate particular positions.

Fourth, by working within outmoded notions of objective reporting and analysis, and by being dependent on powerful institutions to provide them with information for their stories, journalists are led to work within confined frameworks of understanding that exclude alternative possibilities. As Bennett (1983, p. 7) argues, "the news avoids wide-ranging coverage of diverse viewpoints and experiences in favor of extensive coverage of official positions and mainstream perspectives. This preoccupation with 'normalcy' creates the impression that there are few serious alternatives to mainstream politics and life styles." The effect is similar to that discussed in Thomas Kuhn's (1974) critique of positivism's claims for natural science. In particular, Kuhn's idea of "normal science" suggests that most scientific work takes place within the boundaries of taken-for-granted epistemological positions toward which critical reason is suspended. Also, Kuhn shows how scientists, working within epistemological straitjackets, often ignore or explain away experimental results that are inconsistent with accepted theories. Journalists, too, tend to work within straitjackets in their "preoccupation with 'normalcy.'" They rely on routine sources within powerful institutions for most of their stories. Guaranteeing access to such routine and useful sources means that journalists, whether consciously or not, must often suspend truly critical judgments of the powerful institutions that these sources serve. As a result of such mutually reinforcing relationships, one journalist has gone so far as to refer to the news media as "stenographers to power" (Hertsgaard, 1988).

In the end, reliance on a masculine notion of objectivity is, in many ways, reliance on taken-for-granted analyses of the world, which, as we have seen, excludes many people—perhaps the majority—from the news world. The effect of the male presence in the news media has been to set off a bounded space of acceptable male interpretation of reality while devaluing critical alternatives.

Conclusion

The combination of two realities—the numerical dominance of the news media by a particular type of male and the dominance of the male perspective in the values and techniques employed by news media personnel—has resulted in news that contributes to the undermining of the democratic value of diversity. More specifically, in its quest for objectivity and expert knowledge, the news media tends to sanction a particular narrow view of the world—that of elite white males. It legitimizes the worldview of a tiny segment of our society, granting a particular elite the power of authorship of reality for millions of news viewers and readers. This sort of undemocratic privileging of one experience over those of women, people of color, and political dissenters is counter to the notion of a free press.

Men clearly dominate the news media. But men—perhaps the majority of men—are also potentially constrained by the narrowly defined images of sanctioned male roles presented by the news media. These images portray a particular type of both male perspective and male behavior that may not be resonant for a vast number of men. Men who are not white, or who are not part of the culture of power, will find little in the news media to validate their experience. Instead, these men, like women and others who are generally excluded from the halls of power, must contend with a news media that often helps to disguise power as truth.

Notes

1. We calculated the early appearance rate by dividing the number of appearances before the first commercial break by the total number of appearances.

2. Race was identifiable for 80% of the guests.

3. We use the term *radical* here very loosely, only to distinguish this strain of critique from the *liberal* feminist critique, which, in the context of science, has been primarily concerned with the number of scientists, their status, the subjects and problems chosen for research, and the equation of the male perspective with the human perspective (Abel & Abel, 1983). We in no way attempt to do justice to the finer nuances that exist within the radical tradition.

12

Images of Men in Sport Media

The Social Reproduction of Gender Order

DONALD SABO
SUE CURRY JANSEN

Partly in response to the women's movement and growth of feminist scholarship, conventions for representing gender in mass media have come under increasing scrutiny during the past two decades. To date, however, these efforts have been limited in three ways. First, content analyses have focused almost exclusively on women and, as Craig observed in Chapter One, men's roles in media have been tacitly viewed as unproblematic.[1] Second, most studies have relied on mainstream sex-role theory, which assumes that mass media transmit stereotypical gender images that shape role expectations and, in turn, inform behavior and identity. Sex-role theory frequently ignores or underemphasizes power differences between the sexes, the relational processes through which gender identity is socially constructed, and dynamic linkages between gender images and larger systems of social stratification and ideology. Third, very few studies have focused on gender images in sport media, which is somewhat remarkable, given the omnipresence of sport programming and athletic imagery in media as well as the fact that sport and masculinity have been culturally equated in North American society (Sabo & Runfola, 1980).

Sport imagery and athletic events are prominent features of U.S. electronic and print media. Indeed, the growth of mass spectator sports and mass media during the twentieth century is characterized by increasing interdependence (Coakley, 1986). In their study of the media coverage of the Summer Olympic Games between 1956 and 1984, for example, Lucas and Real (1984) found that television networks came to rely on coverage of the Games for revenues and program content. Reciprocally, the International Olympic Committee received progressively more lucrative television revenues (more than $20 million from its share of the 1984 Los Angeles games) and thus has become largely dependent on media sponsorship for continuance of its expanding operations. The media-dependent sports industry now produces its schedules, structures its formats, and sometimes even changes the rules of the games in order to deliver the largest audiences to advertisers. Indeed, the Super Bowl, an event created for television, annually generates the highest cost-per-second advertising revenues in network television. The symbiotic relationship between the sport industry and mass media is further reflected by the growing presence of sports coverage in newspapers since 1900 (Lever & Wheeler, 1984). Today the sports section is the most widely read section of major metropolitan newspapers, and more newspaper print is devoted to sports than any other topic, including national and international news (Coakley, 1986; Greendorfer, 1983; Smith & Blackman, 1978).

Millions of sports spectators are regularly assembled by media events in simulated solidarity, for example, the Olympics, the Super Bowl, college football and basketball games, the National Basketball Association (NBA) finals, the Professional Golf Association and Ladies Professional Golf Association tournaments, and Wimbledon or U.S. Open professional tennis tournaments. Mediated sport is a powerful presence in American culture. From the corporate perspective, fans are mainly seen as consumers; NFL management sometimes refers to them as "fannies in the seats" (Meggesey, 1990). Sport media are the major communication apparatus of the expanding sport industry. They are expected to generate a gross national sport product of $121.1 billion by the year 2000; projections for sport advertising revenues on television are $11.5 billion and, for all advertising revenues combined, $25 billion (Rosner, 1989). The combined and usually collaborative efforts of national news, entertainment, and advertising media have stimulated the growth of sport as a major cultural phenomenon and profit center in North America.

In this chapter, we explore emerging research on gender in sport media in order to demonstrate how male images in sport media contribute to the social reproduction of cultural values and structural dynamics of dominance systems within the gender order. Connell (1987) uses the term *gender order* to refer to a "historically constructed pattern of power relations between men and women and definitions of femininity and masculinity" that emerges and is transformed within varying structural contexts (pp. 98-99). Drawing upon both feminist theory and a concept of hegemony loosely derived from Gramsci, we try to identify some of the ways in which sports media contribute to the social constructions of hegemonic masculinity, and enable dominant groups within the gender order to extend their material control to the cultural sectors.

Critical Feminist Analysis of Sport and Media

Messner and Sabo (1990) have outlined the emergence of critical feminist perspectives on the relations linking men to sport and the gender order. By the early 1970s, a multidisciplinary sport studies had blossomed and succeeded in illuminating the relationship between sport and racism, class inequality, nationalism, violence, drug use, and other social issues (Edwards, 1973; Hoch, 1972; Naisen, 1972; Scott, 1971). The concept of gender, however, remained undeveloped in most of these early "radical" critiques of sport. The fact that the institution of sport was constituted from its inception as an exclusive and exclusionary arena of male experience and male relations was ignored or taken for granted as natural. Sport studies' blind spot concerning the fundamental relationship between sport and the social construction of gender resulted in a very incomplete, sometimes distorted, analysis of the historical and contemporary meaning and significance of sport.

In the late 1970s a "feminist critique of sport" emerged; it viewed sport "as a fundamentally sexist institution that is male dominated and masculine in orientation" (Theberge, 1981, p. 342). Feminist analyses examined sex differences in patterns of athletic socialization and aimed at demonstrating how sport as a social institution naturalizes men's power and privilege over women. The marginalization and trivialization of female athletes, it was argued, served to reproduce patriarchal domination of women by men. Feminist analysis of sport began to flourish during the early 1980s, a period that also witnessed the importation of neo-Marxist theory, critical theory, and cultural studies perspectives into sport studies. Adherents of these critical schools commonly conceptualized sport within the frameworks of larger historical critiques of capitalism, the culture industry, or modernity. They linked analyses of inequalities, oppression, and social problems to calls for political action and the creation of liberative strategies for resistance and change in sport and society (Gruneau, 1983; Hargreaves, 1982). As feminist critics pointed out, however, analysis of gender remained tangential to the class-centered agendas of neo-Marxist and cultural studies perspectives (Deem, 1988).

A dialogue between feminist theorists and critical theorists in sport sociology was initiated during the 1980s. Some feminist thinkers increasingly recognized the importance of the concept of hegemony and have used it to examine gender relations (Bryson, 1990; Hall, 1990; Messner, 1988; Sabo, 1990). Some critical theorists also began attributing more importance to gender and exploring linkages between analyses of class, gender, and race inequality (Gruneau, 1983; Hargreaves, 1982; Sage, 1990). One result is the emergence of a "multiple systems of dominance perspective" that is attempting to "explore intersections of class, gender, and racial practices and relations and the way in which they are dialectically related in local community sport rituals" (Foley, 1990).

Within communications studies, broadly conceived, a similar but more tentative and more highly nuanced dialogue between feminist and critical theory has been initiated (Gallagher, 1989; Kuhn, 1982b; Mulvey, 1975; Radway, 1984; Rakow, 1986, 1987; Tuchman, Daniels, & Benet, 1978; and many others). It has been more tentative because mass communication research has not generally ignored gender; it has treated it as a variable, sometimes even as a very significant variable, in research using content analysis. Some of this work has been extremely useful in advancing feminist critiques of mass media (Goffman, 1979; Tuchman et al., 1978).

Nevertheless, communications studies as a field has proven more resistant to integration of feminist perspectives within its theoretical models than other disciplines within the social sciences and humanities (Jansen 1989, 1990). The blind spot that secures this resistance appears to operate at the very basic epistemological level: at the level where foundation metaphors demarcate a vision of how the field is to be conceptualized. The founding metaphors of communication studies, for example, information, sender-receiver, channels, and so on, were borrowed from electrical engineering (Rogers, 1989; Shannon & Weaver, 1964). These terms are used both literally and metaphorically in articulating models of communication processes. Used literally to describe and model the technological constituents, organizational structures, and processes that make dissemination for mass mediated messages possible, they provide useful mappings of the technologies and institutions that function, in George Gerbner's words (1977, p. 147), as "cultural arms" of existing systems of domination (see also Gerbner, 1989). Stripped of their original meanings and elevated to the status of laws of general principles of communication science, these terms no longer simply map systems of domination, they advance them. This blind spot in mainstream communications theory naturalizes and privileges binary logics and principles of hierarchy at levels of abstraction that make their analogue and roots in the gender order very difficult to unpack.

The dialogue between feminist theorists and critical theorists has been more highly nuanced within communication studies than within sports studies because paradigmatic debates among contending critical schools have been more fully articulated and much more contentious (see, for example, Dervin, Grossberg, O'Keefe, & Wartella, 1989). To date, cultural studies perspectives have more thoroughly integrated feminist perspectives within their theoretical core than other critical approaches. Thus, for example, Stuart Hall (1988, p. 29) recognizes, "all social practices and forms of domination—including the politics of the Left—are always inscribed in and to some extent secured by sexual identity and positioning." Moreover, he maintains:

> If we don't attend to how gendered identities are formed and transformed and how they are deployed politically, we simply do not have a language of sufficient explanatory power at our command with which to understand the institutionalization of power to our society and the secret sources of our resistances to change. (p. 30)

We laud this advance but continue to situate our own position within what we call critical feminism. We recognize that critical theory, in its classic Frankfurt School articulations, is both an androcentric and essentializing discourse (Harding, 1989); and we acknowledge that a fully formed critical feminist theory will transform both critical and feminist theory (Jansen, 1983, 1989). We further acknowledge that our moves toward this transformation are, at this juncture, incomplete. However, we believe that Frankfurt-informed critical theory remains a powerful, albeit imperfect, tool for analyzing the sports industry and sports media (Jansen, 1983; Sabo, 1990).

Within this theoretical context, mediated sport is understood as a nexus of patriarchal ritual that reproduces hegemonic forms of masculinity and femininity as well as competitive values and achievement ideologies that are closely tied to class ideology. We regard mediated sport as a cultural theater where the values of larger society are resonated, dominant social practices are legitimized, and structured inequalities are reproduced. Gender is thus viewed as a linking concept, which draws analytical attention to a wider configuration of structural, ideological, institutional, as well as psychological processes that, in part, compose the American gender order.

The Gendering of Sport Media

In sport media men predominate in numbers and prevail in presence. Men outnumber women in general television by three or four to one in prime-time television dramas; in children's cartoons, males outnumber females by 10 to one (Gerbner, 1990). Television sports programming is, however, virtually an all-male world with rare excursions into the worlds of women's sports. "News" coverage of sports replicates these programming practices. Woolard (1983) found that 85% of newspaper coverage of sport was devoted to men's sports, while Coakley (1986) estimates that 95% of total sports coverage deals with males. The message was clear in a Federal Express commercial, aired during a post-season bowl game between the Colorado Buffaloes and the Fighting Irish of Notre Dame (January 1, 1991), which depicted a pick-up basketball game among corporate employees designed to "build company morale." The males quickly get serious and aggressive about the game while two females plead from courtside, "Can we get in now?" After their third plea, in full frontal frame, a sweaty and enraged male yells "No, not now!"

The Glorious Presence of Men

Although women have been involved in organized sports in the United States for more than a century and have dramatically increased their presence and virtually revolutionized their performance records since the 1970s, the media spotlight remains firmly fixed on the male athlete. Male athletes are valorized, lionized, and put on cultural pedestals. They are our modern gladiators: the last heroes left in American popular culture. Visual portrayals of male athletes, often filmed in slow-motion and framed from the ground up, are cast against soundtracks of roaring crowds or musical fanfares replete with throbbing bass or thundering drums.

In a study that systematically compared coverage of men's and women's sports, Duncan, Messner, and Williams (1990) found local television conventions for framing sports reportage to be highly gendered. Using both quantitative and qualitative methods of content analysis, they examined 6 weeks of coverage of athletic events carried by a Los Angeles station during the summer of 1989: Coverage encompassed events involving both sexes, including the "Final Four" of the 1989 NCAA women's and men's basketball tournaments and the women's and men's 1989 U.S. Open tournaments. The findings showed that masculinist biases prevailed in television conventions for representation of sporting events. Gender marking was evident in the naming of events. The men's championship game was called "the national championship game," while the women's game was called "the women's national championship game." On-screen graphics were differentially coded blue and pink, representing men's and women's events, respectively. Commentators tended to infantalize women athletes as "girls" or "young ladies," whereas males were afforded adult status as "men" or "young men." Moreover, commentators were significantly more likely to refer to women athletes by their first names. Commentators called women tennis players by their first names 52.7% of the time, men 7.8% of the time. This overall pattern displays a "hierarchy of naming," that is, a set of linguistic practices that naturalize and reinforce prevailing gender-based status differences (Messner, Duncan, & Jensen, 1990).

Duncan, Messner, and Williams (1990) also studied the verbal descriptors applied to men and women athletes. They discovered a recurrent theme of male agency and control as "men were framed as active subjects, women reactive objects" (p. 21). Compared to female athletes, male athletes were more often described in terms of strengths rather than weaknesses, success rather than failure. For example, commentators described "big guys" with "big forehands" playing "big games,"'" whereas the physical strengths of female athletes tended to be neutralized by ambivalent language such as "she's small, but so effective under the boards" (p. 19). In men's basketball, attributions of success outnumbered attributions of failure by more than a five-to-one ratio. In addition, males were more apt to be described with martial metaphors and power descriptors, such as pounds, misfire, force, big guns, fire away, drawing first blood, or battles. For example, a male was said to "attack the hoop," while a female "went to" the hoop. The researchers concluded that:

> The combined effect of focusing more on strength than on weakness, more on success than on failure, and of using many and varied martial metaphors

and power descriptors when describing men athletes has the effect of linguistically weaving an aura of power, strength and human agency around male athletes. (p. 26)

The Trivialization of Women

Two major patterns are evident in the treatment of women in sports: exclusion and trivialization. As we have seen, women's sporting events are generally not covered by sports media. When they are, the skills and strengths of women athletes are often devalued in comparison to cultural standards linked to dominant standards of male athletic excellence, which emphasize the cultural equivalents of hegemonic masculinity: power, self-control, success, agency, and aggression.

When female athletes are discussed in sports media, the coverage is often framed within stereotypes that pertain more to appearance and attractiveness (from the perspective of the male gaze) than to athletic skill (Corrigan, 1972). A content analysis of articles on women athletes in *Sports Illustrated*, from 1964 to 1987, revealed that many articles focused on women in more "sex appropriate" or "feminine" sports, such as figure skating and tennis (Kane, 1988). Similarly, Boutilier and SanGiovanni's (1983) analysis of *Sports Illustrated* found that women were underrepresented in photos, depicted in a narrower array of sports than men, and more likely than men to be posed in passive and nonathletic positions.

Sport media also inferiorize women as sex objects. For example, during Duncan and Messner's 6-week study discussed above, the longest television news segment featuring a woman was on Morgana, the Kissing Bandit, an extraordinarily buxom woman who runs onto baseball fields to kiss players. *Sports Illustrated* fully exploits the "tits and ass" motif of soft pornography to produce its annual swimsuit issue, where women models, not women athletes, make the sport scene. And perhaps most tellingly, after a decade of feminist protest against its publication, this issue remains the best-selling single magazine issue in America. Near-naked women posed languidly in faraway and exotic places do not challenge gender stereotypes and male dominance. This is no accident, K. F. Dyer (1982) indicates, since it is in long-distance swimming where women hold most of the world records and where the mythos of male supremacy is most vulnerable to debunking. The sexualization of female athletes in sport media, such as the case of Katerina

Witt's performances in ice skating at the 1988 winter Olympics, robs women of athletic legitimacy and preserves hegemonic masculinity.

Women's status is further inferiorized in the beer commercials that are commonly grafted to athletic events (Hartley, 1984). When they are represented at all, Wenner contends, women occupy tangential and servile positions in the "sanctum sanctorum of male beer-and-sport commercials" (1991, p. 405). Male viewers do not actually perceive the rituals of sport and beer as vestiges of male culture; ideology is safely dissolved within the suds. In the end, the juxtaposition of dominant males and subservient females reflects the unequal power balances between the sexes, that is, a culturally determined idealization of male dominance (Duncan & Hasbrook, 1988).

Socially Structured Silences

What is not said in sports media reveals as much or more about how hegemonic processes work within the U.S. sports industry *as what is said*. The socially structured silences that the representational conventions cultivated by these media support, legitimize and police the interests of both profit-driven media organizations and the established gender order. The following examples identify a few of the silences supported by the story-telling routines that frame most sports coverage in U.S. media.

The dominant narrative structures in sports media construct and valorize hegemonic masculinity. In doing so, they marginalize and interiorize non-hegemonic forms of masculinity. As Bryson (1990) points out, "Each cultural message about sport is a dual one, celebrating the dominant at the same time as inferiorizing the 'other'" (p. 173). The cultural standardization this dualistic process supports does not reflect the heterogeneity and diversity of men's lives and experiences as athletes or as fans. Alternative or counter-hegemonic masculinities are not ordinarily acknowledged or represented by sports media. For example, a portion of male athletes in all sports are gay and there is a substantial gay presence in some sports such as weight lifting/body-building, yet discussion of homosexuality is virtually taboo in mainstream sports media. The Gay Olympics is almost totally blacked out by sport media. In short, there is little evidence in sports media of what Connell (1990) calls "protest masculinities," men who don't like what's going *on* or *in* the field.

Sport media do not ordinarily focus on men who fail to measure up in sports or life, but rather, they revel in those who succeed. The focus is almost always on success stories or, as a variation on the theme, stories of formerly successful athletes who have fought their way back from adversity, such as injury, academic probation, drug addiction, incarceration, or delinquency. The has-beens, ne'er-do-wells, quitters—in short, the failures—are seldom profiled. For example, the spotlight does not shine on the approximately 60% of NCAA Division I scholarship athletes in football and basketball who fail to graduate after 5 years of college (Eitzen, 1987; Molotsky, 1989). Nor are there frequent portrayals of life after the NBA or NFL for the majority of players whose careers are cut short by injury, lack of enough talent to survive, or corporate decisions. There is no serious discussion of the long-range physical costs of athletic participation as regards increased susceptibility to musculoskeletal problems, reduced life expectancy, or risk for cancers that can result from earlier steroid use or prolonged anti-inflammatory use.

In those relatively infrequent instances when sport scandals do receive extensive media attention, for example, the Pete Rose case, the coverage becomes a site for working out the challenges a fallen hero poses to the legitimacy of dominant cultural values. Sports commentators use crisis frames to examine the transgression from different angles: Sports history (precedence) is explored, for example, Pete is compared to The Babe; the athlete's life in and out of the game is examined; some sports writers present the case against Pete (he was a known gambler), others come to his defense (he was good with kids), and so on. However, the net effect of the extended coverage is to rescue hegemonic masculinity by framing the transgressor as an anomaly, whether as a cheat, an impostor, a tragic victim of flawed judgment, or a compulsive personality.

These narrative structures are not, however, entirely unidimensional. It is common practice for television coverage of athletic events to present brief takes of athletes that show them engaged in community work. Framing of these spots is, however, almost always done in conjunction with public relations agendas (e.g., The National League or the NBA support the United Way in your community). Similarly, coverage of intercollegiate athletic events often includes portrayals of the academic side of the lives of "student-athletes" by depicting young male athletes in laboratories or walking across campus with books in hand. Yet these images do not say as much about athletes' lives as they do about the institutional images of the NCAA or the university that co-sponsors. Moreover, they do not in any way challenge the domination of hegemonic forms of masculinity; to the contrary, they provide free advertising for it.

Conclusion

The gendered narrative structures of sports media and the socially structured silences that support them cultivate the illusion of a shared cultural consensus about what constitutes masculinity, femininity, and appropriate gender relations (Himmelstein, 1984). Hegemonic definitions of masculinity get portrayed as being "normal," "natural," or, as Altheide and Snow (1979) state, "social reality is constituted, recognized and celebrated with media, thus supporting the idea the media present to us what is 'normal' " (p. 12). In sum, the gendered textual conventions of sports media are secured by an unstated but strongly implied subtext that positions portrayals of the sexes within a relational framework in which men are dominant, masculine, and valued, while women are subordinate, feminine, and devalued. This valorization of a highly stylized version of traditional masculinity in sports media also expresses and reinforces hegemonic models of manhood while marginalizing alternative masculinities.

Black Male Athletes: Seen But Not Heard

Sport media tend to cloak all male athletes—regardless of race or ethnicity—in the mantle of hegemonic masculinity. Yet, for black male athletes, the media linkages between athleticism and manliness present peculiar contradictions. Though black men are highly visible and successful at sport, for example, they reside in low-status roles within the hierarchy of the sports industry. Blacks make up 60% of players in professional football, 70% in professional basketball, 17% in professional baseball, as well as widely participating in Olympic-level and intercollegiate sports (especially those with teams that regularly appear on national television). Despite high numbers and visibility as players, however, blacks are scarce in leadership positions. In 1988-1989 only 6 of 27 NBA head coaches were black, and only one of 28 NFL head coaches was black; likewise, blacks were only 7% of front office personnel in both the NFL and the NBA in 1989 (Lapchick & Rodriguez, 1990). Sport media, of course, are not directly responsible for this pattern of institutionalized racism but merely reflect it, yet some research suggests that media practices do systematically represent black male athletes in different and more negative terms than whites.

Black Athleticism and Racial Stereotypes

A second major contradiction in media portrayals of black athletes arises from the fact that many stereotypical traits associated with athleticism (e.g., aggressiveness, brute strength, stupidity) also inhere in racial stereotyping (Edwards, 1969). Franz Fanon, for example, once analyzed the free associations made by his white psychiatric patients to the word "Negro." Characteristics responses included "strong, athletic, potent . . . savage, animal" (1970, p. 118). Likewise, the "dumb jock" stereotype has probably served to intensify existing racial prejudices about the alleged intellectual inferiority of black men (Eitzen, 1987; Sabo, Melnick, & Vanfossen, 1989). A few research studies have shown that sport media play a role in reinforcing these stereotypes.

Rainville and McCormick (1977) analyzed transcriptions of 12 televised NFL games in 1976 in order to explore the extent of racial prejudice in pro football commentators' speech. They found that white players were praised more frequently than black players and were more likely to be described as causal agents. Compared to blacks, whites also received more physical attributions (e.g., "Big John Smith") and positive cognitive attributions (e.g., "Big John is trying to figure out what to do on this one"). Blacks, compared to whites, received significantly more references to past negative professional achievements (e.g., academic probation in college) and were described more as externally moved objects rather than causal agents. The researchers concluded that "announcers are building a positive reputation for white players and a comparatively negative reputation for black players" (p. 179).

Derrick Jackson (1989), a journalist for *The Boston Globe*, conducted a content analysis of 1988-1989 televised sports commentary in basketball and football. Seven college basketball games were recorded, including three NCAA "Final Four" games, as well as five NFL playoff games. Two university researchers were given transcriptions of the commentaries; they had no knowledge of which comments were attributed to which players. All comments were then classified into four categories: "Brawn" (running, leaping, size, strength, and quickness); "Brains" (intelligence, leadership, motivation); "Weakling" (lack of speed and size); and "Dunce" (confused or out of emotional control). The key results indicated marked stereotyping.

- In football, 65% of all comments made about black athletes were about Brawn, compared to 17% for white players.
- Black football players were six times more likely than whites to be classified as Dunces; 12 % and 2%, respectively. In basketball the corresponding figures were 7% and 3%.
- Whereas 77% of comments made about white football players fell into the Brains category, only 22.5% of comments about black players did so. The corresponding figures for basketball were 63% and 15%.

The above studies suggest that racial stereotyping in sport media is covert and systematic; that is, it goes beyond occasional individual pronouncements such as those made by CBS sport broadcaster Jimmy (The Greek) Snyder, who was fired in 1988 for saying that black athletic achievements were owed to selective breeding by slave owners (Smith, 1990). Without further study, however, we do not know either how systematic racial stereotyping is or the extent to which it influences viewer perceptions and attitudes. We do know that stereotypes both flow from and feed prejudice and avoidance behavior, and thus maintain patterns of structured inequality (Kitano, 1985). For whites, then, it would appear that stereotypes of black male athletes can simultaneously shore up hegemonic masculinity and white supremacist sentiments and beliefs. As Ralph Ellison (1964) observed, "The object of the stereotype is not so much to crush the Negro as to console the white man" (p. 58). Nothing is known about the extent to which blacks internalize or resist racial stereotyping in sport media. It is likely, however, that many black men do gravitate to mediated images of hegemonic masculinity in an effort to reclaim a sense of manhood that has been shattered by severe economic dislocation, family disintegration, reduced life expectancy, political marginality, and prejudice (Segal, 1990).

Sport Media as American Dream Machine

Americans believe that sport is a training ground for life. The formula, "succeed in sport, succeed in life," is at the heart of the American sports creed. Athletics are seen as a social theater in which youth learn to aspire higher, work hard and sacrifice, perform with a team, and overcome defeat in their pursuit of the American dream (Sabo, Melnick, & Vanfossen, 1989). The high visibility of blacks in sport media leads to the conclusion that sport is one social vehicle through which the black population has achieved significant upward social mobility. Michael Jordan soars across cereal boxes and television screens, Magic Johnson beams on the cover of *Sports Illustrated*, and many Americans assume that sports provide a gateway to success for minority males.

This optimistic refrain is not borne out by facts. For example, only about 3,000 blacks make their living at professional sports, and this figure includes not only athletes but also coaches and management personnel (Coakley, 1986). Indeed, there is a greater probability for a black high school athlete to become a doctor than a professional athlete (Edwards, 1987). Sport sociologists have generally found no significant relationships between athletic participation and subsequent educational or occupational mobility gains for black males (Howell, Miracle, & Rees, 1984; Sabo, Melnick, & Vanfossen, November, 1989).

The image of the male athlete-celebrity is created and cultivated by sport media. Whether black or white, he exemplifies the self-fulfilled man who has won success, recognition, and occupational achievement within the competitive and risky world of the American economy. Yet, because of racism, it is likely that the successes of black and white male athletes are perceived differently across class and race subgroups. For example, bigoted whites whose racial prejudices make them prone to overgeneralization, may be led to assume that black men *as a class or category* are faring better in the American economy than they really are. Though blacks are generally more skeptical in their appraisals of equal opportunity and social mobility, many working-class and poor black males see sport as a way to prove their "manhood" and as a pathway out of the ghetto (Edwards, 1987). Only a few, of course, will achieve the dream while the masses will continue to contend with the harsh economic conditions and structural constraints.

Conclusion

Media images of black male athletes are a curious confluence of athletic, racial, and gender stereotypes. The intermeshing of racial stereotypes with images of hegemonic masculinity, in effect, reflects and reinforces time-worn racist notions about the sexuality and masculinity of black men. It would therefore appear that sport media are complicit in, not some-how separate from, the larger institutional and cultural processes that reproduce and exonerate white men's domination over black men, and men's domination over women. Furthermore, the curious interplay be-tween images of hegemonic masculinity and racial stereotypes in sport media also seems to promulgate ideologies and perceptions that both flow from and legitimate stratification by class as well as race.

Conclusion: From Gender Emblem to Class Icon

Based upon skill, discipline, training, strategy, competition, and rules of fair play, the sporting event is a pure articulation of the values of a meritocratic system. All players begin the game at the same starting point, but the most talented finish first. The real-world analogue is, of course, capitalist ideology. In the real world, however, all the players, qua laborers, do not begin at the same starting point, teams are not evenly matched, and the scoring system does not necessarily reward skill, training, intelligence, or determination.

Hence, within the changing structure of the postindustrial capitalist order, sport rituals are likely to be just as much a source of achievement ideology as of gender imagery. The emphasis on meritocratic ideologies (e.g., individualism, personal achievement, success striving) is particularly evident in corporate advertising and mass media portrayals of the game (Jhally, 1989). Indeed, it may be that the cultural efficacy of the big-time celebrity athlete is changing from a living symbol of manliness to a meritocratic icon (Sabo & Panepinto, 1990).

The pageantry of the mediated sporting event, with its highly ritualized portrayals of "the thrill of victory and the agony of defeat," reproduces and reaffirms cultural myths regarding democracy, merit, and social mobility. This pageantry validates the privileged position of all males within the gender order, but it also legitimizes and valorizes the special privileges of the winners by making it clear to the losers and their fans that in a man's world, "tough guys" have to be even "tougher." Losers do not always consume this ideological tonic; violence on and off the field, policed by uniformed referees and security guards, is a regular feature of mediated sports. Moreover, mediated simulations of solidarity among winners and losers remain simulations: The victory that brings the "tough guys" in the private boxes and the bleachers together on Sunday afternoon does not last through Monday morning. Sports fans know this; they are not "cultural dopes," not just "fannies in the seats." They are generally aware of the superficiality of the game and the commercialism and fantasy potential that accompany it, and they frequently engage in playful parodies of media hype and the framing conventions that overdramatize the nature and significance of sporting events.

What escapes discernment, however, are the subtle ways that sport media pattern perceptions of group relations and provide legitimacy for structural inequalities between men and women, rich and poor, whites and blacks, and straights and gays. The power of sport media is *not* in its ability to mold individual psychology or gender identity; but rather, it is centered in its capacity to configure individual perceptions of group relations. Sports media locate group relations within the larger blue-prints of structural and cultural hierarchies.

Viewing images of men in sports media from the perspective of critical feminism is not simply one more variation on a theme that contributes to completing the inventories of content analysis and representational conventions. To the contrary, in a world where politics has become entertainment and entertainment has become politics, critical feminist analysis provides entry to a set of discourse practices that appear to be prime sites for playing out struggles for dominance and legitimation.

Note

1. The work of Gerbner (1977, 1990) and his associates (Gerbner, Gross, Morgan, & Signorelli, 1986) is a significant exception to this general practice. It conceives of television violence as cultivating a "mean world syndrome" and it sees white males as the primary agents of violence in television drama; it also takes into account the ways that violence is used against women, minorities, and the foreign born. In sum, it is, at least implicitly, exploring the operations of what we call the gender order and hegemonic masculinity in prime-time television dramas.

13

Redesigning Men

Hegemonic Masculinity in Transition

ROBERT HANKE

Culture is a struggle for meanings as society is a struggle for power.

John Fiske (1987a)

The struggle for meaning is here, and it is a struggle of and for
political criticism . . .

Stephen Heath (1990)

This chapter attempts to think through some issues pertaining to the
critical cultural analysis of the representation of men and masculinity
on American prime-time television. There are many pitfalls that arise
in such an endeavor, and there is a need to be reflexive about the location
from which one (in my case, as a white, male, heterosexual academic)
speaks and writes about masculinity, or as Tulloch (1990, p. 6) has put
it, the "desires, practices, assumptions and discourses which make up
one's agency as an author," lest we reproduce the hegemonic (masculinist) culture we seek to interrogate, challenge, and transform. Nevertheless,

AUTHOR'S NOTE: I would like to thank Steve Craig, Larry Gross, and DeLana Browning
for their help with this chapter.

such work is necessary and vital if we are to advance our understanding of the *gender regime* of television and questions of male power.[1]

The main difficulty that male scholars face is similar to the one Richard Dyer has elucidated in his work on the representation of whiteness as an ethnic category in mainstream film: "White power secures its dominance by seeming not to be anything in particular," "whiteness" is constructed as the norm against which non-dominant groups are defined as "other" (Dyer, 1988). "Masculinity," like "whiteness," does not appear to be cultural/historical category at all, thus rendering invisible the privileged position from which (white) men in general are able to articulate their interests to the exclusion of the interests of women, men and women of color, and children.

Since Williams (1977) and Gitlin (1987) first explored the operations of cultural hegemony, there has been a substantial body of feminist and nonfeminist scholarship on television and gender from a variety of theoretical perspectives and methodological approaches (for an overview, see Buck & Newton, 1989). While Gitlin (1987) stressed that hegemony "is reasserted in different ways at different times, even by different logics," his main goal was to examine these processes in relation to liberal capitalism and consumer, bourgeois ideology. However, if we are to advance the theory of cultural hegemony, it is clear that we need to give separate attention to questions of the relations between television and gender, to analyze the expression of patriarchal ideology and gender/sexual politics on its own terms. Any theory of cultural hegemony must also take account of the cultural studies perspective on the audience, specifically, the thesis that subordinate members of the audience are able to resist the hegemonic thrust of media culture. It is not my intention to offer a synthesis of the theory of hegemony and the theory of resistance, but rather to suggest some revisions in the theory of hegemony in order to conceptualize a "moving state of play in meanings, which is then articulated to a state of play in the field of power" (Hall, 1989, p. 51). This revision entails drawing upon the critical study of men and masculinities (see Hearn & Melechi, this volume; Hearn & Morgan, 1990). More specifically, I would like to consider whether the concept of "hegemonic masculinity" can be usefully employed to analyze the dialectics of domination and resistance that characterize television culture and its discursive construction of masculinity.

Media studies has not considered masculinity as a problematic or historically troubled category until recently (Penley & Willis, 1988). Grossberg and Treichler (1987) suggest that studies of media and gender

have largely been oriented toward "the 'depiction' (picturing) of females on television in relation to presumed cultural realities and norms."
For the most part, as Fejes's (1989) review indicates, most empirical
research on men and the media utilized and was limited to the sex-role
framework of functionalist sociology, addressing the nature and effects
of stereotyped male and female role portrayals. Feminist theory and
scholarship has, for obvious reasons, concentrated on women's devaluation in communication processes, the social construction of femininity, and women's efforts and abilities to resist or challenge patriarchal
ideology, in order to account for women's subordination or oppression
and women's cultural experience (cf. Brown, 1990; Rakow, 1990; Steeves,
1987). While much more work on these issues remains to be done, there
is also a need for media scholars to examine and analyze how media
institutions, through their specific representational forms and practices,
are involved in the production and re-production of masculinity as a
cultural category. How, in short, is masculinity itself defined and redefined in order to secure a position of dominance for men within the
sex/gender system? Is there a single, unified masculine discourse, which
constructs masculinity in opposition to a (usually subordinated) femininity, or, as Hall (1989, p. 51) suggests, are discursive systems always
the product of articulations, always contradictory, containing possibilities for transcoding and decoding the dominant definitions? In this
chapter, following Connell's (1987) work, I explore hegemonic, conservative, and subordinated masculinities in three areas: gender and genre,
the "new view of manhood," and heterosexual ideology. Television's representation of "femininized" masculinity as well as homosexuality will
be taken as "indicative features of what the hegemonic process has in
practice had to work to control" (Williams, 1977, p. 113).

Gender and Genre

According to Gitlin (1987), genres are one of the concrete forms
through which cultural hegemony operates. Perhaps the most sophisticated treatment of the "engendering work" of television has been
Fiske's (1987a, 1987b) examination of gendered genres. From an ethno-
graphically informed, structuralist-accented, cultural studies perspective, Fiske offers a comparative, dialectical analysis of the basic narrative form of soap opera and cop adventure programs that includes
evidence from ethnographic studies of viewing practices. Fiske argues

that television helps to produce a "crucial categorization of its viewers into masculine and feminine subjects" (1987a, p. 179) through particular generic conventions and the negotiated or oppositional readings they invite. In his view, soap opera lends itself to resistant readings by women, who occupy a subordinate position within patriarchy, while the conventions of cop adventure shows, which are designed to address men, primarily reinforce dominant gender ideology through the articulation of gender differences (such as sensitive/tough, domestic/professional, and so on). For example, Fiske argues that masculinity in programs like *Magnum, P.I.*, is primarily defined along two dimensions: self-sufficiency and assertiveness, yet different subordinated groups (boys, black men, and women) will negotiate masculine ideology toward their interests. For Fiske, the "polysemy" of media texts and the heterogenity of audiences thus explains why hegemonic ideology is always under "threat," why television, as popular culture, makes possible a kind of semiotic democracy.

Fiske does avoid the categoricalism of a purely structuralist analysis of gender, since he shows how masculine ideology overlaps with ideologies of race and nation. Yet, further analysis within the category masculinity seems necessary since masculinity is inflected not only by race and nationality, but also by class, ethnicity, generation, and sexual preference (Mouffe, 1983). Not only are women exscribed out of masculine narratives, but gay men (and lesbian women) are as well; heterosexual masculinity is also defined, in part, by its distance from homosexuality (Kimmel, 1987b).

Fiske also acknowledges that other programs combine masculine and feminine forms, and that genres evolve historically, suggesting perhaps that the meanings of masculinity and femininity cannot be easily reduced to a system of binary oppositions. Other scholars have noted the ways in which particular texts, performers, or forms have blurred the boundaries of masculinity and femininity (cf. Aufderheide, 1986; Modleski, 1990; Wernick, 1987). Fiske suggests that even within masculine narratives, there is evidence of the destablization of "masculinity" as a category, which may allow male viewers to experience the "feminine" pleasures that contradict, if not deconstruct, the dominant ideology. He claims, for instance, that the image of men in shows like *Miami Vice*, while conforming to the masculine ideology of action-oriented genres, has redefined masculinity as appearance, concluding that "*Miami Vice*'s challenge to the meaning of masculinity may be the most insidious and politically effective because it occurs not at the level of *what* is represented but *how* it is represented" (p. 222). However, from the point of view of cultural hegemony, *Miami Vice*'s re-coding of masculinity and the "pleasures of style, look, and appearance" it offers may be less of a challenge to patriarchal values, less of an opportunity for men to interrogate those values, than a construction of a masculine consumer subject. As Ebert (1988) has argued from a postmodern feminist cultural perspective:

> The differentiations between masculine and feminine increasingly collapse under the pressure of capitalism, yet patriarchy finds new ways to perpetuate male privilege, make sure that wages, property ownership, control over production and political power remain largely gender differentiated. (p. 21)

In Fiske's analysis, exactly how *Miami Vice*'s contradictory image of men articulates with any specific social formation and the larger context of postindustrial, transnational consumer capitalism is not examined.

From Fiske's perspective (and possibly that of U.S. cultural studies as a whole), hegemonic ideology appears to have great difficulty inserting itself into our everyday, cultural experiences in a way that would define most people's commonsense understandings of the gender regime. Fiske, for example, concludes that "despite the power of ideology to reproduce itself in its subjects, despite the hegemonic force of the dominant classes, the people still manage to make their own meanings and to construct their own culture within, and often against, that which the industry provides them" (1987b, p. 286). This conclusion seems to contradict his earlier claim that oppositional viewers would be unlikely to watch popular TV programs (p. 266). Budd, Entman, and Steinman (1990) have also recently pointed out other difficulties with the thesis that audiences routinely resist the hegemonic thrust of media content as often as cultural studies proposes. Moreover, in this formulation "men" appear to be characterized as members of the "dominant classes" who hold power over women, although not all "masculinities" have the same relation to discourses and institutions of power (Penley & Willis, 1988). These considerations, as well as other criticisms of "ludic postmodern" theory (see Zavarzadeh, 1991) or "resistance" theory (see Sholle, 1990), lead us to ask whether the cultural studies' conceptualization of the hegemonic process in television is adequate to the task of a critical cultural analysis of television and gender.

Hegemonic Masculinity

The concept of "hegemonic masculinity" originates within recent work in the sociology of gender. Carrigan, Connell, and Lee (1987) and Connell (1987) argue that hegemonic masculinity should not be understood as the "male role" but as a particular variety of masculinity to which women and others (young, effeminate, or homosexual men) are subordinated. For Carrigan et al. (1987), hegemonic masculinity is a question of "how particular men inhabit positions of power and wealth and how they legitimate and reproduce social relationships that generate dominance" (p. 179). Hegemonic masculinity thus refers to the social ascendancy of a particular version or model of masculinity that operates on the terrain of common sense and conventional morality that defines "what it means to be a man," thus securing the dominance of some men (and the subordination of women) within the sex/gender system. The ascendancy of men as a ruling bloc within capitalist patriarchy is achieved not only through violence and coercion but also through a cultural process in which masculinism, the dominant ideology of patriarchy, meets with resistance and challenge. For this reason, the analysis of hegemonic masculinity is also a question of how oppositional gender ideologies (such as liberal feminism or gay/lesbian politics) becomes absorbed, contained, and rearticulated. Moreover, as Connell (1987) argues, the "justifying ideology for the patriarchal core complex and the overrall subordination of women requires the creation of a gender-based hierarchy *among men*" (p. 110). This hierarchy has three elements: hegemonic masculinity, conservative masculinity, and subordinated masculinities. While this hierarchy is supported and maintained by a variety of institutions of patriarchy, it is the institutionalized cultural expression of this hierarchy in the mass media, and prime-time television in particular, that concerns me here.

Some scholars have begun to focus on the patterns of hegemonic masculinity in prime-time television. For example, the male-oriented action-adventure genre has evolved to the point where women figure more directly into the plot (as the hero's buddy or love interest); however, these "tales are still very much male-dominated and male-defined: In fact, most feature an aggressive masculinity, expressed through guns, tanks, armed helicopters, and other instruments of death. Emphasis is placed on the male body, its musculature and strength, and its ability to withstand torture and to kill efficiently" (Marchetti, 1989, p. 191). This analysis supports Connell's claim that patriarchal power "requires the construction of a hypermasculine ideal of toughness and dominance" (1987, p. 80). Moreover, in the 1980s, these definitions of masculinity were aligned with the politics of the New Right. Schwichtenberg (1987), for example, suggests how *The A-Team*'s encoding of masculinity and femininity enabled the Right to align "what it means to be man" with a notion of "the will of the people" and the "national interest." These representations of masculinity secure ruling-class hegemony by neutralizing class antagonisms and harnessing working-class resistance to authoritarian ends. This form of gender stereotyping, as a number of analysts have pointed out, was a cultural expression of the attempt to restore the loss of masculine authority in the post-Vietnam era.

The action-adventure genre clearly represents a popular genre that continued to define men in relation to power, authority, aggression, and technology. Other television genres express the values of hegemonic masculinity as well. Sports programming represents men in relation to competition, strength, and discipline, while news programming features men in relation to achievement, leadership, and control. Even the television Western, which defines masculinity in terms of the cowboy images and the myth of the West, has been revived in prime time (e.g., *Young Riders*, *Guns of Paradise*).

The relationship between such genres, the hegemonic principles they articulate, and audiences is, of course, complex. According to Cantor (1990), images of gender vary according to genre and the intended audience; the dominating, authoritive male is uncommon in domestic comedy. Her analysis suggests a pattern of continuity and change in the portrayal of men as fathers and husbands, one that perpetuates the myth of female dominance and the loss of male authority as well as the myth of fatherhood. In Cantor's view, domestic comedy is a vehicle for cultural myths, portraying men in roles in the TV world they do not occupy in the real world. However, against this functionalist thesis, some cultural analysts have argued that "myths" of female dominance, as part of feminine discourse, may appeal to women and men who reject paternal stereotypes (e.g., *Coach*) and some aspects of traditional sex roles (e.g., *Who's the Boss?*). A more complex view of the relationship between hegemonic principles and popular fictions, such as situation comedy, is suggested by Woollacott (1986). According to her, only historical analysis can specify whether situation comedies work to stabilize existing subjectivities, or whether they "come to provide a nexus through which ideologies may be actively reorganized, shifting the subjectivities at their core" (p. 217). Indeed, the '80s "sensitive man" seems to provide an opportunity to explore this question further.

Conservative Masculinity

Some popular critics have focused on changing images of men and have hailed the advent of images of "liberated" masculinity on television. Lehrer's (1989) selective examination of male characters in *thirty-something*, *L.A. Law*, and the short-lived series *Men*, leads him to wonder whether "themes of male liberation" have become a staple of television drama (Lehrer, 1989). According to him, *thirtysomething*, broke "new ground in portraying the conflicts and feelings of its male characters," presenting a "new view of manhood" in which "sensitive, nurturing men, aware of themselves and their feelings, take the spotlight" (Lehrer, 1989). While this reading implies a reconstruction of masculinity that is not marked by the repudiation of the feminine, there are at least two difficulties with such generalizations. First, the critic mistakes the synchronic variety of images of men for diachronic change. From a historical perspective, there have always been images of men who do not fit the hegemonic pattern (just as there have always been images of women who do not fit conventional femininity). Second, as with much popular criticism, the critic fails to acknowledge that unreconstructed male characters have not disappeared from prime-time television with the advent of liberated male characters (Tankel & Banks, 1990). Furthermore, while television may offer a range of images of men, such redemptive readings do not address the ideological work that exceptions to the hegemonic pattern do, within a relatively stable framework of patriarchal codings of gender roles and relations, marriage, and the family.

These codings of masculinity also intersect with social class in ways that express the tension between the gender regime and the social class structure. In this regard, it is important to keep in mind Aronowitz's (1989) argument that the representation of working-class males disappeared in the mid-1970s as "working class identity was displaced to other upwardly mobile occupations (e.g. police, football players, and other sites where conventional masculine roles are ubiquitous)" (p. 141). According to Butsch (1991), the numbers of working-class domestic situation comedies peaked in the mid-1950s and the early 1970s; middle-class series predominated throughout the 1980s, despite the recent revival of working-class series (e.g., *Family Matters, Roseanne, The Simpsons*, and *Married with Children*). Images of white-collar professionals and managers define the particular "masculinity" of upwardly mobile, white, liberal, middle-class men. In middle-class domestic comedy series, as well as in some dramas, (eg., *L.A. Law*), middle-class codes valorize the construction of images of "soft" men.

For example, the series *thirtysomething* represents a form of domestic situation melodrama that discursively constructs an image of men that clearly deemphasizes signs of dominance and authority. Middle-class codes of therapeutic culture valorize the expression of emotions, an openness to domestic concerns, and greater responsiveness to interpersonal relationships. *thirtysomething*'s "new view of manhood" entails a version of masculine discourse that incorporates elements of the critique of domestic patriarchy, enabling it to more efficaciously address the social situation of white, middle-class, professional, heterosexual members of the "baby boom" generation living within dual- career marriages. As Loeb (1990) suggests, the notion of "provider" is "defined to include sensitivity, support, and commitment to the emotional needs of the family"; yet, the images of quasi-equality between men (and women) in *thirtysomething* support and maintain core elements of patriarchal ideology. Unlike traditional melodrama, which problematizes female sexuality, the series is crucially concerned with male (hetero)sexuality (Torres, 1989). In fact, the regular male character (Gary Sheppard) who was the most politically liberal, who occasionally gave voice to the critique of the dominant mode of male sexuality (and therefore might have been seen as being on the side of women's desires), was killed in the February 12, 1991, episode. In this way, *thirtysomething* constructs a conservative masculinity that remains complicit with patriarchal ideology, masking and displacing real gender inequalities, and effacing any further critique of dominant gender ideology.

In Hall's terms, this form of televisual discourse works hegemonically to produce an "achieved complementarity between hegemonic and subordinate classes and their cultures" (1982, p. 334). In *thirtysomething*, the relations between the genders are made sense of not in terms of male domination and female subordination, but in terms of the organization of affect—feelings of solidarity and jealousy among friends and married and unmarried couples—and relations of compatibility and incompatibility with other members of the professional, managerial class. Moreover, there is a close correspondence between *thirtysomething*'s definition of gender relations and the reorganization of work within an expanding postindustrial economy. As more and more people are employed in the managerial-service sector, more of us do work that depends on emphatic communication and for which therapy serves as a model rather than a contrast (Bellah, Madsen, Sullivan, Swidler & Tipton, 1986, p. 123). Furthermore:

> The same sort of interpersonal communication runs the gamut from work to love and back again. Co-workers "give each other therapy" to cement teamwork. Individuals who meet only on the job make use of intimacy as a method to become more effective as a working "unit." Their sensitive and caring conversation is not a break from the job. It's part of the job (Bellah et al., 1986, p. 123).

The middle-class verbosity of *thirtysomething*'s characters, and the mediations they typically engage in at home or at work, symbolically condense and displace the whole field of organizational and professional politics into the domain of personal motivations and feelings. In this way, *thirtysomething*'s image of manhood is complementary with postindustrial capitalism and the changing organization of work.

So while the men of *thirtysomething* appear to be less sexist than their more macho counterparts in masculine narratives, the series perpetuates the myth that middle-class, professional men are less sexist than working-class men or third world men (Brod, 1987). Moreover, according to Hearn (1987), the professions are one of the four major institutions of patriarchy (along with hierarchic sexuality, fatherhood, and the state). The "new view of manhood" is the expression of the cultural ascendancy of the professional/managerial class, that is to say, white, middle-class, men's concerns, on the terrain of yuppie common sense.

Subordinated Masculinity

Having considered hegemonic and conservative masculinity, I shall now turn to a brief discussion of television's construction of subordinated masculinity, through its images of gay men.

In the case of gay men (and lesbian women), hegemonic ideology works through exclusion (Gitlin, 1987), or what Gross (1989) and others have termed "symbolic annihilation." By and large, gay men (and lesbian women even more so) are rarely featured as regular major characters in prime-time television series. More than likely, as Gross argues, gay men are negatively stereotyped as villains or victims of ridicule (e.g., *In Living Color*).

However, there have been some exceptions to this pattern of invisibility that suggest that hegemonic masculinity operates through inclusion as well as exclusion: *Love, Sydney; Dynasty; Hooperman; Doctor Doctor; Roseanne*; the cable television show *Brothers; The Tracey Ullman Show*; and *thirtysomething* have featured regular major or minor gay male characters. For example, the series *thirtysomething* featured one minor gay character, and his positioning as the friend of one of the regular, single, female characters appeared to add an element of urban realism to the courtship situation of single women searching for single, heterosexual men. Instead, this portrayal perpetuates the stereotype that only people involved in the art world maintain friendships with homosexuals. Other series' subplots have involved the one-time appearance of gay male characters; for instance, *L.A. Law* has had subplots dealing with an AIDS-related "mercy killing" and the issue of "outing," referencing real-life stories in the news. There has also been the occasional gay story in made-for-TV movies (e.g., *An Early Frost, Welcome Home Bobby*). Such representations of gayness, however, do not necessarily assume a gay perspective. In fact, as Henry (1987) points out, such programming "typically takes the point of view of straights struggling to understand" and constructs gay masculinity as a "moral" problem that causes considerable anguish and pain for straight characters. Gay (and lesbian) characters rarely appear when his/her gayness is not a problem, a subject of controversy, or associated with AIDS. In general, while the appearance of some gay male characters or themes may suggest a certain level of acceptance of homosexual individuals, the way in which gayness is constructed tends to define homosexuality as a negative symbol of masculine identity.

Conclusions

The above analysis should be considered preliminary. I have tried to suggest that the process of cultural hegemony may be far more expansive than the analyses of action adventure or law enforcement/crime genres have suggested. Television works hegemonically, not only by imposing dominant (masculinist) ideology but also by "articulating the relations between a series of ideologies (subordinate as well as dominant),

overlapping them on to one another, so as to bring about certain movements and reformations of subjectivity" (Bennett & Woollacott, 1987,
p. 5). Thus, one way in which conflicts in gender relations may be
handled and defused is through the construction of a social definition
of masculinity (sensitive, nurturing, emotionally expressive) that is
more open to the work of maintaining interpersonal relationships and
child rearing and more accommodating of traditionally feminine connotations and values. The key question is not whether such a version of
masculinity is more modern or less (hetero)sexist than traditional, hegemonic conceptions of the male role (naturalized in the form of the hero
or hero team), but how masculinity is defined and re-defined in order
to *remain* hegemonic (see Gitlin, 1987). As Brittan (1989, p. 187) has
argued, "hegemonic masculinity is able to defuse crisis tendencies in
the gender order by using counter and oppositional discourses for its
own purposes."

Hegemonic masculinity thus works through a variety of representational strategies, including images of feminized masculinity and the
construction of negative symbols of masculinity, in order to win the
consent of male and female viewers, who, as social agents, may be
situated very differently. The gender regime of television is marked by
a degree of instability and contradiction; however, hegemonic masculinity must continually be reconstituted through specific representations of masculinity, and the strategies by which hegemonic masculinity
is achieved, and ideological consent won or lost, varies.

As some structuralist-thinking analysts have shown, patriarchal ideology in television is encoded through the representation of clear-cut
differences that define masculinity and its characteristics as "strong,"
and femininity and its characteristics as "weak." Hegemonic masculinity may also work through the *inversion* of differences, as it does in
popular culture expressions of antifeminist ideology. As Ehrenreich
(1983, p. 163) states, "New Right ideology inverts the traditional imagery
of gender roles: Men are 'passive,' 'fragile'; while women are 'active'
and 'can do everything.'" Or, as I have tried to suggest here, hegemonic
masculinity can work through the *leveling* of some gender differences,
by constructing feminized men who are more open to domestic concerns
and interpersonal relationships. This form of masculine/feminine discourse represents male and female interests as basically identical.
Finally, the hegemonic process also operates through the *exclusion*, as
well as *inclusion*, of subordinated masculinities, thus supporting and maintaining a gender hierarchy among men that justifies and legitimizes the

(often violent) oppression of gay men. The overall cultural effect of this ongoing process is that questions of power, real gender inequities, capitalist work relations, and sexual politics are glossed over. Apparent modifications of hegemonic masculinity may represent some shift in the cultural meanings of masculinity without an accompanying shift in dominant social structural arrangements, thereby recuperating patriarchal ideology by making it more adaptable to contemporary social conditions and more able to accommodate counter-hegemonic forces, such as liberal- feminist ideology and gay/lesbian politics.

This analysis is a tentative step towards understanding television's discursive construction of masculinity. The exact relationship between hegemonic, conservative, and subordinated masculinities cannot be determined by textual analysis alone; whether television works ideologically to stabilize (or modify) gendered subject positions can only be determined through historical analysis. We might expect, perhaps, that these social definitions of masculinity may be ignored, negotiated, or resisted by some viewers and not others; different strategies of representational practice may articulate in different ways to historically specific "subject" positions, social identities, or social formations. However, if Press's (1989) work is any indication, it appears that hegemonic ideology reaches male and female viewers in class (and other socially) specific ways.

Finally, following Ebert's (1988) advice, male scholars seeking to advance the critical study of gender and the media should be careful to avoid falling prey to the "progressive" fallacy in which any changes in images of male and female characters are taken as the displacement of dominant gender ideologies. In this regard, Galperin (1988) notes that the "feminization" of prime-time is unlikely and "that prime-time soaps such as *Dallas* and *Dynasty* actively mitigate the revolutionary currents of their daytime counterparts . . ." (p. 160). Significant social change in the direction of gender equality will require more than the "new view of manhood" offered by prime-time television. There is also a need for male scholars to engage in counter-hegemonic "readings" and political critiques of television's ideological practices in order to better understand television's role in the reproduction of power relations—the power of men over women, or the power of heterosexuals over homosexuals. For male scholars interested in the relationship between television and gender, this will not be possible as long as "masculinity" remains invisible to ourselves.

Note

1. The term *gender regime*, which refers to the "state of play in gender relations in a given institution," is from Connell (1987).

14

Gaze Out of Bounds

Men Watching Men on Television

CLAY STEINMAN

Men still have everything to say about their own sexuality.

Hélène Cixous (Jardine, 1987, p. 60)

If sexual orientation is a way of feeling, always unfixed and remade, what happens when, watching television, a heterosexual man's gaze alights on a male image it finds attractive? How do shows on commercial television (en)gender desire for heterosexual males? How do they make sexual roles and identities seem absolute, if they are in flux?

AUTHOR'S NOTE: I began this work as a result of having had the good fortune to hear the late Dennis O'Donovan (1988) discuss men's fears concerning gender and the damage they cause. Tom Banks, Mike Budd, Chris Berry, Steve Craig, Michael Cudney, Bob Entman, Lynn Garrett, Richard Garrett, Keith Kelly, Shannon Kratz, Margaret Montalbano, and Deborah Whitworth suggested several improvements after reading earlier drafts. I am grateful, as I am for the conversations we have had over the years that have helped shape my work in this area. Edwin Barton, Merry Pawlowski, and Jorge Yviricu each generously shared several substantial ideas with me, which, I am pleased to acknowledge, added to the argument. My comments about men and sports arose primarily from conversations with Michael Flachmann. Steve Carter, Jane De Bracey, Kim Flachmann, Glenda Hudson, Monte Jewell, Victor Lasseter, Jeff McMahon, Ernie Padilla, Joanne Schmidt, Jeffry Spencer, and Janet Vice also read drafts of this chapter and offered helpful suggestions. Earlier versions of portions of this chapter were presented at the 1988 and 1990 meetings of the Speech Communication Association.

A look at a late-1990 episode of *Evening Shade*, a situation comedy with Burt Reynolds on CBS, might illuminate these processes. It might clarify how society maintains gender, with all of its separations and its discrepancies in power and privilege. Aimed for commercial reasons at women and men, *Evening Shade* offers advertisers access to both. In doing so, the show provides its viewers with a more flexible representation of maleness than do most programs targeted at one sex. Yet, also for commercial reasons, heterosexism limits what *Evening Shade* can do.

I make several assumptions. I take *masculine* as a term of history and culture, not of biology. It designates a cluster of connotations, an "ensemble of multiple effects" (Penley, 1988, p. 20), commonly linked to those born male in this patriarchal culture.[1] These connotations are terms within a discursive system in which the meaning of *masculine* is based on its difference from *feminine* (and vice versa). In other words, we can identify no such "thing" as masculinity, only unevenly shared ways of understanding behavior (of males or of females) as masculine. As Anthony Easthope (1986) says, "Men and women, male and female, masculine and feminine are . . . compartmentalized, sorted into opposite categories and assigned to separate places" (p. 111).

Differentiations of this kind pervade culture in ways that are hegemonic but also unstable, contradictory, and shifting at crucial points. "Inevitably the strategy comes apart at the seams" (Easthope, 1986, p. 111). In film and television, attempts to contain sexual difference shape not only images of gender but imaging of gender as well. They affect how sexual difference is constructed by the organization of narrative, by sights and by sounds (Doane, Mellencamp, & Williams, 1984; Kuhn, 1982b; Modleski, 1988). Patriarchy regulates not only what is seen on the screen, but also the "axis of vision itself," which includes the ways spectators enjoy and make sense of what is presented to them (Doane et al., 1984, p. 6). Nearly two decades of psychoanalytic studies guided by feminism have shown that the "primary motivating force" in mainstream movies has been the "narrative and symbolic problem" of characters winding their way toward their authorized place in terms of gender (Penley, 1988, p. 3). With stories that tease and flatter viewers' sense of sexual differentiation, films also offer socially sanctioned "erotic ways of looking and spectacle" (Mulvey, 1975, p. 6). Offering ostensibly for free what movies sell (Smythe, 1977), mass-audience television takes up these tasks at least as successfully. In the United States, television tends to be more commercial than film has ever been because its economics require far more consumers to be profitable. Early in television's history, the broadcast industry assigned its programs the same fundamental mission it had asked of its radio shows: not to sell themselves but to provide conducive environments for commercials (Williams, 1974). What Laura Mulvey (1975) wrote of classical cinema applies even more to ordinary broadcasting, with its determined congeniality: It has "coded the erotic into the language of the dominant patriarchal order" (p. 8). Configurations on screen and in the minds of spectators tend to resemble, legitimate, and reinforce each other—at least sometimes, at least in part (Smith, 1989, pp. 100-101)—because "the unconscious of patriarchal society has structured film form" (p. 6).

Discussing pleasure in watching film in ways that apply to television, Mulvey argued that the "determining 'male gaze' projects its phantasy on to the female figure which is styled accordingly" (p. 11). Meanwhile, "curiosity and the wish to look mingle with a fascination with likeness and recognition: the human face, the human body, the relationship between the human form and its surroundings," the (mis)recognition of oneself in an ideal image (p. 9). This "male gaze," rather than a rocksolid aspect of what many men are, is a vantage point, a position men slip into and out of, sheer and comfortable enough to remain invisible, despite nearly two decades of feminist expose.

Looking in this sense would seem to work differently for men with same-sex and heterosexual erotic orientations. Yet these orientations are themselves uncertain. Scholars in gay studies have shown that homosexuality as currently conceived is itself a comparatively recent cultural form, whatever causes the sexuality of an individual. And, of course, without homosexuality as its Other, heterosexuality has no meaning.[2] Simon Watney (1987) puts it plainly: "Without gays, straights are not 'straight' " (p. 26).

As conceptions of desire become fluid in theory, even as patriarchal order strives to keep sexuality in line, maleness, masculinity, and like terms become all the more elusive. Although for Mulvey (1975) male seems to mean heterosexual (p. 12), her analysis does not seem driven by essentializing conceptions of gender (for a different view, see Rodowick, 1982). Rather her concern is with the "masculinisation of the spectator position" (1981, p. 12) within the "ambivalent sexuality of any individual" (1988, p. 73). Still, reading masculine where she wrote male only defers the problem. For example, some men in contemporary gay culture consider themselves both masculine and homosexual (Kleinberg, 1987). Others consider themselves simultaneously masculine, homosexual, and pro-feminist, just as there are those whose mixed feelings about feminism some women find quite masculine (see, e.g., Morrison, 1990, for a discussion of the Gay Masculist Coalition, and, for a critical response, Hinton, 1990). Perhaps, recasting a phrase of Jeffrey Weeks (1985), there are masculinities, not a single masculinity (p. 179).

As a result, *masculine gaze* remains problematic. A compromise might be *"male gaze,"* connoting containment of sex within gender while sidestepping both essentialism and some of the complications of masculinity as an analytical term. Although occupants of this position surely tend to be male and to identify themselves as heterosexual, its label should stress more the experience than the gender or sex of its beholder. Recognizing the continuum of sexual orientations through which men live, we might view the "male gaze" as an inconsistent regulator of gendered experience, as well as an apparatus for domination of women. In this light, texts configured for it will be as revealing in their representation of men as they have been for feminist criticism in their representation of women.

To illustrate this, I will look at the configuring of Burt Reynolds for the camera in a recent episode of *Evening Shade*. Helpful in this regard has been Richard Dyer's (1982) analysis of male pin-ups and the instability surrounding the male image as an erotic object for women and for men. For Dyer, this instability exists both within the gaze of men and within the text of the pin-up itself. To be an image of masculinity, he argues, the male pin-up cannot be posed as women conventionally are for men, as passive objects of an active look. Instead, the model must refuse his status as an object of others' pleasure or he will risk, in patriarchal terms, appearing feminine. Think of how action-oriented Arnold Schwarzenegger is in the fictional movies in which his body is most displayed. "Images must disavow . . . passivity if they are to be kept in line with dominant ideas of masculinity-as-activity" (Dyer, 1982, p. 66). Similarly, for Mulvey (1975), "Man is reluctant to gaze at his exhibitionist like" (p. 12). The emphasis in many such images on hardness, on muscularity, or, occasionally, on facial hair (Flitterman, 1985; King, 1990) seems designed to ward off feminine affect.

This fear of the feminine would seem to have several effects on relations between the "male gaze" and male images. To look at another man's exhibitionism is to risk admitting pleasure in the sight, to risk imagining glances exchanged, to risk being thought out of line. At the same time, the exhibitionist image threatens to become an object of identification, and as such may trigger fear that it might represent a feminine aspect of the viewer himself. In either case, male heterosexual spectators seem to need constant reassurance that they are different (from women, from gay men), as if on some level they know their masculinity cannot be guaranteed. As Easthope (1986) says, "The masculine ego has to defend itself from 'the enemy within,' and this mainly takes the form of its own femininity" (p. 104). This may explain why explicitly homo-erotic images, whether in the photographs of Robert Mapplethorpe or on *thirtysomething*, and openly homoerotic behavior, such as two men kiss-ing on the street, produce in so many heterosexual men such fierce reactions, physical reactions, even violent reactions. It may explain how anyone might take comfort in seeing AIDS as a "symbolic extension of some imagined inner essence of being, manifesting itself as disease" (Watney, 1987, p. 8). Aside from victimization, mainstream culture's only authorized nonmasculine male behavior is comic (e.g., Liberace's later performances), behavior that offers straight male audiences plea-sure and a sense their difference is taken seriously. Risk is low, since parody is not erotic (Bersani, 1987, p. 208).

As a consequence, the last thing many heterosexual men expect to encounter in commercial entertainment is a challenge to their sexual security. Cultural and economic forces restrict the representation of men on television: In the early 1990s, mass-audience television (or main-stream movie theaters, newspapers, or periodicals, for that matter) allows few images of men that male heterosexuals might find threatening (Goldstein, 1990).[3] This is hardly a recent development, nor is it a function only of the more obvious commercial requirements of television. Media industries and patriarchal differentiations work hand in hand to keep gender in line. Andrew Britton (1983), in his valuable study of gender and the image of Cary Grant, repeated the story that "studio executives were at one time so worried about Grant's image, particularly after he began to share a house with Randolph Scott, that they set out expressly to manu-facture publicity which would build up Grant's 'virility' " (p. 11).

Reynolds himself appeared as a pin-up in *Cosmopolitan* in the early 1970s, evidently enhancing his appeal with at least some female audi-ences. Doing so seems not to have hurt his popularity with most men. Indeed, my recollection is that, in both public and private, heterosexual men took pride in Reynolds as their representation and were not threat-ened by the well-publicized image of him nude. Despite his presence in what many men might take as an unmanly position, he seems not to have become Other. Part of this has to do with the insistent heterosexuality of *Cosmopolitan* and the fact that Reynolds did not choose to appear in male pin-up magazines whose buyers include many men. More, I suspect, has to do with the specifics of Reynolds' media persona, which consistently cast him in roles that at the time were as conventionally masculine as those of, say, Clint Eastwood. These roles tended to be comic in ways Eastwood's were not. They allowed Reynolds to kid his sexual stature without questioning it, to put it beyond question precisely by kidding it. In film after film, the character Reynolds played remained invulnerable to all attempts to emasculate him. His triumphs were so constant, his resistance to any form of domestication so strong, that even by the early 1970s, all he had to do was wink, giggle, or grin to reassert his masculine autonomy. Women and gay men might well have viewed it otherwise, but for heterosexual men, my guess is that Reynolds' body tended to be seen in the context of his screen image. This gave the pin-up an irony consistent with Reynolds' persona, an irony strong enough to recuperate the image, shifting it from passive to active in the heterosexual eye, for which Reynolds remains a regular guy after all (Barthes, 1972, p. 40).

In the series, *Evening Shade*, Reynolds stars as a high school football coach with a winning family and a losing team in a small Southern town. Trading with older viewers on his performances in *The Longest Yard* (1974) and *Semi-Tough* (1977), and perhaps on his college football record in Florida, Reynolds here plays a former football star. Reynolds trades, too, on what has been his film persona for nearly two decades. Exemplified by *W.W. and the Dixie Dancekings* (1975), this role casts Reynolds as a good-spirited, athletic, kind, rebellious loner, a Rainmaker among men, the ego ideal, who arrives to rekindle the colorless lives of ordinary fellows, figures with whom audience members might identify. Taking charge with a smile, he redeems them, frees them to play, to live out their old hearts' delight, to become themselves. What could be more desirable in a friend? What could be more flattering as masculinity? What could be better news? Offered the chance, Reynolds shares his magic generously; he does not discriminate. Except for the unusually misogynistic *The Longest Yard*, in his films he acts at ease, unafraid with women as well as men, and nonthreatening as well. This accounts, I think, for his popularity among both sexes.

Reynolds plays a similar role in *Evening Shade*, which exploits his wide appeal by featuring an unusual mix of ads aimed at women and at men. This mix may be one reason CBS was willing to pay a premium license fee to cover the $800,000 budget per episode—$100,000 more than the average sitcom—even though the show had yet to crack the top 20 (Lippman, 1991, p. D6; Wallace, 1991, pp. 3, 90). According to

Andrew Wernick (1987), advertisers in several media have begun responding to changes in the economy and iconography of gender with more "fluid, labile categories" and strategies (p. 293; also see King, 1990). For example, as Diane Barthel (1988) has observed, the March 1987 cover of *GQ* asked, "Are you man enough for mousse?" (p. 176).

With his appearance in *Cosmopolitan* and his guest host spots on *The Tonight Show*, Reynolds years ago established himself as a master of what Mark Crispin Miller (1986) calles "routine autosubversion" (p. 215), the habitual mocking of social roles in the moment of acquiescing to them (cf. Barthes, 1972, pp. 41-42). The strategy is part of the "ridicule of all by all" that has become the "very essence of the modern sitcom" (Miller, 1986, p. 214), and Reynolds would seem to be its avatar. The wonder is that it took the networks nearly two decades to figure this out and put him in an appropriate vehicle. Like Reynolds' action movies and adventure series, *Evening Shade* tests and restores his virility in an entertaining way and as such appeals to straight men watching at home. But, true to the sitcom formula, it does so without violence and with more laughs, and more quips for its main female characters (played by Marilu Henner and Elizabeth Ashley). As such it provides images meant to draw heterosexual women thought unlikely to watch an action show.

Combining audiences with contradictory traits goes back at least to *All in the Family*. That show owed its high ratings to its appeal to the Right as well as to the Left, an appeal rooted in the different readings the show made possible for different audiences, who saw it as a confirmation of their politics (Vidmar & Rokeach, 1974). With its stress on gender in an era in which markets are more segmented, *Evening Shade* may exemplify a new form of commercial television in the United States, designed to couple male and female rating points, even in households where men tend to regulate the remote control or tuner (Crain, 1989; Lull, 1982, 1988; cf. Morley, 1986, 1988, for research on viewing in Great Britain). This form may become more prevalent as the broadcast networks frantically scurry to combat ever-larger losses of viewers, in particular affluent viewers, to cable networks and videocassettes. This topic deserves more than I can devote to it here. Crucial are the ways masculinity aimed at both women and men differs in its traits (its inclusion of gentleness and warmth) from masculinity pointed either at male audiences, such as adventure shows or the Rambo movies (see Lippe & Jacobowitz, 1986; cf. Willis, 1989), or at female audiences, such as soap operas.

On a particular episode of *Evening Shade*, commercials alternated and combined appeal. The first group of ads, for example, opened with a commercial for Hot and Spicy Kentucky Fried Chicken, with actors playing a multi-ethnic jazz group (with one woman) on a food break. Although food ads typically are targeted at women, both men and women could be susceptible to this pitch. The second ad, for Degree antiperspirant, was intended for women. It featured a narrator saying, "When life turns up the heat, Degree has you covered," while the visual images constructed a brief story about a woman's fear of being close to men. The third ad was for Hanes Activewear and featured Joe Montana, "male gaze" and all, wearing the clothes and acquiring a convertible and "blonde" companion in the process. Although many men's clothing ads are aimed at women, this one seemed clearly aimed at least as much at men.

Reynolds' role as Wood Newton on *Evening Shade* may prove as successful as Carroll O'Connor's as Archie Bunker on *All in the Family* in creating a bimodal response, although for different reasons. Where O'Connor played a figure of contradictory identification and loathing, Reynolds plays the male who is willing to change—up to a point. This quality would seem to appeal to women and men who want to see men more open to gender fairness. At the same time, more men than we might like to think might revel in the thought that Reynolds is faking it when he acts like a New Man.[4]

Yet otherwise the plan of the show accords its star customary authority. In that sense, in Raymond Williams' term, it "flows" with the commercials I have mentioned. No matter its target audience or product, each ad was narrated by a man, like 91% of the ads broadcast during prime time, according to one count (Craig, 1990; for more on ad/program flow, see Altman, 1987; Browne, 1984; Budd, Craig, & Steinman, 1983; Williams, 1974). In the program, no one else is as funny as Reynolds' character, as filled with adventurous schemes. The only flaw ascribed to him is the record of his football team, which has lost 30 games in a row. This lack creates a space for Reynolds-Wood[5] to be kidded and to kid himself, to participate in the ritual "ridicule of all by all." It also may help viewers feel more at home with the character. ("When were you ever humiliated?" Reynolds is asked. "I'm humiliated every Friday night at the football stadium," he replies, and the audience laughs.) Such a flaw is common to Reynolds in his movies as well; it helps make sure spectators can admire him, even feel in some way superior.

As a commodity image, this pass at imperfection strengthens Reynolds. Like his persona's self-mockery, it "immunizes" him, as Roland Barthes

(1972) would say. Then again, without this lack, by no means minor in the calculus of this culture's masculinity, the perfection of the Reynolds character might leave no room for comedic tension. Even with it, no other man in the show is as conventionally attractive, no adult as physical, and none controls the narrative or the video camera frame as he does. Mulvey (1975) suggests that the problem of men watching men is elided by the function of the male star: His "glamorous characteristics are . . . not those of the erotic object of the gaze but those of the more perfect, more complete, more powerful ideal" (p. 12). Yet her argument seems to depend upon a strict division of labor by sex and sexual orientation. A compelling image of masculinity might be indiscriminately attractive. If so, it would confound any sexual division. And so it must, like the pin-up, be allowed no risk of causing mixed feelings in those who find it such a pleasure to watch. So in the same way that he cannot turn out to be, say, a cokehead, or a spouse- or child-abuser, Reynolds-Wood must be, by every indication, a real man, masculinity undoubted. Even with his skills at autosubversion, this is not so easy, given his character's soft edge and warmth toward men. What sets up this situation is precisely the show's interest in attracting women as well as men.

It is an interest that has complicated structures of gender in Hollywood films as well, at least since the 1920s. It was then that the U.S. motion picture industry made the films of Rudolph Valentino, which were, according to Miriam Hansen (1986), the first "explicitly addressed to a female spectator, regardless of the actual composition of the audience" (p. 6). Unlike the male-oriented classical cinema analyzed by Mulvey (1975), "female-addressed Hollywood films [focused] spectatorial pleasure on the image of a male/hero performer" (Hansen, p. 10). Situating the male star as an object of visual pleasure in itself involves a "feminization of the actor's persona" (p. 10; also see Neale, 1983, pp. 14-15; for a critique of the "feminization" argument, see Smith, 1989). This complicates Dyer's pin-up analysis. It gives mainstream films aimed at women a special assignment: They must both eroticize male stars and preserve their masculinity, which threatens to disperse every moment men are configured as passive objects for women's eyes. Hansen concentrated on the implications of this different form for women, but her work remains important regarding male spectators as well. What happens to the "male gaze" when it meets a male star whose presence has been eroticized? The film doesn't distinguish among its spectators. Do otherwise heterosexual men ignore the image's seduction?

These questions call for a close look at specific films that takes seriously the strategies of feminist film studies even if it questions them (see, e.g., Smith, 1989). From Hansen's work, a critical aspect of any seduction would seem to have to do with point-of-view shots and cuts on glances (p. 15). Yet these are mostly absent from such three-camera comedies as *Evening Shade*. Although it includes shots set up for one camera, most of the show seems to be made in the normal three-camera format of sitcoms. This format makes point-of-view structures difficult (difficult, not impossible—there is one point-of-view insert of a newspaper in the show). How the three-camera system affects the arguments of Mulvey (1975, 1981), Neale (1983), Hansen (1986), Smith (1989), and others who stress the complex system of glances in classical cinema and its relation to identification and pleasure has yet to be explored systematically.

Still, we can see several processes of gender construction at work in *Evening Shade* by looking at two short segments of the episode:

1. In the opening sequence, as a voice-over narrator (Ossie Davis) tells us that "Wood Newton loves any sort of competition," Reynolds-Wood sits sprawling on a front porch set, stogie in mouth, right leg hosted over the furniture, reading a paper. After a dissolve to an establishing shot of a large house, the show cuts to a shot of him sitting not dissimilarly in the kitchen-dining area. His wife, Ava (Marilu Henner), serves two children, and speaks of another child who worries her, while Reynolds-Wood eats toasts and reads. When he speaks, he commands the camera. Three of the 11 shots in the sequence feature him alone, a privilege no other actor/character is given until later in the show. He dominates conversation, is served like a king by his wife, and is given the lion's share of the frame when the two of them are in a shot together. He gets the punch lines. In the show's credits, "Starring Burt Reynolds" fades into view precisely on a dissolve to a successful football play. As it fades out, "Also Starring Marilu Henner" fades into its place, on a dissolve from the football play to a cheerleader going through her paces. Although the show kids these roles, especially Reynolds', it never strays far from the tale of hero and fan the credits establish.

So far, except for references to the losses in football, the show has followed conventional codes of gender. As it continues, Ava, by gesture and remark, repeatedly certifies the heterosexuality of Reynolds-Wood. He in turn stakes out his manhood by his differentiation from her. He is the father: When she is alone with their high-school-age son, she controls their relationship; when the three are together, she retreats to second place.

2. The next sequence begins after Reynolds-Wood is told that his friend Herman, the assistant coach (Michael Jeter), wants to have a man-to-man talk with him and Reynolds-Wood quips, "Why not? We're both men." He dominates the space of his office as if it were his lair. Indeed, the opening shot of the sequence has him sitting much like he did in the opening shot of the show, this time with feet up on his desk, leaning back, his arms clasped behind his neck. The cigar is there, too, though it's sagging at about a 30-degree angle from his mouth. Jeter—assign-ed the nerdy name "Herman" and an affect to match—seems cast to em-phasize Wood's physicality. Reynolds, not a tall man, towers over Jeter, and the performances accentuate the differences: Herman slumps when he walks; Reynolds-Wood stands erect. As a foil, Herman tries with gestures and remarks to achieve masculinity, but he fails, becoming a figure of parody, not so much of masculinity as of those who don't have but are desperate for it.

"Teach 'em to mess with us," he snarls as he hitches up his pants.

"Aww-right!" he howls, initiating a high-five salute—and then miss-ing the oncoming hand.

This differentiation helps construct the image of Wood's gender, of Wood the natural, "just as Fred Astaire was made to look 'masculine' by the casting of Edward Everett Horton as his 'auntie' sidekick"— David Marc's description of George Bush's pairing with Dan Quayle (1990, p. 24). Near the end of the show, standing in purple and scarlet light, Herman says, "I got an idea for a charade" based on a movie title. He puts on a prom queen's crown. "*The Lady in Red*," guesses Reynolds-Wood (it's *Carrie*).

As well as supplying a sidekick, Herman's role parallels that of the ordinary men Reynolds enlivens in his films. In viewers' search for pleasure, identifications shift and split, sometimes in contradictory ways (Willis, 1989, p. 18). Some may identify with Herman, or Reynolds-Wood, or both at the same time. Within the fiction, viewers can easily believe that Herman adores Wood, that Wood is his ego ideal. He wishes he could have played with him when they were younger, could have joined his gang in their unlikely, boyish exploits, like demolishing an Interna-tional House of Pancakes with a 400-pound snowball.

"I was never part of the in crowd," Herman says. "You probably did stuff like that all the time."

"My wife doesn't understand," says Wood of his pranks. "She thinks I'm immature."

"Silly woman," Herman replies, another time saying, "Teach me. I'm new at all this."

The scenes mimic the structure of legion pornographic films, gay and heterosexual male, that wind around narratives of erotic initiation. But this is commercial television—money shots don't pay. Neither does ambiguity of gender. Still, with men as well as women eroticized as stars, and with sexual orientation never sealed, "male homosexuality is constantly present as an undercurrent, as a potentially troubling aspect," as Neale has said of mainstream cinema (1983, p. 15; see also Wood, 1987).

Here the sublimated clincher comes toward the end of the office sequence, when Reynolds-Wood walks over to Herman and puts his hands on his shoulders and begins to plan another stunt. Whatever its intention, the dialogue flashes with sexual innuendo.

"It's gotta be so big that we become immortal," says Reynolds-Wood as he rubs Herman's shoulder.

"You got me all keyed up," Herman says.

After missing the high-five, Herman makes the low-five and spins around, bending over as he turns his back. A moment later, he turns back around again.

"Whatever it is," he says, "just remember I'm with you all the way. It's kinda like that song."

And then he speaks-sings the love song's lyrics: "There's someone/Walking behind you/Turn around/Look at me."

Reynolds-Wood deflects the affection, his tone so dismissive it threatens to overturn his friendly character.

Of course he can't return the affection. Identifications may be "multiple, fluid, at points even contradictory" (Neale, 1983, p. 4). Still, Reynolds-Wood must remain an object of identification more than the object of a desire that might "feminize" him (Neale, 1983, p. 15). Could many men in the audience continue to identify with a star, even Reynolds with his ironic bravado, who happily acknowledged being the object of male desire, let alone the subject of desire for another man? No commercial TV producers in their right minds would allow Burt Reynolds to be seen in either relationship.[6] Nor would many give the Herman character a masculine name and have him played by an actor with an affect gendered like Reynolds', making him a more conventional object of attraction. Would Reynolds-Wood be allowed to rub the shoulder of

Tom Selleck, and not play it for laughs? Would Tom Selleck be allowed to serenade Reynolds with a love song?

But perhaps men are eroticized in film and television in ways unlike women for the "male gaze," ways whose pattern is experienced and found pleasurable by men but not usually thought of as erotic. Paul Smith (1989) has cataloged a "little 'semiotics' of the heroized male body," specific compositions and camera movements in the films of Don Siegel and Clint Eastwood and other directors of action movies (p. 95). But I do not find these applicable to three-camera sitcoms. More relevant here is the way men are shown playing together, physically, especially when men play *with* and not *against* each other. Sports competition permits men to touch each other in order to win, to establish difference through dominance. This is most graphically embodied in high school and college wrestling, where otherwise taboo groin-touching is allowed to occur. The object is to pin one's opponent, on his back, winner on top. Unconsciously, the culture seems aware enough of the sport's sexuality.[7] Unless compelled by federal law, adults tend not to permit wrestling between boys and girls. I suspect this is not only because with girls and boys together, no ritual of male differentiation would recuperate the contact. The sight of men on television at play without competing, however, may offer a desirable vision of prepubescent plenitude in which boys could be friends and find pleasure in being together, requiring no cover, not yet needing to test their masculinity at each other's expense, not yet so conscious of the borderline of affection that awaits them as adults.

According to Eve Kosofsky Sedgwick (1985), crucial to patriarchy has been the segregation of *homosocial* from *homoerotic* relations among men, the former on guard against erotic possibilities. Separating out the two in experience is tricky; they are not inherently distinct. For many women today, Sedgwick argues, the homosocial includes the homosexual: "An intelligible continuum of aims, emotions, and valuations links lesbianism with the other forms of women's attention to women: the bond of mother and daughter, for instance, the bond of sister and sister, women's friendship, 'networking,' and the active struggles of feminism" (p. 2).

For most men, however, dividing the continuum is a minefield crossed only with the closest attention to the authorized codes, of what feelings shall pass and in what form, under what name. *Evening Shade* covers this minefield, and although it still knows where it can and cannot step, it strays more than the average sitcom. Reynolds-Wood strides through homosociality with men on the show (and in the audience). Arguably, the farther he goes the more appealing the show can be, but if he or any other character begins to step out of bounds, the ideological-industrial complex will begin to "claw back" the gesture (Fiske & Hartley, 1978, p. 87). Could Wood say to Herman, "Look, I love you, too, but I'm married, and I'm monogamous"? Could Reynolds say that to Tom Selleck? And yet, no matter the dialogue, no matter the succession of scenes, the multivalence of the show's images and sounds may sustain alternative experiences for viewers predisposed to find them (Budd, Entman, & Steinman, 1990). For Mulvey (1988), such structures, "supply visible, material expression to the invisible erotic scenarios that construct the concept of sexual different in a given historic/symbolic order, and thus also construct deviances" (p. 74).

This seems more true of this episode of *Evening Shade* than it is of other sitcoms I have seen susceptible to similar readings (*Cheers*, *Three's Company*). But what makes it exceptional is not its general character, which seems typical, but its specific details, which make that character unusually clear. Whatever the contingent circumstances, on this show contradictory forces normally contained by the culture somehow edged closer to the surface, however they affected different groups of viewers. At the very end of the episode, Ossie Davis resumes the narration, offering one of the morals of the story: "And a man can let a little boy hidden inside leap out once again to laugh and play." As Davis begins the sentence, we are given a reprise of the video portion of the high-five/low-five scene, the moment when Herman is about to face Reynolds-Wood and begin singing "Turn Around, Look at Me." As Davis says, "let the . . . boy hidden inside leap out," the image dissolves to a shot from the middle of the show: Herman and Reynolds-Wood, sitting next to each other on the porch of the opening scene, smiling, together crossing their legs in time, crossing to a gender-bending, knee-over-knee position. The choreography creates an affectionate leap partway across the homosocial continuum. As first shown Herman followed up the gesture by putting his hand on Reynolds-Wood's forearm. Now, in the reprise, the image dissolves before Herman can move. Instead, the show presents a new shot on the porch, with Reynolds-Wood hugging his wife, she precisely in the place in the frame where Herman, now absent, had sat.

The "claw back" could not be more sure. Far less certain is its erasure of what already has passed. For male viewers, the instability Dyer (1982) describes would seem to be a fact of life to the extent their gender consciousness has been conventionally shaped. It is part of the process of viewing. For them, *Evening Shade* would seem to construct an attractive image of masculinity, both on screen and in themselves, through its parade of differentiations. The show helps viewers in tune with patriarchy keep their gaze within bounds while allowing them the pleasure of its experience. Viewing affirms a subjectivity that validates desire for a certified star, but has no truck with acknowledging homoeroticism on screen. For heterosexuals, viewing denies its own eroticism. In that sense, both the show and its spectators remain prisoners of gender, bonded by chains that could be broken only if first they could be seen.

Notes

1. As Judith Butler (1990) and others have argued, conceptualizing patriarchy—a system of "power relations in which women's interests are subordinated to the interests of men" (Weedon, 1987, p. 2)—as a universal form "overrides or reduces distinct articulations of gender asymmetry in different cultural contexts" (p. 35) and risks minimizing issues of class and race. It also elides the implications of women and men struggling for new arrangements. Here I will concentrate on this culture's complex system of male-dominated differentiations organized around gender and sexual orientation, differentiations that seek to construct and valorize certain sexualities at the expense of others.

2. On this basis, David M. Halperin (1990) argues for a break with the "modern medical/forensic/social-scientific category of homosexuality (with its essentializing, psychologistic implications)" (p. ix). In analyses like Halperin's, sexual orientation (heterosexual, homosexual, bisexual) ceases to signify a specific, discernible state of mind or an internally defining characteristic of self. A classical scholar, Halperin says the study of sexual life in antiquity reveals homosexuality, heterosexuality, and even sexuality itself to be culture-specific forms of erotic life—"not the basic building blocks of sexual identity for all human beings in all times and places, but peculiar and indeed exceptional ways of conceptualizing and experiencing desire" (p. 9). In the late nineteenth century, for example, "heterosexual" for some meant what "bisexual" does now (Halperin, 1990, p. 159n). This supports Simon Watney's (1987) argument that: "Our most basic classificatory systems for making sense of sex are grossly inadequate to the task, in so far as they delimit any possible understanding of sex to a single, monolithic binary opposition" (p. 28).

3. Curtis Hanson's *Bad Influence* (1990) is an intriguing exception. Rob Lowe plays a character who excites the otherwise heterosexual protagonist (played by James Spader) and then threatens to destroy his ordered life. The role is similar to Hart Bochner's in Martin Donovan's more adventurous *Apartment Zero* (1988). Both films are worth analyzing in terms of the experience they offer heterosexual spectators. The value of their successful plays on gender, however, would seem to be contradicted by their association of ambiguous sexuality with evil.

4. Television shows featuring "the unreconstructued male and the woman who isn't having any," with their contradictory appeals to men and women, seem to have been especially common in the mid-1980s (Tankel & Banks, 1990, p. 289).

The Reynolds persona I describe below provides an intriguing contrast, offering his admirers joy (and his producers a larger audience). Though he may prod people to take risks in his charge, they have nothing to fear. For an illuminating analysis of the complex pleasures offered many women viewers by a related figure, Tom Selleck in *Magnum, P.I.*, see Flitterman (1985).

5. I use the combined term to mark the presence of Reynolds' established persona in the character.

6. Even without a star such as Reynolds, representing a man loving a man as an ordinary narrative event in a series episode can cost a network upwards of $1 million in lost advertising (Weinstein, 1990).

7. This is not to say that social discourse always denies wrestling's sexuality (or its gender politics). See Ken Russell's 1969 *Women in Love*, or think of the market among men for the spectacle of women wrestling, slick with oil or in the mud, a market (with no role-reversed counterpart) that foregrounds the sadism of the "male gaze."

15

The Transatlantic Gaze

Masculinities, Youth, and the American Imaginary[1]

JEFF HEARN
ANTONIO MELECHI

Talking Pictures

Males and Men

This chapter is about imaging men. In saying *men* we are not referring
to some monolith; we are talking of the social references called men—as
when someone says with ironic certainty, "That's a man, isn't it?" We
are not talking of *males*, which we see as a biological reference, though
itself socially constructed and not biologically determined.[2]

In deconstructing imaging *men* we are writing in a critical relationship to recent practical and theoretical problematizations of *men* and
masculinities. These problematizations have applied to men and masculinities as both social categories and substantive social phenomena. Much
of the impetus for this has come from feminist theory and practice; it has
also come in a different sense from gay scholarship and liberationism, and
from rather limited development of anti-sexist theory and practice by
men. Furthermore, change of and about men has been occurring in the
full range of social arenas, from the international to the national, local,
domestic, and personal, as well as in cultural, media, and academic sites
and forums. It particularly problematizes dominant forms of masculinity and *hegemonic masculinity*.

This chapter focuses on the relationship between the study of men and masculinities and imaging, the (re)production of images. However, despite the historical importance of the visual, especially in the mass media over the last hundred years or more, and the major growth of cultural studies scholarship on images in recent years, the question of imaging has, somewhat surprisingly, not been a major element in the academic problematization of men and masculinities. Instead these recent studies (sometimes known ambiguously and unfortunately as "men's studies" —we prefer "the critical study of men and masculinities"[3]) have been dominated by psychology, social psychology, nonvisual sociological traditions, history, and literature.

The first section sets out the relationship of the primary elements— men, masculinities, youth, and the American Imaginary—from the perspective of the transatlantic gaze. The two subsequent sections explore these relationships in the context of, first, the birth of film and the Western at the turn of the century, and, second, the generation of youth and rock 'n' roll in the fifties. These are portrayed as two particularly significant moments in the construction of the American Imaginary in, through, and by the transatlantic gaze.

Imaging Men and Masculinities

Men and masculinities are talked of, pictured, imaged. To do so invokes *age*, *youth*, and *agedness*. Men and masculinities, whether in image, text, social practice, or social structure, are necessarily about aging, sometimes explicitly so, often implicitly. There is a recurring inseparability in men/masculinities and age/aging. Age is implicated in the construction of men and masculinities—both in the distinction of men from young men and boys, and in the construction of particular masculinities: avuncular, coy, mature, rough, fatherly, athletic, gay, working-class, and so on.

In developing this critique of imaging men and masculinities, we take issue with notions of "images of," whether images of men, or images of masculinity, or images of aging. Rather than speak of specific images of, we see imaging, men, and masculinities as mutually inclusive of one another. Images and imaging involve references to culturally assigned meanings of looking, showing, being looked upon, being shown. The very notion of image rests upon such cultural processes of looking and showing, which themselves rest upon dominant forms of men/masculinities, which themselves look upon images. Thus we are concerned as much with the gendering of imaging as we are with the imaging of gender. Moreover, these processes of representation and signification are not limited to the formal media and institutional forms of communication; they exist in all forms and instances of social practice. They apply not only in imaging gender; they are themselves gendered. For what is important is not what images are (in some idealist sense), but rather who produces images, and by whom and how they are consumed. Images are (only) produced in their consumption, so that looking and imaging are inseparable and equally gendered.

Imaging America

Processes of imaging are nowadays characteristically international. Globalization of imaging represents a relatively recent consolidation of power of men in imaging, in both production and display. In this international organization of imaging, the United States has a special significance. Indeed from the vantage point of the United Kingdom, it is almost impossible to talk of imaging, and especially the mass media, without recourse to America. This is particularly clear in the international organization and domination of *visual* mass media, especially film, television, and photography. In the United Kingdom, film connotes Hollywood and America. This association even persists in the very construction of the United States as "America." This semantic expansion is in some ways the inverse of the construction of the United Kingdom as "England," as is common among Americans. In the first case, a nation grows to become two continents; in the second, a nation reduces to one of (at least) four constituent parts. This former's continental imperialism mirrors its place in the New World—the world of youth and young men. These New World systems of imaging are themselves controlled very largely by men through the economic structuring of imaging, in hierarchical, capitalist, patriarchal organizations. These combinations of imaging, the visual, America, and men are so intense that modern culture itself may sometimes equate with imaging American men as businessmen, film stars, cowboys, rock singers, superheroes, he-men, crooners, "fancy men," city slickers, and sexual deviants.

In writing about images in talking pictures, we are also necessarily making reference to the connotations of the word and the visual, both in geography and in gender. To put this simply, we are writing in English, the English language, the language of Britain and America, about images of America, the American image. While the United Kingdom, even

England, retains a delicate authority through language, history, and historical imperialism, America retains and expands its authority over image, the present, and contemporary imperialism, including imperialism of the visual. This applies to both America as frontier and America as film. Talking pictures here is "English talking American pictures." However, in case this contrast appears too simple, just as (Great) Britain is the land of heritage, unspoken traditions, and the far-flung former Empire, so America is the land of the written constitution, and the power of the pen—America writes itself.

The Transatlantic Gaze

Not only are we "talking pictures," "Englishing America," we are also looking *at* America *from* England, caught in the familiar (to us) transatlantic gaze. We are indulging in a kind of international tourism—a tourism that is cultural and transcendental, involving no physical movement. It is a psychological *virtual reality* that requires no immediate technology, though for its existence, it relies on the mass media technology of film, video, and telecommunications. Like the tourist gaze, the transatlantic gaze deploys notions of being "home" and "away." In looking at American men in this way, we are at home, looking at them away—they are different to us, they are shown to be bigger, stronger, fitter, younger, healthier, better-looking, sexier, more tanned, more famous, and they are usually white. Not only is America the "hyperreal,"[4]American men are hyperreal. We are moving from imaging to the imaginary.

America as the Imaginary: The American Imaginary

The idea of the *Imaginary* has been developed in French psychoanalysis, most visibly by Jacques Lacan (1977a, 1977b). It refers to "the world, the register, the dimension of images, conscious or unconscious, perceived or imagined" (Sheridan, 1977, p. ix).

The *Imaginary* is not seen in isolation, but in a three-way relationship with the *Symbolic* and the *Real*. For Lacan, the Imaginary does not refer specifically to images; rather it is the realm of the ego, its identifications, before and beyond the language. The Symbolic does not specifically refer to symbols, rather it is the realm of language. The Real does not refer to some basic reality; rather it is the realm (the moment of impossibility) onto which both the symbolic and the imaginary are grafted, the point of that moment's endless return (Rose, 1982, p. 31). Thus the Imaginary is not to be confused with that which is simply imagined. The Imaginary is a structure of subjectivity acquired, like the unconscious, by the infant at the mirror phase—the pre-oedipal identification of the infant with its mirror image, an identification guaranteed by the gaze of the mother holding the child to the mirror. This stage is pre-language; it involves the splitting of the ego into the I which is watching and the I that is watched, such that identification with the mirror image is imaginary; and although, according to Lacan, the process is genderless, it marks the beginning of the acquisition of gendered subjectivity. It is the realm of interpersonal and narcissistic identifications of the ego and its "other."

The concept of the imaginary has been developed in rather different ways in French psychoanalytic feminist theory, and particularly by Luce Irigaray to stand for female strength and identity. In *Speculum de l'Autre Femme*, Irigaray (1985) argues that the imaginary is a possible means to the transformation of ideology with its basis in the erotic memory for the pre-oedipal mother. Thus there are both pre-gendered and gendered accounts of the imaginary.[5] Indeed, gendered accounts could be developed in relation to both mother and father, rather than simply the mother. We see both the pre-gendered and gendered interpretation of the imaginary as relevant to our present purposes.

What has all this to do with masculinities, youth, and America? In the context of British culture, as we write, we are referring to America *as the Imaginary*—hence, the American Imaginary. We are identifying the American Imaginary, both as a reference to the restimulation of infant processes, and as a model of (adult) engagement with images and identification. Thus to the transatlantic gaze, America is the world, the dimension of images, the realm of identifications. The American Imaginary refers to the pre-oedipal experience and process of difference and sameness: It is beyond language; it may be erotic (Irigaray) or beyond the erotic (Lacan). The American Imaginary, may be seen as pre-gendered (following Lacan) or gendered (following Irigaray) or both (as we would prefer). Accordingly, looking at American men in terms of the American Imaginary may refer to the fundamental pre-gendering and/or gendering of sameness and difference. American men appear as ("in touch with") representations we know directly *without explanation of reference to meaning* and that is of their appeal, erotic or otherwise. Looking at American men we are looking at or looking for all those qualities and identifications that appear asocial, apparently primordial, erotic or otherwise.

These processes of the American Imaginary thus refer to a range of complex and sometimes contradictory identifications. In its immediate form, the identification of American youth culture may naturally often refer to men's culture, as in the equation: modern culture = America = youth = men. Less concretely, these processes may be both gendered and pre-gendered. For example, to the British, America does not have the heaviness of traditional (European) civilization. In this way, its dream-like quality refers us back to a pre-modern, pre-oedipal erotic memory, simultaneously and paradoxically fleetingly male/female and naturally male/female—both postmodern and pre-modern. Looking at American men may similarly invoke both postmodern/pre-modern, gendered/pre-gendered, and male/female.

The Birth of Film and the Western at the Turn of the Century

If America is the world of images and representations in modern culture, youth and men stand distinctively within that imaginary. This imaginary is itself historical—as in the very phrase *The New World*, named after a European explorer. To the European, America is about youth (newness) and men (explorers). The discovery of America, itself a Eurocentric historical view, was historically and culturally overlain by the continuing movements both to the frontiers and of those frontiers. There is now a widespread recognition of the historical significance of the frontier and pioneering for the changing forms of masculinity at the end of the nineteenth century (Dubbert, 1979; Filene, 1986; Gerzon, 1982; Kimmel, 1987b; Mangan & Walvin, 1987; Pleck & Pleck, 1980). The frontiersman was himself a new man of his times. He was young by association with young land, tough and reliant, a true man. The frontier was young (man). In contrast Great Britain was the world of old men.

While these associations apply in all the expanding mass media at the end of the nineteenth century, the essential medium of the frontier, youth and America, of youthful American men, was film.[6] Indeed film was itself a new, youthful frontier. Invented in the late 1880s, film soon moved onto popular showings, with the first public event in the United States at Koster and Bial's Music Hall, New York, in April 1896 (Brownlow, 1973, p. 2; Wenden, 1975, p. 10). From the beginning films were not just gendered, but often media for showing off men and heterosexuality, as in *The Kiss* (1896); *Fatima* (1897), featuring a Coney Island belly dance; *Dolorita in the Passion Dance* (1896), which brought the first demands for film censorship; and *The Kiss in the Tunnel* (1899). By the 1900s genres of sexual adventure films (*Wife Away, Hubby Will Play; Physical Games*) and "blue movies" were being produced. By 1907 Chicago had introduced local censorship, and other American cities soon followed (Wenden, 1975, p. 23, pp. 117-18), so beginning an intense dialectic between sexualization and restraint.

From the beginning film was the model medium of projection and gazing—the huge mirror in the dark vacuum. Film, like America itself, is a mirror of the transatlantic gaze. America and film are both fundamental references of sameness and difference. Film, the great mirror, the screen of projection, the "kingdom of shadows" (as Maxim Gorky called it), was a new, youthful, total environment, a dream in a dream palace, decorated *as woman*—a site of escape, fantasy, addiction, distress, seduction, sexuality, pleasure, desire, a site of identifications. It was also America. Within this (pre-oedipal) world, men and masculinities, especially as youthful adventurers, could rise and fall. This subtext of sexuality and age existed as a new medium of the masses, both in and through a language of *images* (especially before the coming of the talkies in 1926-1927). Film also provided information on the American, white, Anglo-Saxon world to East European, Italian, Jewish, and other immigrants. Ironically, some of these immigrants pioneered the American film industry itself. Samuel Goldfish (Sam Goldwyn), Cecil B. de Mille, Adolf Zukor, and many others were central in creating this American dream, Hollywood, and even the Western itself.

American film's (American Imaginary's) power as "object of desire" is perhaps clearest in the rise of the stars, both women and men. Fan and film magazines, like *Photoplay*, indicated that stars were becoming major influences in the public's emotional lives, starting in about 1916-1918 (Izod, 1988, p. 45). By the twenties and thirties, technical innovations facilitated the production of shorts with softly lit, strangely glowing *faces*: your own "dream" (boy or girl)—famous, beautiful, first seen at the first-run cinemas—the "shot" of the new face.

Men as viewers and fans gazed on women and men in film, just as men stars gazed on the women on film. Within this broad structure there were many variations. Romantic heroes and tough male villains contrasted with the city-dwelling antiheroes of Lloyd, Chaplin, Keaton— often founded on anonymity, loneliness, clowning, sexual ordinariness, even sexual coyness. Identifications were available to men as either remote stars beyond reach or ordinary "guys like me."

Furthermore, such portrayals of men were themselves often located within the "male sexual narrative [of the] male hero" (Dyer, 1985). This applied in both serials, which became a favorite form that combined capitalist marketing and sexualized excitement in the problematic rescue of the heroine, like *Perils of Pauline* (1914), and longer feature films, which after 1910 expanded from two or three reels to five. "Male sexual narrative" involved an idealized male (hetero)sexist ordering of events operating in a continuous stream of movement and adventures, usually involving the chase, the entanglement, the climax, the world seen and "shot" through the eyes of the "heterosexual male" (Dyer, 1985). It figured in romance films, crime and thriller genres, and the early vice movies, themselves forerunners of modern pornography. *Traffic in Souls* (1913) portrayed the white slavers' capture of immigrant girls and the familiar chase and rescue of the "pure white girl." While women were left for rescuing (virgins?) or showing as villainesses (whores?), men had a vast array of social and technological inventions to play with and within: the chase, the gang, the posse, the crash, the train, the car, the car driving into walls or through buildings, the hero hanging onto moving trains, the runaway train, and so on. These devices were used in both adventure and humorous films. Men may form primal bands and bonds, chase other men, rescue women, or elope with them (perhaps by car as in Harold Lloyd's *The Joy Rider*).

These themes of frontier, film, youth, men, and sexuality were brought together in the genre of the Western—a particularly powerful set of sexual/violent/aged/masculine images, including the cult of violence and gun law (Kimmel, 1987c); this provided numerous opportunities for various forms of vicarious pseudo-frontiering, adventuring, and identifications (Mellen, 1977). After the "West" had been "won," the Western tells not just of the frontier and the frontiersmen themselves as the loss or presumed loss of the frontier (in America). Thus the frontier, after it had been presumed "lost," took on the qualities of conquest and escape. Man was on the edge of Nature, be it "Indian Territory" or "the Wilderness." This gazing into the frontier and simultaneous loss of the frontier has remarkable similarities with the process of Lacan's mirror stage. At this stage the infant identifies with the image of its physical form, in the mirror. In so doing the "I" is split between the watcher and the watched. Similarly, the frontier, the source of plenitude, is simultaneously gained and lost—like the self in the mirror stage, like cowboys galloping toward the sunset.[7]

The frontier (nature) has been lost, but the cowboy (man) could be created—in literature and in film. Western white man fought Eastern black man, except the latter were native to the West, and were not seen as black. The struggle of the West (Occident) and the East (Orient) was reproduced within the New West of "America" in the reversal of the Eastern (white) Seaboard and the Western/Indian/native/black/Frontier. On the Western Frontier "Western" white men from the East Coast fought "Eastern" (black, but not seen as black) Indian men: (white) man fought (black) natives/nature. The origin of the black/Indian Natives was literally on the *other* side of the world, from Canada, Alaska, Siberia, Asia. These were the *other* native black men, as opposed to the directly brought black men of Africa. This is all the *Western*.[8] And moreover, this white man, this non-native, was a cowboy, an animal and a *young* man in one. This period coincides with the beginning of film such that, to the transatlantic gaze, the Western film is America, and the birth of the Western is paradoxically the birth of modern America. The Western, the West-ern, the Occidental (cf. Said, 1978) is the American genre.

Early vignettes included *Cripple Creek Bar-room* (1898) and *The Life of an American Cowboy* (1902). In 1902 Owen Wister's novel, *The Virginian*, was published as the first genuine Western novel, with 15 reprintings in less than a year, and 8 years of dramatizations (Filene, 1986, p. 94). The film, *The Great Train Robbery* (1903), was probably the first effectively organized piece of dramatic fiction on film, with the robbery, the chase, and the triumph of justice all on one reel. One of the members of the outlaw band, Max Aaronson, was to become, as "Bronco Billy" Anderson, the first star of Westerns—a cowboy hero in a long series of one- and two-reelers.

The typical Western brings together a number of elements of masculinity, sometimes in contradiction. The whole plot may be founded on the "male [hetero?]sexual narrative" (Dyer, 1985) "structured around pursuit, the man chasing the woman, that type of narrative that elides love, seduction, possession and rape." In this, men and masculinities, the cowboy, the Indian, the sheriff, the baddies, and the goodies are but elements in the structure of the narrative. This kind of narrative is also very much about age, aging, and youthful pursuit.

The Western can also be seen in a rather different way, as combining male (hetero)sexual narrative and the homosexual subtext (Wood, 1987) of homosocial groups of men,[9] as in the portrayal of posses, engaged in their own (sexual) pursuit of other men. The meeting point of these two subtexts is often the saloon, where men "lose themselves in drink and . . . triumph over each other at the gaming tables," and where there is "usually . . . if only by implication, a brothel upstairs." Both the brothel/saloon and Hollywood "cater in mass entertainment, in glamour, in a narcissistic titillation . . . which ends in dissatisfaction; both trade in the decorative and in fantasies of disguise; and both in attempting to appease phantoms of desire, create a thousand more" (Rhode, 1976, pp. 217-18).

Such American fantasies were brought closer to home, indeed concretized, in the generation of youth and the marketing of dress in fifties Britain.

The Generation of Youth: Rock 'n' Roll and the Spectacle of Difference

The spectacular formation of postwar youth in Britain finds its much chronicled genesis in the mid-fifties, when the burgeoning influx of American film and music came to constitute the cultural space of teenage leisure, where the generational difference of youth would be consumed. While the influence of the American media in this period stands mythologized across the sonic shock waves of rock 'n' roll, we are more generally concerned with this historic moment (1955-1957) as the primal scene of the transatlantic gaze: the birth of modern youth and the beginning of a *visible* relation between British youth and the American Imaginary—from where the multifarious guises of modern youth styles, from Rocker to B-Boy, have been appropriated. In examining these conspicuous signs of youth in terms of the construction and consumption of masculinities, we intend to broadly focus on two areas: (a) the relationship between white youth and the sexuality of the black performer in rock 'n' roll, and the significance of black alterity as a signifier of the generation gap; and (b) the sexuality of the transatlantic male gaze and the desires that inform fashionable identification with American stars.

Black Images/White Gaze

The screening of *The Blackboard Jungle* in the cinemas of South London in the winter of 1955 marked an important moment in determining the use and the meaning of rock 'n' roll for its British consumers. The film's representation of juvenile delinquency in a New York high school, set against Bill Haley's "Rock Around the Clock," incited Britain's first pop riot as metropolitan cinema audiences slashed seats and danced in the aisles and on the streets. In effecting the connection between youth, discord, and rock 'n' roll, *The Blackboard Jungle* is particularly notable in that it featured the black actor Sidney Poitier in a lead role. Poitier plays Miller, the boy from the ghetto, who, in an unlikely alliance with the moronic white hoodlum West (Vic Morrow), fronts the chorus of classroom dissent against the benign liberalism of newly posted teacher Rick Dadier (Glenn Ford):

> In this film Poitier was a delinquent first and a black character second. This was an important breakthrough because it put a black character on a par with Jim Stark in *Rebel Without a Cause*. It is no longer necessary to think of Gregory Miller, the character Poitier played in *The Blackboard Jungle*, in terms of race any more than one is consciously reminded throughout *Rebel Without a Cause* that Jim is white. (Pettigrew, 1986, p. 125-26).

The irony of one white critic's positive response to Miller reflects both the recuperation of black resistance within the film's treatment of delinquency, and the ethnocentrism of Pettigrew's color blindness: commending Poitier's "breakthrough" into a psychological reality beyond black and white. While *The Blackboard Jungle* finally achieves a conciliation as Miller turns against West to side with Dadier, the original alliance of black and white defiance foregrounds the process, apparent in various subcultures, whereby white youth appropriate the symbolic possibilities of black culture. Miller's resentment of the educational "white system" is in this way assimilated within the dominant frame of deviancy, negating the political specificity of black marginality, which stands merely as a figure of youthful difference.

When rock 'n' roll was exposed to a larger audience with the showing of *Rock Around the Clock* (which featured tracks from black rock 'n' roll performers Chuck Berry and Little Richard) in the summer of 1956, the disturbances that *The Blackboard Jungle* had aroused were now repeated in provincial cinemas, prompting Watch Committees in Belfast, Bromwich, Smethwick (Birmingham), and many other towns to ban the film. The waves of commotion that received the performance of *Rock Around the Clock* provoked a moral panic in the national press, which, in the brief duration of the hysteria, imagined the possession of teenage audiences throughout Britain, who, "seduced" by the black spirit of rock 'n' roll, were abandoned to its "primal" beat:

Frenzied "rock 'n' roll" fans snatched up fire hoses and sprayed Mr. Tom Boardman, manager of Gaiety Cinema, Manchester, during the first showing of *Rock Around the Clock*. . . . He had been trying to stop a mob of youths from "jiving" on stage in front of the screen where they had climbed to get away from the attendants and the police. . . . Young people at the back of the cinema, when they were not giving vent to their emotion by stretching their arms out to the screen like savages drunk with coconut wine at a tribal sacrifice . . . chanted the songs and banged the persistent beat. ("Frenzied fans," 1956)

The otherness of youth, perceived to have "turned sharply from the outlook of its elders . . . in its whole way of thinking, feeling and reacting" (Fyvel, 1961, p. 14), was in this way refracted through a colonial fantasy of black culture—the law of the jungle. The response, in the above account, to the unthinkable hedonism incited by rock 'n' roll, echoes a racist mythology of orgiastic pleasure and bacchanalian excess, which formed the rhetoric of British imperialism in its incursion into the "Heart of Darkness." Yet, while the public reaction to rock 'n' roll in 1956 served to briefly displace newly resurrected hostilities with the arrival of black (mainly Afro-Caribbean) immigrants in Britain, rock 'n' roll provided an imaginary space for white youth to identify and exalt the very physicality that the press sought to vilify; to appropriate blackness as a signifier of their own difference and symbolically place themselves at the margins of their own culture.

The celebration of black rock 'n' roll performers in the pop journalism of Nik Cohn (1989), which claims that white rockers, bar Elvis, were generally less impressive than their black counterparts, provides a textual space in which to examine the meaning of the black image as object of the white gaze. Much of the language that Cohn uses to describe his favorite black rock 'n' rollers reproduces the hegemonic stereotyping of the black man: Carl Gardner from The Coasters is described as a "natural born hustler." Chuck Berry displays the "smoothness and the cool of a steamboat gambler" and Fats Domino exhibits a "lazy" and "good-humoured" avuncularity. While Cohn champions the black presence in rock 'n' roll, the terms in which he describes the appeal of these artists reiterate the ideological construction of black masculinities, young and old—from the street-wise ghetto cool of the maverick black hipster to the droll affability of Uncle Tom.

For Cohn the originality and excitement of rock 'n' roll lay in (a) the sexuality and aggression that displaced the "mushiness" of white music, and (b) its ability to function as a private "teen code," which was incomprehensible to adults. It is significant that in these terms the essential attraction of rock 'n' roll echoes the white fascination in black masculinity, where the rampant hypersexuality of the black machismo meets the subterranean homosociality of black kinship, street talk, and brother love. However, if the white consumption of the black image generally fixed the black performer in a mythology of super-masculinity, this ideological containment was not absolute. The most striking resistance to this stereotyping was to be realized through the phenomenon of Little Richard, who was particularly popular in Britain in the mid-fifties:

> He looked beautiful. He wore a baggy suit with Elephant trousers, twenty-six inches at the bottom, and he had his hair back-combed in a monstrous plume like a fountain. Then he had a little toothbrush moustache and a round totally ecstatic face. . . . He'd scream and scream and scream. He had a freak voice, tireless, hysterical, completely indestructible. (Cohn, 1989, p. 74)

Little Richard was quite literally "something else": a black performer who transcended the traditional codification of the black man, defying assimilation into a white imaginary where black masculinity is the natural embodiment of untrammeled heterosexual desire. The manic energy of the "freak voice," the senseless scream, is paralleled at a visual level in the sublime confusion of conflicting sexual signifiers: the "monstrous plume" belies the zoot suit; eyeliner and mascara contradict the pencil-thin moustache. While the frantic intensity of Little Richard's showmanship singled him out as a unique performer, it was the "look" that signaled the spectacle of an ambivalent sexual identity, playing the hyperactivity of "the wildman of rock and roll" against the burlesque of "the Bronze Liberace."

Moving into the space of the British pop scene in the late eighties and early nineties, a number of images of black masculinity have displaced the archetypal sexuality of the hipster, as artists like Michael Jackson, George Benson, and Luther Vandross have, as Mercer and Julien note (1988), explored the "softer side" of black sexuality. At the same time as these artists have explored emotional and sensitive versions of masculinity (for which many have been subject to allegations of compromising their cultural and sexual identity), the late eighties saw the rise of Rap and Hip-Hop in Britain as Run D.M.C., Public Enemy, and Tone Loc advanced a radically different form of black identity, based on a sometimes politicized version of black machismo. With roots in the

Bronx, Rap and Hip-Hop represent a more traditional imaging of black urban masculinity for white subculture, where the male bonding of the street crew combines with misogyny ("That Girl Is a Slut") and phallic egoism ("Dick Almighty").

Beyond both these forms of black masculinity, represented at their extremes by Michael Jackson and N.W.A., it is Prince who, more than any other black performer, has magically circumvented the fixity of sexual identity—black or white. In the tradition of Little Richard, Sly Stone, and David Bowie, Prince represents an ambivalent and open-ended sexuality, being "anything he or we want him to be" (Reynolds, 1990, p. 50). Polymorphously exploring a field of undifferentiated desires in his songwriting ("Sister," "Jack U Off," "If I Was Your Girlfriend") Prince frames himself as an object of desire, whether pictured on the cover of "Dirty Mind" in mac, knickers, suspenders, and ankle boots; or in classically feminine passivity in his nude pose on the cover of "Love-sexy." The games that Prince plays with the imaging of sexual difference emerge in a ludicrous spectacle of masculinity—Gay? Androgynous? Transvestite? Bisexual?—suspending desire and identity in the uncertain irony of surface, masquerade, and simulation.

Ad(dressing) Desires

To fully assess the significance of these fragments of the American Imaginary, we need to move from a discussion of the text of the image, to the dialectic of the gaze, and the process of identification.

The psychoanalytic model of the mirror phase provides a means of theorizing this relation between British youth and the American media around questions of desire and identity. In its original formulation by Jacques Lacan, the mirror phase marks the inauguration of the Imaginary as the infant (a non-subject) perceives, identifies, and merges with the image: either its specular like or the real presence of an/other, which provides the fiction of bodily unity and autonomy. In the Imaginary relation of the mirror phase, "there is only identity and presence . . . no sense of separate self since the self is always alienated in the other" (Moi, 1985, pp. 99-100).

The constitution of proper subjectivity is effected when the child takes its place in the language of the *symbolic order*, where the representation of self necessitates the recognition of difference—the other. It is with the repression of imaginary plenitude, the infantile absorption in the other, that the subject is fractured into lack: the primal repression, which opens up the unconscious and the endless displacement of desire. So, while the *symbolic order* calls for the essential fixity of self, the legacy of the Imaginary remains in the flux of desire and the want of the other.

In this sense the psychoanalytic account of subjectivity provides a particularly fruitful approach to film, music, and fashion as the privileged space of imaginary relations, where the cultural ordering of difference and identity is eclipsed by the "image as a means to regain visual access to the lost object" (Pollock, 1988, p. 147)—where the self slides into the other. The spectacle of the postwar (p)leisure industry, dominated by the American image, can in this sense be seen to market a form of specular bliss, the return of the repressed, through the desire for identification with the screen-like, where "The question of identity is never the affirmation of a pre-given identity, never a self-fulfilling prophecy, it is always the product of an image of identity and the transformation of the subject in assuming the image" (Bhabha, 1986, p. xvi).

The psychoanalytic notion of identity, which represents the decentered subject as an effect of identification, finds its tangible expression in the philosophy of modern fashion, which consciously constructs and markets the self in the consumption of the "image" and the "look." The birth of modern fashion in this sense coincides with the popularization of the American Imaginary as the rapture of the transatlantic gaze foregrounds the desire to identify with, and reconstruct oneself in, the image of American stars.

The transatlantic influence on British fashion manifested itself in the transformation of Britain's first postwar folk devils: the teds. Emerging in South London in the early fifties, the teddy boys represented the public face of youthful differences through the spectacle of style, forming a readily identifiable look based on a working-class appropriation of aristocratic Edwardian dress: waisted jacket with narrow lapels, slim-fitted trousers, embroidered waistcoat, toe-capped shoes, shirts with cutaway collars, and knitted ties worn with a Windsor knot. The ted uniform soon underwent subtle transformations as the style became embellished with American signifiers, such as string ties and Western belts drawn from the Hollywood gunfighters. When, in the late summer of 1956, the screening of *Rock Around the Clock* brought rock 'n' roll to the attention of British youth, the ted style was further subject to transatlantic influences: swapping the somber hues of the Edwardian suit for red, green, and pink; donning those legendary blue suede "creepers";

sculpting the heavily greased "D.A." hairstyle with its exaggerated sideburns. The popularization of rock 'n' roll in this way effectively marked the demise of the original teddy boy subculture, as working-class teenage fashion attempted to recreate the image of transatlantic icons Elvis Presley, James Dean, Eddie Cochran, and their sanitized British counterparts, Cliff Richard and Billy Fury. Thus the American media's influence on British youth style, which had been limited to the Edwardian excess of the original teddy boys, saw the development of a popular market founded on the "American Look" and the reciprocal pleasures of looking (voyeurism) and being looked at (narcissism).

The Male Gaze

The relation between the gaze of the male spectator and its male object has been theoretically addressed in Laura Mulvey's (1975) key essay, "Visual Pleasure and Narrative Cinema," which postulates that the ideology of patriarchy ensures that "the male figure cannot bear the burden of sexual objectification. Man is reluctant to gaze at his exhibitionist like. . . . A male movie star's glamorous characteristics are thus not those of the erotic object of the gaze, but those of the more perfect, more complete, ideal ego conceived in the original moment of recognition in front of the mirror" (Mulvey, 1975, p. 12).

While Mulvey's thesis has been subject to criticism and revision, the logic of the male gaze prevails in various contemporary discussions of masculinities and men's relation to pop and fashion, reducing the consumption of images of men to the *desire for identification*. The problems with this conceptualization of the male gaze are twofold: (a) the hetero-centrism of its "repressive hypothesis" (Foucault, 1979), which approaches homosexual desire as the barred subtext of the image; and (b) perhaps more crucially the very dichotomy that psychoanalysis preserves between homosexuality and heterosexuality as mutually exclusive. Instead of thinking of the spectacle of film, pop, and fashion as complicit with the hegemony of sexual difference, we conceptualize this popular imaginary as a space in which fantasy can unfix the status of sexual identity, collapsing the binary oppositions between masculine/feminine, homo/hetero, and narcissism/voyeurism into polymorphous desires. It is precisely in this sense that there is no text of masculinity. In the imaginary, the dialectic of the gaze, there is always difference, where the subject is consumed and reproduced in and through a multiplicity of desires.

Masses of Connections

The turn of the century and the fifties are two particularly significant moments in the construction of the American Imaginary. In the first case the frontier was lost, film was born, and the frontier of film was created. The Western was an icon of this process. The possibility of the cultural masses was created; film retrieved the specular plenitude and lost space of the frontier—a first mirror phase of the masses.

The fifties were a different kind of cultural frontier, a new frontier of youth, and a new mass market. Rock 'n' roll and pop culture and fashion were icons of this process. The fifties presented a second mirror phase, generated both in contrast to and within the first, and in and through this frame further variations were elaborated, as, for example, between the teds and the "American Look."

Some of these connections persist now. The transatlantic gaze and the American Imaginary continue to construct one another. In addition, cultural changes, particularly around television, music, and video, appear to have assisted the fragmentation of age and masculinities. Contemporary reworkings of American classics in film, television, and advertising abound (the retro trend), both as references and as reformulations—in space adventures, technological thrillers, gangster and crime movies, fantasy and science fiction, dance and "teen" movies, fifties re-creations, and their television equivalents.

These are some of the masses of connections—between the cultural, historical, spatial, and psychological—in imaging American men.

Notes

1. This chapter is a development of the paper, "Representations and Images of Men and Masculinity in the Mass Media," presented at the Centre for the Study of Ageing/ *Theory, Culture and Society*, International Seminar at Teesside Polytechnic, August 1989.

2. These separations of *sex* and *gender*, *males* and *men*, themselves exist in culture.

3. For further discussion of these debates, see Hearn, 1989.

4. See, for example, Baudrillard, 1983, 1988; Eco, 1986; Kroker and Cook, 1988.

5. Relevant recent feminist commentaries include Weedon, 1987; Grosz, 1989.

6. Further discussion of the relationship of early film and masculinities are included in Hearn, 1988, 1992.

7. In this perspective, there is a continuing relationship between image/appearance and background/disappearance. The desert/horizon is the place/space of emptiness, beyond the frontier, the background to the image in the mirror.

8. Also see Fiedler, 1970, on the relation between black and white men in the American pastoral.

9. Analysis by way of "male sexual narratives" and "homosexual subtexts" has some affinity with the notions of voyeurism/scopophilia and narcissism, respectively (Freud, 1977; Wernick, 1987).

References

Abel, E., & Abel, E.K. (Eds.). (1983). *The signs reader: Women, gender and scholarship.* Chicago: University of Chicago Press.

Action Comics. (1990, November). New York: DC Comics

Allen, R., & Bielby, W. (1979). Blacks' attitudes and behaviors toward television. *Communication Research, 6*(4), 437-462.

Altheide, D. L., & Snow, R. P. (1979). *Media logic.* Beverly Hills, CA: Sage.

Althusser, L. (1971). *Lenin and philosophy* (B. Brewster, Trans.). London: Monthly Review.

Altman, R. (1987). Television sound. In H. Newcomb (Ed.), *Television: The critical view* (4th ed.) (pp. 566-584). New York: Oxford University Press.

Amazing Spider-Man. (1990). Issues number 340, 341, 342. New York: Marvel Comics.

Anderson, C. (1987). Reflections on "Magnum, P.I." In H. Newcomb (Ed.), *Television: The critical view* (4th ed.) (pp. 112-125). New York: Oxford University Press.

Andrea, T. (1987). From menace to messiah: The history and historicity of Superman. In D. Lazere (Ed.), *American media and mass culture* (pp. 124-138). Berkeley: University of California Press.

Aronowitz, S. (1989). Working class culture in the electronic age. In I. Angus & S. Jhally (Eds.), *Cultural politics in contemporary America* (pp. 135-150). New York: Routledge.

Atkin, C. K. (1987). Alcoholic-beverage advertising: Its content and impact. *Advances in Substances Abuse (Suppl.) 1,* 267-287.

Atwood, R., & McLean, P. (1983, May). *Demographics, system constraints and sense making: An exploration of information seeking and use.* Paper presented at the International Communication Association Convention, Dallas, TX.

Aufderheide, P. (1986). The look of the sound. In T. Gitlin (Ed.), *Watching television* (pp. 111-135). New York: Pantheon.

August, E. (1985). *Men's studies: A selected and annotated interdisciplinary bibliography.* Littleton, CO: Libraries Unlimited.

Balswick, J. O., & Peek, C. W. (1976). The inexpressive male: A tragedy of American society. In D. S. David & R. Brannon (Eds.), *The forty-nine percent majority: The male sex role* (pp. 55-57). Boston: Addison-Wesley.

Barcus, F. E. (1983). *Images of life on children's television: Sex roles, minorities and families.* New York: Praeger.

Barkley, R. A., Ullman, D. G., Otto, L., & Brecht, J. M. (1977). The effects of sex typing and sex appropriateness of model behavior on children's imitation. *Child Development, 48,* 721-725.

Barthel, D. (1988). *Putting on appearances: Gender and advertising.* Philadelphia: Temple University Press.

Barthes, R. (1972). *Mythologies* (A. Lavers, Ed. and Trans.). New York: Hill & Wang. (Original work published 1957).

Barthes, R. (1974). *S/Z* (R. Miller, Trans.). New York: Hill & Wang.

Barthes, R. (1975). *Pleasure of the text* (R. Miller, Trans.). New York: Hill & Wang.

Basinger, J. (1986). *The World War II combat film: Anatomy of a genre.* New York: Columbia University Press.

Batman. (1990). Issue number 456. New York: DC Comics.

Baudrillard, J. (1970). *La societé de consommation: Ses mythes, ses structures* [Consumer society: Its myths, its structures]. Paris: S.G.P.P.

Baudrillard, J. (1983). *Simulacra and simulations* (P. Foss, P. Patton, & P. Bertchman, Trans.). New York: Semiotext(e). (Originally published 1981).

Baudrillard, J. (1988). *America* (C. Turner, Trans.). London & New York: Verso.

Baumrind, D. (Ed.). (1973). Authorization vs. authoritative parental control. In M. Scarr-Salapatek & P. Salapatek (Eds.), *Socialization.* Columbus, OH: Charles Merrill.

Bellah, R. N., Madsen, R., Sullivan, W., Swidler, A., & Tipton, S. (1986). *Habits of the heart: Individualism and commitment in American life.* New York: Harper & Row.

Bennett, T., & Woollacott, J. (1987). *Bond and beyond: The political career of a popular hero.* New York: Methuen.

Bennett, W. L. (1983). *News: The politics of illusion.* New York: Longman.

Berry, G. (1982). Research perspectives on the portrayals of Afro-American families on television. In A. Jackson (Ed.), *Black families and the medium of television.* Ann Arbor: University of Michigan Press.

Bersani, L. (1987). Is the rectum a grave? *October 43,* 197-222.

Bhabha, H. (1986). Foreword in F. Fannon (Ed.), *Black skin, white masks* (C. Lom, Trans.). London: Pluto.

Blue, C. (Ed.). (1989). Structuralist analysis: Bill Cosby and recording ethnicity. In M. Real, *Super media: A cultural studies approach.* London: Sage.

Boehm, H. (1984, September). Superheroes, super sellers. *Madison Avenue,* pp. 16, 18.

Boutilier, M. A., & SanGiovanni, L. (1983). *The sporting woman.* Champaign, IL: Human Kinetics.

Bowser, B., & Hunt, R. (1981). *Impact of racism on white Americans.* Beverly Hills, CA: Sage.

Brabant, S., & Mooney, L. (1986). Sex role stereotyping in the Sunday comics: Ten years later. *Sex Roles, 14*(3/4), 141-148.

Bretl, D. J., & Cantor, J. (1988). The portrayal of men and women in U.S. television commercials: A recent content analysis and trends over 15 years. *Sex Roles, 18*(9/10), 595-609.

Brittan, A. (1989). *Masculinity and power.* New York: Basil Blackwell.

Britton, A. (1983). *Cary Grant: Comedy and male desire.* Newcastle upon Tyne: Tyneside Cinema.

Brod, H. (1987). Introduction: Themes and theses of men's studies. In H. Brod (Ed.), *The making of masculinities: The new men's studies.* Boston: Allen & Unwin.

Brooks, T., & Marsh, E. (1981). *The complete directory to prime time network TV shows: 1946-present* (rev. ed.). New York: Ballantine.

Brooks-Gunn, J., & Schempp, W. (1979). *He & she: How children develop their sex-role identity.* Englewood Cliffs, NJ: Prentice-Hall.

Broughton, I. (Ed.). (1986). *Producers on producing: The making of film and television.* Jefferson, NC: McFarland.

Brown, D., & Bryant, J. (1990). The manifest content of pornography. In D. Zillman & J. Bryant (Eds.), *Pornography: Research advances and policy considerations* (pp. 25-56). Hillsdale, NJ: Lawrence Erlbaum.

Brown, J. D., & Campbell, K. (1986). Race and gender in music videos: The same beat but a different drummer. *Journal of Communication, 36*(1), 94-106.

Brown, M. E. (1990). *Television and women's culture: The politics of the popular.* Newbury Park, CA: Sage.

Browne, N. (1984). The political economy of the television (super) text. *Quarterly Review of Film Studies 9*(3), 175-182.

Brownlow, K. (1973). *The parade's gone by . . . .* London: Abacus.

Bryson, L. (1990). Challenges to male hegemony in sport. In M. A. Messner & D. Sabo, *Sport, men, and the gender order: Critical feminist perspectives* (pp. 173-184). Champaign, IL: Human Kinetics.

Buck, E. B., & Newton, B. (1989). Research on the study of television and gender. In B. Dervin & M. Voigt (Eds.), *Progress in communication sciences, Vol. IX* (pp. 1-41). Norwood, NJ: Ablex.

Budd, M., Craig, S., & Steinman, C. (1983). "Fantasy Island": Marketplace of desire. *Journal of Communication, 33*(1), 67-77.

Budd, M., Entman, R., & Steinman, C. (1990). The affirmative character of U.S. cultural studies. *Critical Studies in Mass Communication, 7*, 169-184.

Bukatman, S. (1988). Paralysis in motion: Jerry Lewis's life as a man. *Camera Obscura, 17*, 195-205.

Busby, L. J. (1985). The mass media and sex-role socialization. In J. R. Dominick & J. E. Fletcher (Eds.), *Broadcasting research methods* (pp. 267-295). Boston: Allyn & Bacon.

Butler, J. (1990). *Gender trouble: Feminism and the subversion of identity.* New York: Routledge.

Butler, M., & Paisley, W. (1980). *Women and the mass media: Sourcebook for research and action.* New York: Human Sciences.

Butsch, R. (1991). *Class and gender in four decades of TV families: Plus ça change. . . .* Unpublished manuscript.

Cantor, M. (1980). *Prime-time television: Content and control.* Beverly Hills, CA: Sage.

Cantor, M. G. (1990). Prime-time fathers: A study in continuity and change. *Critical Studies in Mass Communication, 7*(3), 275-285.

Caputo, P. (1978). *A rumor of war.* New York: Ballantine.

Carpenter, R. H. (1990). America's tragic metaphor: Our twentieth-century combatants as frontiersmen. *Quarterly Journal of Speech, 9*, 1-22.

Carrigan, T., Connell, B., & Lee, J. (1987). Hard and heavy: Toward a new sociology of masculinity. In M. Kaufman (Ed.), *Beyond patriarchy: Essays by men on pleasure, power and change* (pp. 139-192). Toronto: Oxford University Press.

Cashmore, E. E. (1984). *No future: Youth and society.* London: Heinemann.

Chambers, I. (1985). *Urban rhythms: Pop music and popular culture.* New York: St. Martin's Press.

Chapman, R., & Rutherford, J. (Eds.). (1988). *Male order: Unwrapping masculinity.* London: Lawrence & Wisehart.

Check, J.V.P., & Guloien, T. H. (1989). Reported proclivity for coercive sex following repeated exposure to sexually violent pornography, nonviolent dehumanizing pornography, and erotica. In D. Zillman & J. Bryant (Eds.), *Pornography: Research advances and policy considerations* (pp. 159-184). Hillsdale, NJ: Lawrence Erlbaum.

Cheles-Miller, P. (1975). Reactions to marital roles in commercials. *Journal of Advertising Research, 15*(4), 45-49.

Chodorow, N. (1978). *The reproduction of mothering: Psychoanalysis and the sociology of gender.* Berkeley: University of California Press.

Christenson, P. G., & Peterson, J. B. (1988). Genre and gender in the structure of music preference. *Communication Research 15*(3), 282-302.

Christenson, S., & Redmond, S. (1990, July/August). The image. *American Photography,* p. 82.

Coakley, J. J. (1986). *Sport in society: Issues and controversies.* St. Louis: Times Mirror/Mosby.

Cobb, N., Stevens-Long, J., & Goldstein, S. (1982). The influence of televised models on toy preference in children. *Sex Roles, 8*(10), 1075-1080.

Cohn, N. (1989). *Ball the wall: Nik Cohn in the age of rock.* London: Picador.

Comstock, G., & Cobbey, R. (1979). Television and the children of ethnic minorities. *Journal of Communication, 29*(1), 104-115.

Condit, C. M. (1989). The rhetorical limits of polysemy. *Critical Studies in Mass Communication 6*(2), 103-122.

Connell, R. W. (1987). *Gender and power: Society, the person and sexual politics.* Palo Alto, CA: Stanford University Press.

Connell, R. W. (1990). *Love fast and die young: The construction of masculinity among young working-class men on the margin of the labour market.* Unpublished manuscript, Department of Sociology, Macquarie University, Australia.

Considine, J. D. (1990, April). The sons of Aerosmith. *Metal Musician,* p. 62.

Copeland, G. A. (1989). Face-ism and primetime television. *Journal of Broadcasting and Electronic Media, 33*(2), 209-214.

Cordua, G. D., McGraw, K. O., & Drabman, R. S. (1979). Doctor or nurse: Children's perception of sex-typed occupations. *Child Development, 50,* 590-593.

Corrigan, M. (1972). *Societal acceptance of the female athletes as seen through the analysis of content of a sports magazine.* Unpublished manuscript (cited in Boutlier & SanGiovanni, 1983).

Courtney, A. E., & Whipple, T. W. (1974). Women in TV commercials. *Journal of Communication, 24*(2), 110-118.

Craig, S. (1987, March). *Marketing American masculinity: Mythology and flow in the Super Bowl telecasts.* Paper presented at the annual meeting of the Popular Culture Association, Montreal.

Craig, S. (1990, November). *The male image in network television commercials: A content analysis comparing three day parts.* Paper presented at the convention of the Speech Communication Association, Chicago, IL.

Crain, M. (1989). Home, home on the remote: Is male fascination with TV technology creating male domination of family entertainment? *Media & Values, 48,* 2-5.

Crescenti, P., & Columbe, B. (1985). *The official Honeymooners treasury.* New York: Perigee.

Dates, J. (1980). Race, racial attitudes and adolescent perceptions of black television characters. *Journal of Broadcasting, 24*(4) 549-560.

David, D. S., & Brannon, R. (Eds.). (1976). *The forty-nine percent majority: The male sex role*. Boston: Addison-Wesley.

Davies, B., & Harré, R. (1990). Positioning: The discursive production of selves. *Journal for the Theory of Social Behavior, 20*(1), 43-63.

Davis, J. (1982). Sexist bias in eight newspapers. *Journalism Quarterly, 59*(3), 456-460.

De Lauretis, T. (1987). The technology of gender. In T. De Lauretis (Ed.), *Technologies of gender: Essays on theory, film and fiction* (pp. 1-30). Bloomington: Indiana University.

Deem, R. (1988). "Together we stand, divided we fall": Social criticism and the sociology of sport and leisure. *Sociology of Sport Journal, 5*(4), 342-354.

Denski, S. (1990). *An examination of popular music preferences and functions by the contemporary popular music audience.* Unpublished doctoral dissertation, Ohio University.

Denski, S. (1992). Music, musicians, and communication: A personal voice in a common language. In J. Lull (Ed.), *Popular music and communication* (2nd ed., pp. 33-48). Newbury Park, CA: Sage.

Dervin, E., Grossberg, L., O'Keefe, B. J., & Wartella, E. (1989). *Rethinking communication* (vols. 1 & 2). Newbury Park, CA: Sage.

Detective Comics. (1990). Issues number 622, 623. New York: DC Comics.

Doane, M. A., Mellencamp, P., & Williams, L. (1984). Feminist film criticism: An introduction. In M. A. Doane, P. Mellencamp, & L. Williams (Eds.), *Re-vision: Essays in feminist film criticism* (pp. 1-15). Los Angeles: American Film Institute.

Dohrmann, R. (1975). A gender profile of children's educational TV. *Journal of Communication, 24*(2), 110-118.

Dominick, J. R. (1979). The portrayal of women in prime time, 1953-1977. *Sex Roles, 5*, 405-411.

Dominick, J. R., & Rauch, G. E. (1972). The image of women in network TV commercials. *Journal of Broadcasting, 16*, 259-265.

Donald, R. (1990). Conversion as persuasive convention in American war films. In P. Loukides & L. Fuller (Eds.), *Beyond the stars II: Plot convention in American popular film* (pp. 36-52). Bowling Green, OH: Popular Press.

Donnerstein, E., Linz, D., & Penrod, S. (1987). *The question of pornography: Research findings and policy implications*. New York: Free Press.

Donohue, T. (1975). Black children's perceptions of favorite television characters as models of anti-social behavior. *Journal of Broadcasting, 19*(2) 153-167.

Donohue, W., & Donohue, T. (1977). Black, white, white gifted and emotionally disturbed children's perceptions of the reality in television programming. *Human Relations, 30*(7), 609-621.

Downing, M. (1974). Heroine of the daytime serial. *Journal of Communication, 24*(2), 130-137.

Downs, A. C. (1981). Sex-role stereotyping on prime-time television. *The Journal of Genetic Psychology, 138*, 253-258.

Downs, A. C., & Gowan, D. C. (1980). Sex differences in reinforcement and punishment on prime-time television. *Sex Roles, 6*(5), 683-694.

Drabman, R., Robertson, S., Patterson, S. J., Jarvie, G. J., Hammer, D., & Cordua, G. (1981). Children's perception of media-portrayed sex roles. *Sex Roles, 7*, 379-389.

Drozdowski, T. (1990, April). Monsters of guitar. *Metal Musician*, p. 49.

Dubbert, J. (1979). *A man's place: Masculinity in transition*. Englewood Cliffs, NJ: Prentice-Hall.

Duck, S. (1983). *Friends for life: The psychology of close relationships*. New York: St. Martin's Press.

Duckworth, M., Lodder, L., Moore, M. O'D., Overton, S., & Rubin, J. (1990, July/August). The bottom line from the top down. *Columbia Journalism Review*, pp. 30-32.

Duncan, M. C., & Hasbrook, C. A. (1988). Denial of power in televised women's sports. *Sociology of Sport Journal, 5*, 1-21.

Duncan, M. C., & Messner, M. A., & Williams, L. (1990). *Gender stereotyping in televised sports*. Los Angeles: The Amateur Athletic Association of Los Angeles.

Durkin, K. (1985a). Television and sex-role acquisition 1: Content. *British Journal of Social Psychology, 24*, 101-113.

Durkin, K. (1985b). Television and sex-role acquisition 2: Effects. *British Journal of Social Psychology, 24*, 191-210.

Durkin, K., & Hutchins, G. (1984). Challenging traditional sex-role stereotypes via careers education broadcasts: The reactions of young secondary school pupils. *Journal of Educational Television, 10*, 211-222.

Dworkin, A. (1981). *Pornography: Men possessing women*. New York: Perigree.

Dyer, G. (1987). Women and television: An overview. In H. Baeher & G. Dyer (Eds.), *Boxed in: Women and television* (pp. 6-16). New York: Pandora.

Dyer, K. F. (1982). *Challenging the men*. New York: University of Queensland.

Dyer, R. (1982). Don't look now—the male pin-up. *Screen, 23*(3-4), 61-73.

Dyer, R. (Ed.). (1984). *Gays and film*. New York: Zoetrope.

Dyer, R. (1985). Male sexuality in the media. In A. Metcalf & M. Humphries (Eds.), *The sexuality of men* (pp. 28-43). London: Pluto.

Dyer, R. (1988). White. *Screen, 29*(4), 44-65.

Easthope, A. (1986). *What a man's gotta do: The masculine myth in popular culture*. London: Paladin/Grafton.

Ebert, T. (1988). The romance of patriarchy: Ideology, subjectivity, and postmodern feminist cultural theory. *Cultural Critique, 10*, 19-57.

Eco, U. (1986). *Travels in hyperreality*. London: Picador.

Edwards, H. (1969). *The revolt of the black athlete*. New York: Free Press.

Edwards, H. (1973). *The sociology of sport*. Homewood, IL: Dorsey.

Edwards, H. (1987). Race in contemporary American sports. In A. Yiannakis, T. McIntyre, M. Melnick, & D. Hart (Eds.), *Sport sociology: Contemporary issues* (pp. 194-197). Dubuque, IA: Kendall/Hunt.

Ehrenreich, B. (1983). *The hearts of men: American dreams and the flight from commitment*. New York: Anchor.

Eisenstock, B. (1984). Sex-role differences in children's identification with counter-stereotypical televised portrayals. *Sex Roles, 10*(5/6) 417-430.

Eisner, J., & Krinsky, D. (1984). *Television comedy series: An episode guide to 153 TV sitcoms in syndication*. Jefferson, NC: McFarland.

Eitzen, D. S. (1987). The educational experiences of intercollegiate student-athletes. *Journal of Sport and Social Issues, 11*(2), 15-30.

Eitzen, D. S., & Baca Zinn, M. (1989). The de-athleticization of women: The naming and gender marking of collegiate sport teams. *Sociology of Sport Journal, 6*, 362-370.

Ellison, R. E. (1964). *Shadow and act*. New York: Random House.

Epstein, C. F. (1988). *Deceptive distinctions: Sex, gender, and the social order*. New Haven: Yale University Press; New York: Russell Sage.

Fanon, F. (1970). *Black skin, white masks*. London: Paladin. (Original work published 1952.)

Fantastic Four. (1983, 1985). New York: Marvel Comics.

Farhi, P. (1988, November 9). For sale: A stable of superheroes. *Washington Post*, p. B1.

Farrell, W. (1974). *The liberated man*. New York: Random House.

Farrell, W. (1976). The politics of vulnerability. In D. S. David & R. Brannon (Eds.), *The forty-nine percent majority: The male sex role*. Boston: Addison-Wesley.

Fasteau, M. (1976). Vietnam and the cult of toughness in foreign policy. In D. S. David & R. Brannon (Eds.), *The forty-nine percent majority: The male sex role*. Boston: Addison-Wesley.

Fejes, F. (1989). Images of men in media research. *Critical Studies in Mass Communication, 6*(2), 215-221.

Ferrante, C. L., Haynes, A. M., & Kingsley, S. M. (1988). Images of women in television advertising. *Journal of Broadcasting and Electronic Media, 32*(2), 231-237.

Fiddick, T. (1989). Beyond the domino theory: Vietnam and metaphors of sport. *Journal of American Culture, 12*, 79-88.

Fiedler, L. (1970). *Love and death in the American novel*. London: Paladin.

Filene, P. (1986). *Him/her/self. Sex role in modern America* (2nd ed.). Baltimore/London: Johns Hopkins University Press.

Finn, T. A., & Strickland, D. (1982). A content analysis of beverage alcohol advertising, #2: Television advertising. *Journal of Studies on Alcohol, 43*, 964-989.

Finn, T. A., & Strickland, D. (1983). The advertising and alcohol abuse issue: A cross media comparison of alcohol beverage advertising content. In M. Burgeon (Ed.), *Communication yearbook* (pp. 850-872). Beverly Hills, CA: Sage.

Fiske, J. (1986). Television: Polysemy and popularity. *Critical Studies in Mass Communication 3*(4), 391-408.

Fiske, J. (1987a). *Television culture*. London: Methuen.

Fiske, J. (1987b). British cultural studies and television. In R. Allen (Ed.), *Channels of discourse* (pp. 254-289). Chapel Hill: University of North Carolina.

Fiske, J., & Hartley, J. (1978). *Reading television*. London: Methuen.

Flanagan, B. (1984, September). Heavy metal superheroes. *Musician*, p. 58.

Flitterman, S. (1985). Thighs and whiskers: The fascination of "Magnum, P.I." *Screen, 26*(2), 42-58.

Foley, D. E. (1990). The great American football ritual: Reproducing race, class, and gender inequality. *Sociology of Sport Journal, 7*(2), 111-135.

Foucault, M. (1979). *The history of sexuality. Volume one*. New York: Vintage. (Original work published 1976).

Foucault, M. (1980). *The history of sexuality, volume I: An introduction* (R. Hurley, Trans.). New York: Vintage.

Frayser, S. G. (1985). *Varieties of sexual experience: An anthropological perspective on human sexuality*. New Haven, CT: Human Relations Area Files Press, Inc.

Frenzied rock 'n' roll fans snatched up fire hoses. (1956, September 10). *Manchester Guardian*.

Freud, S. (1977). *On sexuality: Three essays on the theory of sexuality and other works* (A. Richards, Ed.). Harmondsworth, England: Penguin.

Freudiger, P., & Almquist, E. M. (1978). Male and female roles in the lyrics of three genres of contemporary music. *Sex Roles, 4*(1), 51-65.

Friesen, B. (1989, August). *Functional aspects of adolescent socialization through deviant subcultures: Field research in heavy metal*. Paper presented at a meeting of the American Sociological Association, San Francisco.

Frueh, T., & McGhee, P. E. (1975). Traditional sex-role development and amount of time spent watching television. *Developmental Psychology, 11*, 109.

Furnham, A., & Schofield, S. (1986). Sex-role stereotyping in British radio advertisements. *British Journal of Social Psychology, 25*, 165-171.

Furnham, A., & Voli, V. (1989). Gender stereotypes in Italian television advertising. *Journal of Broadcasting and Electronic Media, 33*(2), 175-185.

Fyvel, T. R. (1961). *The insecure offenders: Rebellious youth in the welfare state.* Harmondsworth, England: Penguin.

Gaines, J. (1986, Fall). White privilege and looking relations: Race and gender in feminist film theory. *Cultural Critique,* 59-79.

Galligher, M. (1989). A feminist paradigm for communication research. In E. L. Dervin, B. Dervin, L. Grossberg, B. O'Keefe, & E. Wartella (Eds.), *Rethinking communication, vol. 2: Paradigm exemplars* (pp. 75-87). Newbury Park, CA: Sage.

Galperin, W. (1988). Sliding off the stereotype: Gender difference in the future of television. In E. A. Kaplan (Ed.), *Postmodernism and its discontents* (pp. 146-162). London & New York: Verso.

Gans, H. (1979). *Deciding what's news.* New York: Vintage.

Garfinkel, P. (1985). *In a man's world: Father, son, brother, friend, and other roles men play.* New York: New American Library.

Gerbner, G. (1972). Violence in TV drama: Trends and symbolic functions. In G. A. Comstock & E. A. Rubinstein (Eds.), *TV and social behavior* (vol. 1). Washington DC: Government Printing Office.

Gerbner, G. (1977). Television: The new state religion? *Etcetera,* pp. 145-150.

Gerbner, G. (1989). A generalized graphic model of communication. In J. Corner & J. Hawthorn (Eds.), *Communication studies* (pp. 17-18). London: Edward Arnold. (Original work published 1956).

Gerbner, G. (1990). *Media, censorship and democratic values: Challenges for the 1990's.* Panel and workshop presentations, Muhlenberg College, Allentown, PA.

Gerbner, G., Gross, L., Morgan, M., & Signorelli, N. (1986). *Television's mean world: Violence profile, No. 14-15.* Philadelphia: The Annenberg School for Communications of Pennsylvania.

Gerzon, M. (1982). *A choice of heroes. The changing faces of American manhood.* Boston: Houghton Mifflin.

Gilbert, J. (1986). *A cycle of outrage.* New York: Oxford University Press.

Gilly, M. C. (1988). Sex role in advertising: A comparison of television advertisements in Australia, Mexico and the United States. *Journal of Marketing, 52,* 75-85.

Gitlin, T. (1983). *Inside prime time.* New York: Pantheon.

Gitlin, T. (1986). We build excitement. In T. Gitlin (Ed.), *Watching television* (pp. 136-156). New York: Pantheon.

Gitlin, T. (1987). Prime time ideology: The hegemonic process in television entertainment. In H. Newcomb (Ed.), *Television: The critical view* (pp. 507-532). New York: Oxford University Press.

Goffman, E. (1979). *Gender advertisements.* New York: Harper & Row. (Originally published 1976).

Goldin, M. (1990, January). Father time: Who's on the op-ed page? *Mother Jones,* p. 51.

Goldstein, R. (1990, December 18). Free MTV!: It's not the nipple. Madonna's new clip threatens the sexual order of music video. *Village Voice,* p. 52.

Gray, H. (1986). Television and the new black man: Black male images in prime-time situation comedy. *Media, Culture and Society, 9*(2), 223-242.

Green, I. (1984). Malefunction: A contribution to the debate on masculinity in the cinema. *Screen, 25*(4-5), 36-48.

Greenberg, B., & Atkin, C. (1978). *Learning about minorities from television.* Paper presented at the Association for Education in Journalism Convention, Seattle, WA.

Greenberg, B., & Neuendorf, K. (1980). Black family interactions on television. In B. Greenberg (Ed.), *Life on television: Content analysis of U.S. television drama* (pp. 173-181). Norwood, NJ: Ablex.

Greenberg, B., Richards, M., & Henderson, L. (1980). Trends in sex-role portrayal on television. In B. Greenberg (Ed.), *Life on television: Content analysis of U.S. television drama* (pp. 65-88). Norwood, NJ: Ablex.

Greenberg, B., Simmons, K., Hogan, L., & Atkin, C. (1980). The demographics of fictional TV characters. In B. Greenberg (Ed.), *Life on television: Content analysis of U.S. television drama* (pp. 35-46). Norwood, NJ: Ablex.

Greendorfer, S. (1983). Sport and the mass media: General overview. *Arena Review, 7*(2), 1-6.

Gregg, N. (1987). Relections on the feminist critique of objectivity. *Journal of Communication Inquiry, 11*(1), 8-18.

Gross, L. (1989). Out of the mainstream sexual minorities and the mass media. In E. Seiter, H. Borchers, G. Kreutzner, & E. Worth (Eds.), *Remote control: Television, audiences and cultural power* (pp. 130-149). London: Routledge.

Grossberg, L., & Treichler, P. (1987). Intersections of power: Criticism, television, gender. *Communication, 9*, 273-287.

Grosz, E. (1989). *Sexual supervisions: Three French feminists.* Sydney: Allen & Unwin.

Gruneau, R. S. (1983). *Class, sports, and social development.* Amherst: University of Massachusetts Press.

Gunter, B. (1986). *Television and sex role stereotyping.* London: John Libbey.

Hacker, G. A., Collins R., & Jacobson, M. (1987). *Marketing booze to blacks.* Washington, DC: Center for Science in the Public Interest.

Hacker, H. (1957). The new burdens of masculinity. *Marriage and Family Living, 19*, 231.

Hall, M. A. (1990). How should we theorize gender in the context of sport? In M. A. Messner & D. Sabo, *Sport, men, and the gender order: Critical feminist perspectives* (pp. 223-240). Champaign, IL: Human Kinetics.

Hall, S. (1980). Encoding/decoding. In S. Hall, D. Hobson, A. Lowe, & P. Willis (Eds.), *Culture, media, and language: Working papers in cultural studies, 1972-79* (pp. 128-138). London: Hutchinson.

Hall, S. (1982). Culture, the media and the ideological "effect." In J. Curran, M. Gurevitch, & J. Wollacott (Eds.), *Mass communication and society* (pp. 315-348). Beverly Hills, CA: Sage.

Hall, S. (1988). Brave new world. *Marxism Today*, pp. 24-29.

Hall, S. (1989). Ideology and communication theory. In B. Dervin, L. Grossberg, B. O'Keefe, & E. Wartella (Eds.), *Rethinking communication (vol. 1): Paradigm issues* (pp. 40-52). Newbury Park, CA: Sage.

Halperin, D. M. (1990). *One hundred years of homosexuality: And other essays on Greek love.* New York: Routledge.

Hanke, R. (1990). Hegemonic masculinity in *thirtysomething. Critical Studies in Mass Communication, 7*(3), 231-248.

Hansen, M. (1986). Pleasure, ambivalence, identification: Valentino and female spectatorship. *Cinema Journal, 25*(4), 6-32.

Harding, S. (1989). *The science question in feminism.* Ithaca, NY: Cornell University Press.

Hare, N. (1986, March). An interview. *The Crisis, 93*(3), 30-35, 45.

Hare, N., & Hare, J. (1984). *The endangered black family: Coping with the unisexualization and coming extinction of the black race.* San Francisco: Black Think Tank.

Hargreaves, J. A. (Ed.). (1982). *Sport, culture and ideology*. London: Routledge & Kegan Paul.

Harris, P. R., & Stobart, J. (1986). Sex role-stereotyping in British television advertisements at different times of the day: An extension and refinement of Manstead & McCulloch (1981). *British Journal of Social Psychology, 25*, 155-164.

Hartley, J. (1984). Encouraging signs: TV and the power of dirt, speech, and scandalous categories. In W. Rowlands & B. Watkins (Eds.), *Interpreting television: Current research perspectives* (pp. 119-141). Beverly Hills, CA: Sage.

Hartley, R. (1976). Sex-role pressures and the socialization of the male child. In D. S. David & R. Brannon (Eds.). *The forty-nine percent majority: The male sex role*. Boston: Addison-Wesley.

Hatchett, D. (1986). A conflict of reasons and remedies. *The Crisis, 93*(3), 36-41, 46-47.

Hearn, J. (1987). *The gender of oppression: Men, masculinity, and the critique of Marxism*. New York: St. Martin's Press.

Hearn, J. (1988, March). *Speaking the unspeakable: The historical development of organizations and men's sexuality in the public domain*. Paper presented at the British Sociological Association Annual Conference, Edinburgh, Scotland.

Hearn, J. (1989). Reviewing men and masculinities—or mostly boys' own papers. *Theory, Culture & Society, 6*(4), 665-689.

Hearn, J. (1992). *Men in the public eye. The construction and deconstruction of public men and public patriarchies*. London/New York: Unwin Hyman/Routledge.

Hearn, J., & Morgan, D. (Eds.). (1990). *Men, masculinities & social theory*. Boston: Unwin Hyman.

Heath, S. (1990). Representing television. In P. Mellencamp (Ed.), *Logics of television: Essays in cultural criticism* (pp. 267-302). Bloomington: Indiana University Press.

Henderson, L., & Greenberg, B. (1980). Sex typing of common behaviors on television. In B. Greenberg (Ed.), *Life on television: Content analysis of U.S. television drama* (pp. 89-96). Norwood, NJ: Ablex.

Henley, N. M. (1987). The new species that seeks new language: On sexism in language and language change. In J. Penfield (Ed.), *Women and language in transition* (pp. 3-27). Albany: State University of New York Press.

Hennessee, J., & Nicholson, J. (May 28, 1972). NOW says: TV commercial insults women. *The New York Times Magazine*, pp. 13, 48-51.

Henry, W. (1987, April). That certain subject. *Channels*, p. 43f.

Hertsgaard, M. (1988). *On bended knee: The press and the Reagan presidency*. New York: Farrar, Straus & Giroux.

Hibbard, D. J., & Kaleialoha, C. (1983). *The role of rock*. Englewood Cliffs, NJ: Prentice-Hall.

Himmelstein, H. (1984). *The television myth and the American mind*. New York: Praeger.

Hinton, C. (1990, November 21). No more masculists, please! [Letter to the editor]. *San Francisco Sentinel*, p. 8.

Hoch, P. (1972). *Rip off the big game*. New York: Anchor.

Hoch, P. (1980). School for sexism. In D. F. Sabo, Jr., & R. Runfola, (Eds.), *Jock: Sports and male identity*. Englewood Cliffs, NJ: Prentice-Hall.

Howell, F., Miracle, A., & Rees, R. (1984). Do high school athletics pay? The effects of varsity participation on socioeconomic attainment. *Sociology of Sport Journal, 1*(1), 15-25.

Hoynes, W., & Croteau, D. (1989). *Are you on the "Nightline" guest list?* New York: Fairness & Accuracy in Reporting.

Hyden, C., & McCandless, N. J. (1983). Men and women as portrayed in the lyrics of contemporary music. *Popular Music and Society, 9*(2), 19-26.

Irigaray, L. (1985). *Speculum de l'autre femme* [Speculum of the other woman] (G. Gill, Trans.). Ithaca, NY: Cornell University Press. (Original work published 1974).

Izod, J. (1988). *Hollywood and the box office 1895-1986*. London: Macmillan.

Jackson, D. Z. (1989, January 22). Calling the plays in black and white. *The Boston Globe*, pp. A30-A33.

Jacobson, M., Atkins, R., & Hacker, G. (1983). *The booze merchants: The inebriating of America*. Washington, DC: Center for Science in the Public Interest.

Jagger, A. (1983). *Feminist politics and human nature*. Totowa, NJ: Rowman & Allenheld.

Jansen, S. (1983). Power and knowledge: Towards a new critical synthesis. *Journal of Communication, 33*(3), 342-354.

Jansen, S. (1989). Gender and the information society: A socially structured silence. *Journal of Communication, 39*(3), 196-215.

Jansen, S. (1990). Feminist materialism: The challenge of dialogically-based theories of democracy. In *ERIC Clearinghouse on Reading and Communication Skills*. Bloomington: Indiana University Press.

Jardine, A. (1987). Men in feminism: Odor di uomo or compagnons de route? In A. Jardine & P. Smith (Eds.), *Men in feminism* (pp. 54-61). New York: Methuen.

Jeffords, S. (1989). *The remasculinization of America: Gender and the Vietnam war*. Bloomington: Indiana University Press.

Jenkins, H. (1988). Star trek rerun, reread, rewritten: Fan writing as textual poaching. *Critical Studies in Mass Communication 5*(2), 85-107.

Jhally, S. (1989). Cultural studies and the sports/media complex. In L. A. Wenner (Ed.), *Media, sports and society* (pp. 70-93). Newbury Park, CA: Sage.

Johnson, R. (1988, February). TV's top mom and dad. *Ebony*, pp. 29-34.

Johnson, S., & Christ, W. G. (1988). Women through time: Who gets covered? *Journalism Quarterly, 65*(4), 889-897.

Johnston, J., & Ettema, J. (1982). *Positive images: Breaking stereotypes with children's television*. Beverly Hills, CA: Sage.

Kalisch, P., & Kalisch, B. (1984). Sex-role stereotyping of nurses and physicians on prime-time television. *Sex Roles, 10*(7/8), 533-553.

Kane, M. (1988). Media coverage of the female athlete before, during, and after Title IX: *Sports Illustrated* revisited. *Journal of Sport Management, 2*, 87-99.

Kaplan, E. A. (1987). *Rocking around the clock: Music television, postmodernism & consumer culture*. London: Methuen.

Karras, A. (1985). The real men on TV—and the wimps. *TV Guide*, pp. 4-8.

Kaufman, M. (1987). *Beyond patriarchy: Essays by men on pleasure, power and change*. Toronto: Oxford University Press.

Keller, E. F. (1983). Feminism, science, and democracy. *Democracy, 3*(2), 50-58.

Kelly, R. (1981). *The Andy Griffith Show*. Winston-Salem, NC: John F. Blair.

Kimmel, M. (Ed.). (1987a). *Changing men: New directions in research on men and masculinity*. Newbury Park, CA: Sage.

Kimmel, M. (1987b). The contemporary "crisis" of masculinity in historical perspective. In H. Brod (Ed.), *The making of masculinities: The new men's studies* (pp. 121-153). Boston: Allen & Unwin.

Kimmel, M. (1987c). The cult of masculinity: American social character and the legacy of the cowboy. In M. Kaufman (Ed.), *Beyond patriarchy: Essays by men on power, pleasure and change* (pp. 235-249). Toronto: Oxford University Press.

Kimmel, M. (1987d). Rethinking "masculinity": New directions in research. In M. S. Kimmel (Ed.), *Changing men: New directions in research on men and masculinity* (pp. 9-24). Newbury Park, CA: Sage.

King, S. B. (1990). Sonny's virtues: The gender negotiations of *Miami Vice*. *Screen, 31*, 281-295.

Kitano, H. L. (1985). *Race relations*. Englewood Cliffs, NJ: Prentice-Hall.

Klapp, O. E. (1962). *Heroes, villains, and fools: The changing American character*. Englewood Cliffs, NJ: Prentice-Hall.

Kleinberg, S. (1987). The new masculinity of gay men, and beyond. In M. Kaufman (Ed.), *Beyond patriarchy: Essays by men on pleasure, power, and change* (pp. 120-138). Toronto: Oxford University Press.

Knill, B. J., Peach, M., Pursey, G., Gilpin, P., & Perloff, R. M. (1981). Still typecast after all these years: Sex role portrayals in television advertising. *International Journal of Women's Studies, 4*, 497-506.

Komisar, L. (1976). Violence and the masculine mystique. In D. S. David & R. Brannon (Eds.), *The forty-nine percent majority: The male sex role*. Boston: Addison-Wesley.

Kostelnik, M., Whiren, A., & Stein, L. (1986, May). Living with He-Man. *Young Children*, pp. 3-9.

Kroker, A., & Cook, D. (1988). *The postmodern scene: Excremental culture and hyper-aesthetics*. London: Macmillan.

Kuhn, A. (1982a). The body in the machine. In A. Kuhn (Ed.), *Women's pictures: Feminism and cinema* (pp. 109-128). London: Routledge & Kegan Paul.

Kuhn, A. (1982b). *Women's pictures: Feminism and cinema*. London: Routledge & Kegan Paul.

Kuhn, A. (1985). Lawless seeing. In A. Kuhn (Ed.), *The power of the image: Essays on representation and sexuality* (pp. 19-47). London: Routledge & Kegan Paul.

Kuhn, A. (1989). The body and cinema: Some problems for feminism. *Wide Angle 11*(4), 52-61.

Kuhn, T. (1974). *The structure of scientific revolutions*. Chicago: University of Chicago Press.

Lacan, J. (1977a). *Ecrits. A selection* (A. Sheridan, Trans.). London: Tavistock. (Original work published 1966).

Lacan, J. (1977b). *The four fundamental concepts of psychoanalysis* (A. Sheridan, Trans.). (Original work published 1973). London: Hogarth.

Lapchick, R., & Rodriguez, A. (1990). Professional sports: The 1990 racial report card. *Center for the Study of Sport in Society Digest, 2*(2), 4-5.

Lee, E., & Browne, L. (1981). Television uses and gratifications among black children, teenagers and adults. *Journal of Broadcasting, 25*(2), 203-207.

Lee, M., & Soloman, N. (1990). *Unreliable sources*. New York: Lyle Stuart.

Leed, E. (1989). Violence, death and masculinity. *Vietnam Generation, 1*, 168-189.

Leerhsen, C. (1990, Fall). This year's role model. *Newsweek* [Special Issue], pp. 44-47.

Legends of the Dark Knight. (1990). Issue number 12. New York. DC Comics.

Lehrer, J. (1989). The new man: That's entertainment. *Media & Values, 48*, 8-11.

Lemon, J. (1977). Women and blacks on prime-time television. *Journal of Communication, 27*, 70-74.

Lemon, J. (1978). Dominant or dominated? Women on prime time television. In G. Tuchman, A. K. Daniels, & J. Benet (Eds.), *Hearth and home: Images of women in the mass media* (pp. 51-68). New York: Oxford University Press.

Lever, J., & Wheeler, S. (1984). *The Chicago Tribune* sports page, 1900-1975. *Sociology of Sport Journal, 1*(4), 299-313.

Liebow, E. (1967). *Tally's corner*. Boston: Little, Brown.

Lippe, R., & Jacobowitz, F. (1986, Summer/Fall). Masculinity in the movies: *To Live and Die in L.A.. CineAction!*, pp. 35-44.

Lippman, J. (1991, February 7). Is "Cheers" worth $120 million? *Los Angeles Times*, pp. D1, D6.

Livingstone, S., & Green G. (1986). Television advertisements and the portrayal of gender. *British Journal of Social Psychology, 25*, 149-154.

Loeb, J. C. (1990). Rhetorical and ideological conservatism in *thirtysomething*. *Critical Studies in Mass Communications, 7*(3), 249-260.

Lovdal, L. T. (1989). Sex role messages in television commercials: An update. *Sex Roles, 21*(11/12), 715-724.

Lucas, J., & Real, M. (1984). *Olympic television: A descriptive history of the interdependence of media and sports in the Summer Olympic Games, 1956-1984*. Paper presented at the meetings of the American Alliance for Health, Physical Education, Recreation and Dance, Anaheim, CA.

Luebke, B. (1989). Out of focus; images of women and men in newspaper photographs. *Sex Roles, 20*(3/4), 121-133.

Lull, J. (1982). How families select television programs: A mass observational study. *Journal of Broadcasting, 26*, 801-811.

Lull, J. (1988). Constructing rituals of extension through family television viewing. In J. Lull (Ed.), *World families watch television* (pp. 237-259). Newbury Park, CA: Sage.

Lysonski, S. (1985). Role portrayals in British magazine advertisements. *European Journal of Marketing, 19*(7), 37-55.

Maccoby, E. (1990, April). Gender and relationships: A developmental account. *American Psychologist*, pp. 513-520.

MacDonald, J. (1987). *Who shot the sheriff? The rise and fall of the television Western*. New York: Praeger.

MacKinnon, C. (1987). A feminist/political approach: "Pleasures under patriarchy." In J. M. Geer & W. O'Donohue (Eds.), *Theories of human sexuality* (pp. 65-90). New York: Plenum.

Macklin, M. C., & Kolbe, R. H. (1983). Sex role stereotyping in children's advertising: Current and past trends. *Journal of Advertising, 13*(2), 34-42.

Malamuth, N., & Spinner, E. (1980). A longitudinal content analysis of sexual violence in the best-selling erotica magazines. *Journal of Sex Research, 16*, 226-237.

Manes, A., & Melnyk, P. (1974). Televised models of female achievement. *Journal of Applied Social Psychology, 4*(4), 365-374.

Mangan, J., & Walvin, J. (Eds.). (1987). *Manliness and morality: Middle class masculinity in Britain and America, 1800-1940*. Manchester, England: Manchester University Press.

Manstead, A., & McCulloch, C. (1981). Sex-role stereotyping in British television advertisements. *British Journal of Social Psychology, 20*, 171-180.

Maracek, J., Piliavin, J., Fitzsimmons, E., Krogh, E., Leader, E., & Trudell, B. (1978). Women as TV experts: The voice of authority? *Journal of Communication, 28*(1), 159-168.

Marc, D. (1990, December). TV rules: The making of the viewing class [Review of *Television and the crisis of democracy*, *Democracy and the mass media*, and *See how they run: Electing the president in the age of mediaocracy*.] *Voice Literary Supplement*, pp. 23-24.

Marchand, R. (1985). *Advertising the American dream: Making way for modernity, 1920-1940*. Berkeley: University of California Press.

Marchetti, G. (1989). Action-adventure as ideology. In I. Angus & S. Jhally (Eds.), *Cultural politics in contemporary America* (pp. 182-197). New York: Routledge.

Marx, K. (1976). The fetishism of commodities. In P. Connerton (Ed.), *Critical sociology: Selected readings* (pp. 73-89). Harmondsworth, England: Penguin.

Massé, M., & Rosenblum, K. (1988). Male and female created they them: The depiction of gender in the advertising of traditional women's and men's magazines. *Women's Studies International Forum, 11*(2) 127-144.

Matelski, M. (1985). Image and influence: Women in public television. *Journalism Quarterly, 62*(1), 147-150.

Matney, W., & Johnson, D. (1984, July). *America's black population: A statistical view, 1970-1982.* [U.S. Department of Commerce, Bureau of the Census Special Publication]. Washington, DC: Government Printing Office.

McAdoo, J. (1988). The roles of black fathers in the socialization of black children. In H. P. McAdoo (Ed.), *Black families*. Newbury Park, CA: Sage.

McAllister, M. (1990). Cultural argument and organizational constraint in the comic book industry. *Journal of Communication, 40*(1), 55-71.

McArthur, L., & Eisen, S. (1976). Television and sex-role stereotyping. *Journal of Applied Social Psychology, 6*(4), 329-351.

McArthur, L., & Resko, B. (1975). The portrayal of men and women in American television commercials. *The Journal of Social Psychology, 97*, 209-220.

McCormick, T. (1978). Machismo in media research: A critical review of research on violence and pornography. *Social Problems, 25*(5), 544-555.

McGhee, P. (1975). Television as a source of learning sex-role stereotypes. In S. Cohen & T. J. Comiskey (Eds.), *Child development: Contemporary perspectives*. Ithaca, IL: Peacock.

McGhee, P., & Frueh, T. (1980). Television viewing and the learning of sex-role stereotypes. *Sex Roles, 6*(2), 179-188.

McNeil, J. (1975). Feminism, femininity and the television series: A content analysis. *Journal of Broadcasting, 19*, 259-269.

Meehan, D. (1983). *Ladies of the evening: Women characters of prime-time television*. Metuchen, NJ: Scarecrow.

Meggesey, D. (1990, November). *A decade of agency: The challenge of changing sport*. Keynote address at the meeting of the North American Society for the Sociology of Sport, Denver, CO.

Meier, A., & Rudwick, E. (1970). *From plantation to ghetto*. New York: Hill & Wang.

Mellen, J. (1977). *Big bad wolves: Masculinity in the American film*. New York: Pantheon.

Mellencamp, P. (1985). Situation and simulation: An introduction to "I Love Lucy." *Screen, 26*(2), 30-40.

Melton, G., & Fowler, G. (1987). Female roles in radio advertising. *Journalism Quarterly, 64*(1), 145-149.

Mercer, K., & Julien, I. (1988). Race, sexual politics and black masculinity: A dossier. In R. Chapman & J. Rutherford (Eds.), *Male order: Unwrapping masculinity* (pp. 97-164). London: Lawrence & Wishart.

Messner, M. A. (1987). The meaning of success: The athletic experience and the development of male identity. In H. Brod (Ed.), *The making of masculinities: The new men's studies* (pp. 193-209). Boston: Allen & Unwin.

Messner, M. A. (1988). Sports and male domination: The female athlete as contested ideological terrain. *Sociology of Sport Journal, 5*(3), 197-211.

Messner, M. A., Duncan, M. C., & Jensen, K. (1990, November). *Separating the men from the girls: The gendering of televised sports.* Paper presented at the meeting of the North American Society for the Sociology of Sport, Denver, CO.

Messner, M. A., & Sabo, D. (1990). *Sport, men, and the gender order: Critical feminist perspectives.* Champaign, IL: Human Kinetics.

Meyer, B. (1980). The development of girls's sex-role attitudes. *Child Development, 51,* 508-514.

Meyers, R. (1980). *An examination of the male sex role model in prime time television commercials.* (ERIC Document Reproduction Service No. ED 208 437).

Michaelson, J. (1989, February 6). Koppel, producer challenge report, say show is a news program, not equal-access forum. *Los Angeles Times,* VI, pp. 1, 10.

Miles, B. (1975). *Channeling children: Sex stereotyping on prime-time TV.* Princeton, NJ: Women on Words and Images.

Miller, M. C. (1986). Deride and conquer. In T. Gitlin (Ed.), *Watching television* (pp. 183-228). New York: Pantheon.

Miller, M., & Reeves, B. (1976). Dramatic TV content and children's sex-role stereotypes. *Journal of Broadcasting, 20*(1), 35-50.

Miller, S. (1975). The content of news photos: Women's and men's roles. *Journalism Quarterly, 52*(1), 70-75.

Miller, S. (1983). *Men and friendship.* Boston: Houghton Mifflin.

Mills, C. W. (1956). *The power elite.* New York: Oxford University Press.

Mills, J. (1984). Self-posed behaviors of females and males in photographs. *Sex Roles, 10*(7/8), 633-637.

Modleski, T. (1982). *Loving with a vengeance: Mass produced fantasies for women.* New York: Methuen.

Modleski, T. (1988). *The women who knew too much: Hitchcock and feminist theory.* New York: Methuen.

Modleski, T. (1990). The incredible shrinking he(r)man: Male regression, the male body, and film. *differences: A Journal of Feminist Cultural Studies, 2*(2), 55-75.

Moi, T. (1985). *Sexual textual politics: Feminist literary theory.* London: Methuen.

Molotsky, I. (1989, September 10). Graduation rate of athletes below 20% at many schools. *The New York Times,* pp. 45-46.

Montgomery, K. (1981). Gay activists and the networks. *Journal of Communication, 31*(3), 49-57.

Morgan, M. (1982). Television and adolescents' sex-role stereotypes: A longitudinal study. *Journal of Personality and Social Psychology, 43*(5), 947-955.

Morley, D. (1986). *Family television: Cultural power and domestic leisure.* London: Comedia.

Morley, D. (1988). Domestic relations: The framework of family viewing in Great Britain. In J. Lull (Ed.), *World families watch television.* Newbury Park, CA: Sage.

Morrison, J. (1990, November 15). Morrison responds to critics. *San Francisco Sentinel,* p. 10.

Mosher, D. L., & Sirkin, M. (1984). Measuring a macho personality constellation. *Journal of Research in Personality, 18,* 150-163.

Mouffe, C. (1983). The sex/gender system and the discursive construction of women's subordination. In S. Hanninen & L. Paldan (Eds.), *Rethinking ideology: A Marxist debate* (pp. 39-143). New York: International General.

Mulvey, L. (1975). Visual pleasure and narrative cinema. *Screen, 16*(3), 6-18.

Mulvey, L. (1981). Afterthoughts on "Visual pleasure and narrative cinema" inspired by *Duel in the Sun. Framework, 15/16/17,* 12-15.

Mulvey, L. (1988). British feminist film theory's female spectators: Presence and absence. *Camera Obscura, 20-21*, 68-81.

Naisen, M. (1972 July/August). Sports and the American empire. *Radical America*, pp. 95, 96, 107-110.

A national disgrace and a challenge to American parents. (1940, October). *Childhood Education*, 56.

Neale, S. (1982). "Chariots of fire," images of men. *Screen, 23*(3-4), 47-53.

Neale, S. (1983). Masculinity as spectacle: Reflections on men and mainstream cinema. *Screen, 24*(6), 2-16.

NEC Survey. (1990a, Jan/Feb). *New England Comics Newsletter*.

NEC Survey. (1990b, Sept/Oct). *New England Comics Newsletter*.

Newcomb, H., & Alley, R. (1983). *The producer's medium: Conversations with creators of American TV*. New York: Oxford University Press.

New Mutants. (1985). New York: Marvel Comics.

Omi, M. (1988). In living color: Race and American culture. In I. Angus & S. Jhally (Eds.), *Cultural politics in contemporary America* (pp. 111-122) New York: Routledge.

O'Bryant, S., & Corder-Bolz, C. (1978a). The effects of television on children's stereotyping of women's work roles. *Journal of Vocational Behavior, 12*.

O'Bryant, S., & Corder-Bolz, C. (1978b). Black children's learning of work roles from television commercials. *Psychological Reports, 42*.

O'Connor, J. E. (1983). Introduction: Television and the historian. In J. E. O'Connor (Ed.), *American history/American television: Interpreting the video past* (pp. xiii-xliii). New York: Frederick Ungar.

O'Donnell, W., & O'Donnell, K. (1978). Update: Sex role messages in television commercials. *Journal of Communication, 28*(1), 156-158.

O'Donovan, D. (1988, January). *On femiphobia*. Paper presented at the National Conference on the Future of Academic Freedom: Context and Challenge, Gainesville, FL.

O'Sullivan, T., Hartley, J., Saunders, D., & Fiske, J. (1983). *Key concepts in communication*. London: Methuen.

Palys, T. S. (1986). Testing the common wisdom: The social content of video pornography. *Canadian Psychology, 27*, 22-35.

Pecora, N., & Gateward, F. (1989, October). *Superman as social conscience*. Paper presented at the Conference on Culture and Communication, Philadelphia, PA.

Peirce, K. (1989). Sex-role stereotyping of children and television: A content analysis of the roles and attributes of child characters. *Sociological Spectrum, 9*, 321-328.

Penley, C. (1988). Introduction—The lady doesn't vanish: Feminism and film theory. In C. Penley (Ed.), *Feminism and film theory* (pp. 1-24). New York: Routledge.

Penley, C., & Willis, S. (1988). Male trouble. *Camera Obscura, 17*, 4-5.

Perloff, R. (1977). Some antecedents of children's sex-role stereotypes. *Psychological Reports, 40*, 463-466.

Pettigrew, T. (1986). *Raising hell: The rebels in the movies*. London: Columbus.

Pleck, E., & Pleck, J. (1980). *The American man*. Englewood Cliffs, NJ: Prentice-Hall.

Pleck, J. (1982). *The myth of masculinity*. Cambridge: MIT Press.

Poindexter, P., & Stroman, C. (1981). Blacks and television: A review of the research literature. *Journal of Broadcasting, 25*(2) 103-122.

Pollock, G. (1988). *Vision and difference: Femininity, feminism and the histories of art*. London: Routledge.

Postman, N. (1979). *Teaching as a conserving activity*. New York: Delacorte.

Postman, N., Nystrom, C., Strate, L., & Weingartner, C. (1987). *Myths, men and beer: An analysis of beer commercials on broadcast television.* Falls Church, VA: AAA Foundation for Traffic Safety. (ERIC Document Reproduction Service No. ED 290 074).

Potter, W., & Ware, W., (1987). Traits of perpetrators and receivers of antisocial and prosocial acts on TV. *Journalism Quarterly, 64,* 382-391.

Press, A. (1989). Class and gender in the hegemonic process: Class differences in women's perceptions of television realism and identification with television characters. *Media, Culture, and Society, 11,* 229-251.

The Punisher. (1990). Issue number 42. New York. Marvel Comics.

The Punisher War Journal. (1990). Issue number 24. New York: Marvel Comics.

Radway, J. (1984). *Reading the romance: Women, patriarchy and popular literature.* Chapel Hill: University of North Carolina Press.

Radway, J. (1986). Identifying ideological seams: Mass culture, analytical method and political practice. *Communication 9*(1), 93-124.

Ragan, J. (1982). Gender displays in portrait photographs. *Sex Roles, 8*(1), 33-43.

Rainville, R., & McCormick, E. (1977). Extent of covert racial prejudice in pro football announcers' speech. *Journalism Quarterly, 54*(1), 20-26.

Rainwater, L. (1970). *Behind ghetto walls.* Chicago: Aldine.

Rak, D. S., & McMullen, L. (1987). Sex-role stereotyping in television commercials: A verbal response mode and content analysis. *Canadian Journal of Behavioral Science, 19,* 25-39.

Rakow, L. (1986). Rethinking gender research on communication. *Journal of Communication, 36*(4), 11-26.

Rakow, L. (1987). Looking to the future: Five questions for gender research. *Women's Studies in Communication, 10,* 79-86.

Rakow, L. (1990). Feminist perspectives on popular culture. In J. Downing, A. Mohammadi, & A. Sreberny-Mohammadi (Eds.), *Questioning the media: A critical introduction* (pp. 231-241). Newbury Park, CA: Sage.

Raso, A. (1990, May 31). Despite the headaches, Skid Row's not complaining. *Circus,* p. 39.

Reid, P. (1979). Racial stereotyping on television: A comparison of the behavior of both black and white television characters. *Journal of Applied Psychology, 64,* 465-471.

Reiss, D. (1983). *M*A*S*H: The exclusive, inside story of TV's most popular show.* Indianapolis: Bobbs-Merrill.

Reist, N., & Casey, B. C. (1989, May). *Where have all the heroes gone? An analysis of the role of myth in speed metal and the Grateful Dead.* Paper presented at a meeting of the International Communication Association, San Francisco.

Reynolds, S. (1990). *Blissed out: The raptures of rock.* London: Serpent's Tail.

Rhode, E. (1976). *A history of the cinema from its origins to 1970.* London: Allen Lane.

Riemer, J. (1987). Rereading American literature from a men's studies perspective: Some implications. In H. Brod (Ed.), *The making of masculinities: The new men's studies* (pp. 289-299). Boston: Allen & Unwin.

Riesman, D. (1950). *The lonely crowd.* New Haven: Yale University Press.

Roberts, C. (1975). The presentation of blacks in television network newscasts. *Journalism Quarterly, 54,* 50-55.

Robinson, M. (1988). *Superman: Changing to meet the 1980's.* Unpublished manuscript, University of Maryland, College Park.

Rodowick, D. (1982). The difficulty of difference. *Wide Angle, 5*(1), 4-15.

Rogers, E. (1989). Communication: A field of isolated islands of thought. In E. Dervin, L. Grossberg, B. O'Keefe, & E. Wartella (Eds.), *Rethinking communication, Vol. 1: Paradigm issues* (pp. 209-210). Newbury Park, CA: Sage.

Rose, J. (1982). Introduction—II. In J. Mitchell & J. Rose (Eds.), *Feminine sexuality. Jacques Lacan and the ecole freudienne* (pp. 27-57). London: Macmillan.

Rosner, D. (1989). The world plays catch-up. *Sportsinc: The Sports Business Weekly, 1*(1), 6-13.

Ross, A. (1989). The popularity of pornography. In A. Ross (Ed.) *No respect: Intellectuals and popular culture* (pp. 171-208). New York: Routledge.

Rowland, M. (1990, April). If Guns N' Roses are outlawed. *Metal Musician*, p. 32.

Rubin, L. (1985). *Just friends: The role of friendship in our lives.* New York: Harper & Row.

Rugfiero, J., & Weston. L. (1985). Work options for women in women's magazines: The medium and the message. *Sex Roles, 12*, 535-547.

Russo, V. (1987). *The celluloid closet: Homosexuality in the movies.* New York: Harper & Row.

Sabo, D. (1990, November). *Boring from within: The problem of praxis within sport sociology.* Paper presented at the meeting of the North American Society for the Sociology of Sport, Denver, CO.

Sabo, D., Melnick, M., & Vanfossen, B. (1989, November). *The effects of interscholastic athletic participation on postsecondary educational and occupational mobility: A focus on gender and race.* Paper presented at the meeting of the North American Society for the Sociology of Sport, Washington, DC.

Sabo, D., & Panepinto, J. (1990). Football ritual and the social reproduction of masculinity. In M. A. Messner & D. Sabo (Eds.), *Sport, men and the gender order* (pp. 115-126). Champaign, IL: Human Kinetics.

Sabo, D., & Runfola, R. (Eds.). (1980). *Jock: Sports and male identity.* Englewood Cliffs, NJ: Prentice-Hall.

Sabo, D., & The Women's Sports Foundation. (1989). *The women's sports foundation report: Minorities in sports.* New York: The Women's Sports Foundation.

Sage, G. (1990). *Power and ideology in American sport.* Champaign, IL: Human Kinetics.

Said, E. (1978). *Orientalism.* New York: Pantheon.

Saucier, K. (1986). Healers and heartbreakers: Images of women and men in country music. *Journal of Popular Culture, 20*(3), 147-166.

Saunders, C., & Stead, B. (1986). Women's adoption of a business uniform: A content analysis of magazine advertisement. *Sex Roles, 15*(3/4), 197-205.

Saussure, F. de. (1974). *Course in general linguistics.* London: Fontana.

Schechtman, S. (1978). *Occupational portrayal of men and women on the most frequently mentioned television shows of preschool children.* Resource in Education (ERIC Document Reproduction Service No. ED 174 156).

Schneider, K., & Schneider, S. (1979). Trends in sex roles in television commercials. *Journal of Marketing, 43*, 79-84.

Scholz, C. (1985, November 10). Philosophy in a small balloon. *Washington Post: Book World*, p. 18.

Schudson, M. (1984). *Advertising, the uneasy persuasion: Its dubious impact on American society.* New York: Basic Books.

Schwichtenberg, C. (1986). Sensual surfaces and stylistic excess: The pleasure and politics of "Miami Vice." *Journal of Communication Inquiry, 10*(3), 45-65.

Schwichtenberg, C. (1987). Articulating the people's politics: Manhood and right-wing populism in *The A-Team. Communication, 9*, 379-398.

Scott, J. (1971). *The athletic revolution.* New York: Free Press.

Scott, J. (1985). *Violence and erotic material: The relationship between adult entertainment and rape.* Paper presented at the meeting of the American Association for the Advancement of Science, Los Angeles, CA.

Sedgwick, E. K. (1985). *Between men: English literature and male homosocial desire.* New York: Columbia University Press.

Segal, L. (1990). *Slow motion: Changing masculinities, changing men.* Rutgers, NJ: Rutgers University Press.

Seggar, J., & Wheeler, P. (1973). World of work: Ethnic and sex representation in TV drama. *Journal of Broadcasting, 17*, 273-282.

Shannon, C., & Weaver, W. (1964). *The mathematical theory of communication.* Urbana: University of Illinois Press.

Shatan, C. (1989). Happiness is a warm gun: Militarized mourning and ceremonial vengeance. *Vietnam Generation, 1*, 127-151.

Sheridan, A. (1977). Translator's note. In J. Lacan, *Ecrits: A selection* (pp. xii-xvii). London: Tavistock.

Sherrod, D. (1987). The bonds of men: Problems and possibilities in close male relationships. In H. Brod (Ed.), *The making of masculinities: The new men's studies* (pp. 213-239). Boston: Allen & Unwin.

Sholle, D. (1990). Resistance: Pinning down a wandering concept in cultural studies discourse. *Journal of Urban and Cultural Studies, 1*(1), 87-105.

Signorielli, N. (1982). Marital status in television drama: A case of reduced options. *Journal of Broadcasting, 26*(2), 585-597.

Silverman, K. (1989). Fassbinder and Lacan: A reconsideration of gaze, look and image. *Camera Obscura, 19*, 54-85.

Simmel, G. (1978). *The philosophy of money* (D. Frisby, Trans.). London: Routledge & Kegan Paul.

Skelly, G., & Lundstrom, W. (1981). Male sex roles in magazine advertising, 1959-1979. *Journal of Communication, 31*(4), 52-57.

Skidmore, M., & Skidmore, J. (1983). More than fantasy: Political themes in contemporary comic books. *Journal of Popular Culture, 17*(1), 83-92.

Slade, J. (1984). Violence in the hard-core pornographic film: An historical survey. *Journal of Communication, 34*(3), 148-163.

Smith, D. (1976). The social content of pornography. *Journal of Communication, 26*(1), 16-33.

Smith, E. (1990). *The genetically superior black athlete: Myth or reality?* Unpublished manuscript, Washington State University.

Smith, G., & Blackman, C. (1978). *Sport in the mass media.* Ottawa, Ontario: Canadian Alliance for Health, Physical Education and Recreation.

Smith, J. (1975). *Looking away: Hollywood and Vietnam.* New York: Scribner.

Smith, P. (1988). Vas. *Camera Obscura, 17*, 89-111.

Smith, P. (1989). Action movie hysteria, or Eastwood bound. *Differences: A Journal of Feminist Cultural Studies, 1*(3), 88-107.

Smythe, D. (1977). Communications: Blindspot of western Marxism. *Canadian Journal of Political & Social Theory, 1*, 1-27.

Spangler, L. (1989). A historical overview of female friendships in prime-time television. *Journal of Popular Culture, 22*(4), 13-23.

Sporkin, E. (1985, April 10). DC Comics straightens out its superheroes. *USA Today*, p. 1.

Stacey, J., & Thorne, B. (1985). The missing feminist revolution in sociology. *Social Problems, 32*(4), 301-316.

Staples, R. (1978). The myth of the black matriarchy. In D. Wilkerson & R. Taylor (Eds.), *The black male in America* (pp. 174-189). Chicago: Nelson-Hall.

Starker, S. (1989). *Evil influences.* New Brunswick, NJ: Transaction Publishers.

Stearns, P. N. (1979). *Be a man! Male in modern society.* New York: Holmes & Meier.

Steeves, H. (1987). Feminist theories and media studies. *Critical Studies in Mass Communication, 4*(2), 95-135.

Sternglanz, S., & Serbin, L. (1974). Sex role stereotyping in children's television programs. *Developmental Psychology, 10*(5), 710-715.

Stouffer, S. A., Lumsdaine, A. A., Lumsdaine, M. H., Williams, R. M., Jr., Smith, M. B., Janis, I. L., Star, S. A., & Cottrell, L. S., Jr. (1976). Masculinity and the role of the combat soldier. In D. S. David & R. Brannon (Eds.), *The forty-nine percent majority: The male sex role* (pp. 179-183). Boston: Addison-Wesley.

Strate, L. (1989). The mediation of nature and culture in beer commercials. *New Dimensions In Communications, Proceedings of the 47th Annual New York State Speech Communication Association Conference 3*, 92-95.

Strate, L. (1990, October). *The cultural meaning of beer commercials.* Paper presented at the Advances in Consumer Research Conference, New York.

Straw, W. (1989). Characterizing rock music culture: The case of heavy metal. In S. Frith & A. Goodwin (Eds.), *On record: Rock, pop, & the written word* (pp. 97-111). New York: Pantheon.

Streeter, T. (1989). Polysemy, plurality and media studies. *Journal of Communication Inquiry 13*(11), 1-33.

Suls, J., & Gastoff, G. W. (1981). The incidence of sex discrimination, sexual contents and hostility in television humor. *Journal of Applied Communication Research 9*(1), 42-49.

Superman comics. (1980-1984, 1986-1988). Issues number 1, 10, 15, 17, 21, 22, 26, 346, 348, 350, 352, 358, 362, 370, 373, 374, 376, 377, 385, 387, 388, 390, 391, 392, 393, 394, 395, 423. New York: DC Comics.

Superman slipped into Britain aboard ships carrying GIs. (1987, July 8). *Variety*, p. 30.

Tankel, J. D., & Banks, B. J. (1990). The boys of prime time: An analysis of "new" male roles in television. In S. Thomas (Ed.), *Studies in communication: Vol. 4. Communication and culture: Language, performance, technology, and media; Selected proceedings from the Sixth International Conference on Culture and Communication, Temple University, 1986* (pp. 285-290). Norwood, NJ: Ablex.

Taylor, E. (1989). *Prime-time families: Television culture in postwar America.* Berkeley: University of California Press.

Thaler, B. (1987). Gender stereotyping in comic strips. In L. P. Stewart & S. Ting-Toomey (Eds.), *Communication, gender and sex roles in diverse interaction contexts* (pp. 189-199). Norwood, NJ: Ablex.

Theberge, N. (1981). A critique of critiques: Radical and feminist writings on sport. *Social Forces, 60*(2), 341-353.

Thomas, S. (1986). Gender and social-class coding in popular photographic erotica. *Communication Quarterly, 34*(2), 103-114.

Thompson, M. (1989, April 31). The comic industry: 1989. *Comic Buyer's Guide*, p. 58.

Thompson, M. (1990, April 27). The comic industry: 1990. *Comic Buyer's Guide*, p. 104.

Thompson, R. (1990). *Adventures on prime time: The television programs of Stephen J. Cannell.* New York: Praeger.

Tiger, L. (1970). *Men in groups.* New York: Random House.

Torres, S. (1989). Melodrama, masculinity and the family: *thirtysomething* as therapy. *Camera Obscura, 19*, 86-106.

Tuchman, G. (Ed.). (1974). *The TV establishment*. Englewood Cliffs, NJ: Prentice-Hall.

Tuchman, G., Daniels, A., & Benet, J. (Eds.). (1978). *Hearth and home: Images of women in mass media*. New York: Oxford University Press.

Tulloch, J. (1990). *Television drama: Agency, audience and myth*. New York: Routledge.

Twitchell, J. (1989). *Preposterous violence*. New York: Oxford University Press.

Uslan, M. (Ed.). (1979). *America at war: The best of DC war comics*. New York: Simon & Schuster.

VanGelder, L., & VanGelder, L. (1970). The radicalization of the super heroes. *The New Yorker, 3*(42), 36-43.

vanGennep, A. (1960). *The rites of passage*. Chicago: University of Chicago Press.

Veblen, T. (1919). *The theory of the leisure class: An economic study of institutions*. New York: B. W. Huebsch.

Verna, M. (1975). The female image in children's TV commercials. *Journal of Broadcasting, 19*(3), 301-309.

Vidmar, N., & Rokeach, M. (1974). Archie Bunker's bigotry: A study in selective perception and exposure. *Journal of Communication, 24*(1), 36-47.

Vincent, R. C., Davis, D. K., & Boruszkowski, L. A. (1987). Sexism on MTV: The portrayal of women in rock videos. *Journalism Quarterly, 64*(4), 750-755.

Wallace, D. (1991, February 17). The dawn of "Evening Shade." *Los Angeles Times Calendar*, pp. 3, 84, 90.

Wallack, L., Cassady, D., & Grube, J. (1990). *TV beer commercials and children: Exposure, attention, beliefs, and expectations about drinking as an adult*. Washington, DC: AAA Foundation for Traffic Safety.

Wanta, W., & Leggett, D. (1989). Gender stereotypes in wire service sports photos. *Newspaper Research Journal, 10*(3), 105-114.

Ware, M., & Stuck, M. (1985). Sex role messages vis-a-vis microcomputer use: A look at the pictures. *Sex Roles, 13*(3/4), 205-214.

Watney, S. (1987). *Policing desire: Pornography, AIDS and the media*. Minneapolis: University of Minnesota Press.

Weber, M. (1905). *The Protestant ethic and the spirit of capitalism* (T. Parsons, Trans.). New York: Scribner.

Weedon, C. (1987). *Feminist practice and poststructuralist theory*. Oxford: Basil Blackwell.

Weeks, J. (1985). *Sexuality and its discontents: Meanings, myths & sexualities*. London: Routledge & Kegan Paul.

Weinstein, S. (1990, December 22). When gay means loss of revenue. *Los Angeles Times*, pp. F1, F5.

Welch, R., Huston-Stein, A., Wright, J., & Plehal, R. (1979). Subtle sex-role clues in children's commercials. *Journal of Communication, 29*(3), 202-209.

Wells, A. (1986). Women in popular music: Changing fortunes from 1955 to 1984. *Popular Music and Society, 10*(4), 73-85.

Wenden, D. (1975). *The birth of the movies*. London: McDonald.

Wenner, L. (1991). One part alcohol, one part sport, one part dirt, stir gently: Beer commercials and television sports. In L. R. Vande Berg & L. A. Wenner (Eds.), *Television criticism: Approaches and applications*. New York: Longman.

Wernick, A. (1987). From voyeur to narcissist: Imaging men in contemporary advertising. In M. Kaufman (Ed.), *Beyond patriarchy: Essays by men on pleasure, power and change* (pp. 277-297). Toronto: Oxford University Press.

Wertham, F. (1953). *Seduction of the innocent*. New York: Rinehard.

Whitney, D. (1980). Why "Gunsmoke" keeps blazing away. In J. S. Harris (Ed.), *TV Guide: The first 25 years* (pp. 42-43). New York: New American Library.

Whyte, W. H., Jr. (1957). *The organization man*. London: Jonathan Cape.

Williams, F., La Rose, R., & Frost, F. (1981). *Children, television and sex-role stereotyping*. New York: Praeger.

Williams, R. (1974). *Television: Technology and cultural form*. New York: Schocken.

Williams, R. (1977). *Marxism and literature*. New York: Oxford University Press.

Willie, C. (1981). *A new look at black families*. New York: General Hall.

Willie, C., & Greenblatt, S. (1978). Four classic studies of power relationships in black families: A review and look to the future. *Journal of Marriage and the Family, 40*(4), 691-706.

Willis, S. (1989). Disputed territories: Masculinity and social space. *Camera Obscura, 19*, 4-23.

Wolverine. (1990). Issue number 33. New York: Marvel Comics.

Wood, R. (1987). *Raging Bull*: The homosexual subtext in film. In M. Kaufman (Ed.), *Beyond patriarchy: Essays by men on pleasure, power, and change* (pp. 266-276). Toronto: Oxford University Press.

Woolard, H. (1983). *A content analysis of women's and girls' sports articles in selected newspapers*. Unpublished master's thesis, University of Iowa.

Woollacott, J. (1986). Fictions and ideologies: The case of situation comedy. In T. Bennett, C. Mercer, & J. Woollacott (Eds.), *Popular culture and social relations* (pp. 196-218). Philadelphia: Milton Keynes.

X-Factor. (1990). Issue number 59. New York: Marvel Comics.

X-Men. (1990). Issues number 270, 271. New York: Marvel Comics.

Zavarzadeh, M. (1991). *Seeing films politically*. Albany: State University of New York Press.

Zillman, D., & Bryant, J. (1982). Effects of massive exposure to pornography. In N. Malamuth & E. Donnerstein (Eds.), *Pornography and sexual aggression* (pp. 115-138). New York: Academic Press.

Zillman, D., & Bryant, J. (1984). Pornography, sexual callousness, and the trivialization of rape. *Journal of Communication, 32*(4), 10-21.

Zillman, D., & Weaver, J. (1989). Pornography and men's sexual callousness toward women. In D. Zillman & J. Bryant (Eds.) *Pornography: Research advances and policy considerations* (pp. 95-125). Hillsdale, NJ: Lawrence Erlbaum.

Zuckerman, D., Singer, D., & Singer, J. (1980). Children's television viewing, racial and sex-role attitudes. *Journal of Applied Social Psychology, 10*, 281-294.

Author Index

255

Subject Index

About the Contributors

Diane Barthel is Associate Professor of Sociology at the State University of New York at Stony Brook. She is the author of *Putting on Appearances: Gender and Advertising* and *Amana: From Pietist Sect to American Community*. Besides gender and the media, her interests include the cross-cultural study of architectural symbolism and historic preservation, at both the community and societal level.

Venise T. Berry is an Assistant Professor of Journalism and Mass Communication at the University of Iowa. She received her Ph.D. from The University of Texas at Austin, with a major in Radio, Television, and Film and a minor in Ethnomusicology. Her research interests focus on black youth in several areas of concern, such as academic motivation, televised images, and cultural perceptions of the pop and/or rap music experience.

Steve Craig is an Associate Professor of Journalism and Mass Communication at the University of Maine. He received his Ph.D. from Florida State University and has worked professionally in the broadcasting and print media. His research on military broadcasting, media law, and television criticism has appeared in several anthologies and journals. His current interest is in television and gender, and he recently completed a content analysis of gender images in television commercials.

David Croteau is a doctoral candidate in the Department of Sociology at Boston College. He has written and taught about the news media and is a member of Boston College's Media Research and Action Project. His current research is focused on the role of class in contemporary American political culture.

Stan Denski is Director of Telecommunications and Assistant Professor of Communication and Theatre at Indiana University at Indianapolis. He teaches in the area of media theory and video production. He received his doctorate in mass communication from Ohio University. His articles have appeared in *Popular Music & Society* and *Tracking: Popular Music Studies*. He is currently completing work on two books: *Critical Media Pedagogy: Media Studies and the (Re)Production of Culture* (with David Sholle) and *Authenticity in Cultural Studies* (co-edited with Jenny Nelson and David Sholle).

Ralph R. Donald is a Professor of Communication and Chairman of the Department of Communications at the University of Tennessee at Martin. He earned his Ph.D. at the University of Massachusetts, his B.A. and M.A. at California State University, Fullerton. A popular cultural critic, his research centers on themes, issues, and propaganda found in war films. Recent works include such topics as the "conversion" plot convention in war films, the "ugly American syndrome" in Vietnam war combat films, the inversion of American cultural myths in Vietnam war combat films, antiwar themes in narrative war pictures, and a historical reassessment of the symbiotic relationship between Hollywood and Washington during World War II.

Fred J. Fejes received his Ph.D. in communication in 1982 from the Institute of Communication Research at the University of Illinois Urbana-Champaign. He has taught at Wayne State University, the University of Illinois-Chicago and is currently an Associate Professor at Florida Atlantic University in Boca Raton, Florida. He is author of *Imperialism, Media, and the Good Neighbor: New Deal Foreign Policy and United States Shortwave Broadcasting to Latin America* and co-editor with Jennifer Slack of *Ideology of the Information Age*. His current research interests include the role of the media in the construction of gender and social class identity.

Robert Hanke received his Ph.D. in 1987 from the Annenberg School for Communication, University of Pennsylvania. He is currently an Assistant Professor in the Department of Communication at the University of Louisville, where he teaches courses in media studies. He has published articles in *Communication* and *Critical Studies in Mass Communication*, and his research interests include the social dimensions of media culture and cultural politics.

Jeff Hearn is Senior Lecturer in Applied Social Studies, University of Bradford. His publications include *The Gender of Oppression, "Sex" at "Work," The Sexuality of Organization*, and *Men, Masculinities and Social Theory*. He is also Series Editor of Critical Studies on Men and Masculinities (HarperCollins) and Co-Convener of the Violence, Abuse and Gender Relations Research Unit, University of Bradford.

William Hoynes is a doctoral candidate in the Department of Sociology at Boston College and a member of the Boston College Media Research and Action Project. He is the Coordinator of the Communications and Media Studies Program at Tufts University, where he teaches about the news media. His current research examines the politics of public television in the United States.

Sue Curry Jansen is Associate Professor and Head of Communications Studies at Muhlenberg College and Cooperative Professor of Communications at Cedar Crest College, Allentown, Pennsylvania. Her publications include *Censorship: The Knot That Binds Power and Knowledge*.

Antonio Melechi studied Humanities at Manchester Polytechnic and graduated in Critical and Cultural Theory at the University of Wales, Cardiff. He is currently working at the Unit for Law and Popular Culture, Manchester Polytechnic, researching Anglo-Italian cultural relations. He has previously published in *New Statesman and Society* and *Marxism Today*.

Norma Pecora is Assistant Professor of Mass Communication at Emerson College, Boston. Her special interests are in the mass communication and entertainment industry and its place in American culture. In that context, she studies the relationship of children to the media, gender socialization, and the structure of children's entertainment. Her current project is a book on the business of children's television.

Donald Sabo is Associate Professor of Social Science at D'Youville College in Buffalo, New York. His publications include *Jock: Sports and Male Identity* (with Ross Runfola) and *Sport, Men and the Gender Order: Critical Feminist Perspectives* (with Michael Messner).

Diana Saco is a Ph.D. candidate in Political Science at the University of Minnesota. Her research interests include social and political identity, popular culture, and international communications.

David Sholle is an Assistant Professor of Communication at Miami University, Oxford, Ohio. His papers on media studies, popular culture, and critical pedagogy have appeared in *Critical Studies in Mass Communication*, the *Journal of Urban and Cultural Studies*, *The Journal of Film and Video*, and the *Journal of Education*. He is currently completing a book with Stan Denski on media education and critical pedagogy.

Lynn C. Spangler is Assistant Professor in the Department of Communication at the State University of New York, College at New Paltz. She received her doctoral degree in mass communication from Wayne State University in 1983. In addition to her research concerning fictional television relationships, she also writes and directs television documentaries.

Clay Steinman received his Ph.D. from New York University in 1979. He is currently Professor of Communications at California State University, Bakersfield. A recovering journalist, his recent research has focused on gender, racism, and cultural theory. His work has appeared in anthologies and journals, including *The Journal of Film and Video* and *The Nation* and, with Mike Budd, in *Communication Yearbook 15*, *Cultural Critique, Television Studies: Textual Analysis, Critical Studies in Mass Communication* (also with Robert M. Entman), and *The Journal of Communication* (also with Steve Craig).

Lance Strate is Assistant Professor of Communications at Fordham University, Bronx, New York. He is co-author with Neil Postman, Christine Nystrom, and Charles Weingartner of *Myths, Men, & Beer: An Analysis of Beer Commercials on Broadcast Television, 1987*, published by the AAA Foundation for Traffic Safety. He is currently working on a book on the relationship between media environments and concepts of the hero.